More Forgotten Towns
of
SOUTHERN NEW JERSEY

The Clevenger brothers of Clayton held on to the inherited molds, and so Clevenger glass still emerges from the old plant, hidden away at Vine and Lincoln Streets. The late Allie Clevenger (seated) with the veteran glass blowers gathered around him to make Jenny Lind, Booz, and other bottles and pitchers

MORE
FORGOTTEN TOWNS
of
SOUTHERN NEW JERSEY

by

HENRY CHARLTON BECK

RUTGERS UNIVERSITY PRESS
New Brunswick   *New Jersey*

Fifth Printing

Copyright © 1963 by Henry Charlton Beck
Copyright 1937 by E. P. Dutton and Co., Inc.
Library of Congress Catalogue Card Number: 63-18380
Manufactured in the United States of America
by Quinn & Boden Company, Inc., Rahway, N. J.

ISBN: 0-8135-0432-5

Affectionately Dedicated to My Sister
SARAH HATTON BECK

Other books by Henry Charlton Beck:

FORGOTTEN TOWNS OF SOUTHERN NEW JERSEY
JERSEY GENESIS
THE JERSEY MIDLANDS
THE ROADS OF HOME
TALES AND TOWNS OF NORTHERN NEW JERSEY

FOREWORD TO 1963 PRINTING

WHEN *Forgotten Towns of Southern New Jersey* made its appearance in 1936, the late Nathaniel R. Ewan, who in his lifetime was president of both the Camden and the Burlington County historical societies, went hurriedly to the library in Moorestown and borrowed a copy.

It was the policy there, as in most communities dominated by the Society of Friends, to make a charge for books of fiction. Nonfiction could be borrowed free. My friend, Miss Hannah Severns, then the librarian in Moorestown, later confirmed the rumor I had heard, that Nat had read *Forgotten Towns* with what seemed to be incredible speed and had returned the copy to the library almost at once as if by mistake he had taken out a naughty novel. What was more, placing the book with some ostentation before Miss Severns, he also presented a fee.

"But, Mr. Ewan," the librarian quietly protested, "there is no charge—this is nonfiction."

"My money says what it is," replied the man who later became a good friend of mine, and he strode out of the library, fuming.

I have given you the anecdote as I have repeated it publicly many times—and, naturally, without any flight of imagination such as Nat imputed to what was my first book of nonfiction all those years ago. I often have wondered what Nat's reaction was when, only a year later in 1937, *More Forgotten Towns of Southern New Jersey*, the book you are reading now, made its debut.

I must presume that this was adding insult to injury, for soon I began to hear reports, some of which I hope were exaggerated, that Nat Ewan was flavoring his historical addresses here and there with criticism of the *Forgotten Towns* books—and their upstart author. Apparently my besetting sin was making history popular by seeking out and recording New Jersey legends that established historians like to shrug aside. Screwing up my courage, I made an appointment with Nat Ewan and went to see him.

I soon learned that Nat Ewan was an ardent defender of the dry-as-dust school, sworn, sometimes through habit, to accept *nothing* until every "i" is dotted, every "t" crossed, and every detail run to earth no matter what its significance, if any in the end.

"With all due respect," I told Nat Ewan, when he had listed his complaints, "you have no regard for legends at all. Many of your friends are prone to look down their noses at oral tradition. Folklore, what the people say, means nothing to you—unless there is a document, a newspaper clipping, or someone with a *name* to back it up. By implication you are saying that most people consciously have lied to me and that others, when asked questions, have made up what they did not know. But what about the self-trumpeted historians who are determined to keep history for the few by locking it up except on appointed occasions or deliberately making it dull. A few of us are trying to make New Jersey history more alive than it was made for us. . . ." I quickly apologized for my vehemence.

For a long time Nathaniel R. Ewan, may God rest his soul, failed to appreciate such a point of view. He would write me long letters and I would reply, and then, after a while, I think I converted him to the processes of research by trial and error—weaving together the stories of those who are willing to talk and then recording the additions and alterations of others who remember, even if only to compete with others in the family or someone on the other side of town. I told Nat not long before he died that much historical information that he had collected was filed away awaiting fragments that would never turn up—and I feel certain that I was right. Many manuscripts of which Nat spoke to me as "in preparation" have disappeared.

I agreed with Nat on several points, and he agreed, finally, on my cardinal argument that whatever else was in error, forgotten town books were the result of honest reporting, the record of what people handed down because they believed it to be true, one generation to another. In New Jersey it is safer to consider even the tallest story possible, rather than wait for proof that long ago went down an old road or out a little river to the sea.

I asked Nat Ewan if he would prepare for me, page by page, comments on all that he had faulted, and I found his six pages of copy in my overflowing files not long ago. Many of the errors he listed were variants, differences of opinion, and, in some instances, assurances that I had lingered and laughed with the wrong people. It was clear that some who had been friendly to me were on Nat's special annoyance list in the country he knew so well from his days as a salesman of his father's Ewansville products, cider and vinegar.

In his notes on *Forgotten Towns of Southern New Jersey* Nat argued that corn liquor was "not common" in the Ong's Hat region; that there was no evidence of a license granted for an inn at Batsto; that the mansion at Batsto, much remodeled by Joseph Wharton, should not be called "venerable," and that some family names had been misspelled—some of these were typographical errors, but others I had found in graveyards where tombstones in the same family lot bore different spellings. Examining *More Forgotten Towns*, now reissued much to my delight, Nat went on in the same vein, with the exception that by this time he was more inclined to offer additions as well as alterations. I know that I accepted too quickly assertions about the Old York Road, and about a tower that was said to have been a part of old Fort Billings, and bricks that came from England, and I was as confused as the kinsmen of the old forge and furnace operators. I am fully aware that the methods with which I began, and on which, I hope, I have improved with later researches, later books, and still later editions, are not yet perfect. No methods are, and nearly all the authors of printed sources I have consulted have admitted as much.

The important fact now is that, even as Nathaniel R. Ewan all but conceded, history and folklore are closer together than ever in New Jersey. Thousands of newcomers, as well as members of old New Jersey families, are not only displaying an avid interest in the state in which they work and live but are prying open the long-dark cupboards, catching history by its folklore "coattails." I have more than ample proof of this with every day's mail. To have a part in helping the new New Jerseyan see the New Jersey it was given to me to find thirty years ago is a very special honor all by itself.

Henry Charlton Beck

Hillcrest Farm,
Robbinsville, New Jersey
February, 1963

FOREWORD

THE appearance of *Forgotten Towns of Southern New Jersey* was rewarded by a generous and somewhat surprising response. From the time of its publication and during the research for and preparation of *More Forgotten Towns* my letter-box has guarded, until my returning, friendly messages from all parts of New Jersey, as well as from a number of other States—some far away—bearing encouragement, suggestion, and additional information.

Although so many of the old villages seemed destined to die unmourned, many who were born in or near them, or whose forebears called them home, have shown they were not utterly forgotten and that the memories refreshed concerning them make the exciting task worth while. I say "exciting" and I mean just that, for although the work was first begun and continued with the author convinced that he, and a few others, were a bit—potty, shall I say?—on the subject, these letters have shown that our quirkiness is not so exclusive.

I have attempted, insofar as I have been able, to reply to all those who have revealed their interest in the romance of decadent things which, whether they call it that or something else, makes us friends. I hope I have shown my appreciation as best I may in this new book and in others that, *Deo Volente*, I hope to write. As long as there are places and people in danger of being forgotten, when they ought not to be, in spite of whatever change and chance may come, there will be a job to do.

Many have asked, and perhaps will continue to ask, why this town or that has not been included among those recalled in this or the previous book. Such a question has required a variety of answers. Some towns are important today, even though they may have lost some of yesterday's pre-eminence, and the stories of their beginnings are well-known. Some towns are historic outposts and to include them would be merely to rewrite what has been recorded elsewhere, and illustrated, in many cases, by relics and remembrances in the showcases of hard-working historical societies.

At the same time, it is obvious that it would be impossible to restore all the forgotten towns in one book, or even two, and it would be unfair to those in other areas of the State, equally in danger of losing their identity forever, to linger longer in one part. To do so would be to imply that nearly everything in Southern New Jersey is forgotten. I am aware that there are more forgotten towns in the lower Counties, but a number, despite persistent efforts, conceal their past with grim determination so that what we have, for the moment, is fragmentary and elusive.

What is a forgotten town? Well, there are a number of answers to that one, too. From our standpoint a forgotten town is one whose earlier days have seen a part, however small, in the developing life of the nation, one whose present contradicts its past and whose future may lose all contact with its birthright. A forgotten town is one that shrugged its shoulders and smiled, contented that a relative should be honored, when the spotlight centered on its more important neighbors. Most of the towns mentioned in this book will be revealed as those that were on the edge, but not in the midst, of the big doings. Sometimes these were a year or two ahead of the times; sometimes they gave up just a little too soon.

Our methods have been quite simple. Armed with an old map, at least a century yellowing its lines and colors, we have looked for strange names, names that have disappeared, names that have been supplanted by others. Then we have looked through Mr. Gordon's discolored pages to see if there is any counterpart and what brief description follows. Reinforced with a hint or two from a letter, an old pamphlet, or someone who suddenly remembers he was lost somewhere near by, we set out, with eyes wide and ears cocked. Frustrated in tracking down criminals except in the comparative safety of detective novels, I have snatched up such clues as offered and run to earth forgotten towns, forgotten industries, forgotten people, forgotten trails.

I have discovered, since the publication of the earlier "Forgotten Towns" book, that a great number of persons expect a historian to be considerably beyond middle life, stern and fond of big words, and given to propounding material that is brimming with details on continents, discoveries, dates and globe-trotters known the world over. As I have assured them, if a historian is really like that, then whatever I am, it's something else. What we have tried to find is what went on, years ago, in a variety of scattered places, in the words of those we have met to talk to, adding such details of our journeys as we deemed worth sharing. Dates pop up here and there and I have quoted from books not within reach of everybody, but the rest of it provides the balance, I hope.

If historians have led people to believe they have to be as many declare they are, then they have done themselves, and their material untold harm. In stressing the big things and big places they have ignored, or at least overshadowed, the little things and little places without which the canvas could not be complete. So, in a besetting anxiety that much would be lost unless it was sought after and put down as quickly as possible, we have hurried hither and yon, in search of coherent folk lore.

This book aims to fill some of the gaps between the villages of Southern New Jersey included in its predecessor and, at the same time, move along the borders of Central New Jersey. Few localities treated here were mentioned previously, even in passing, and contrary to the stories that were collected on a series of journeys that began with a visit to Ong's Hat and Eli Freed, few of those included here have been published before as newspaper sketches and none in this form. If the book will serve as an invitation to tramp the old trails as we have done, aiding its readers to rediscover treasures about them with as much thrill as comes to those with means to take them far away, I shall be more than gratified.

I cannot stress too much what chance has done to so many of these towns, what changes have come, effacing what could have been seen a year before. In spite of new roads, those who have come after us have found clearings grown up, houses burned down, vegetation grown wild and all-concealing. The crumbling bay shore at Town Bank was very different when we were there last, with honeysuckle reaching out in all directions. Weymouth was all but hidden by a screen of trees. Someone had pushed two of the walls over at Harrisia and the spring was broken down. The Princess House at Union Forge was a blackened ruin and they were tearing down the ruin of the paper mill at Pleasant Mills. Never have the pine woods seemed more colorful than this last year, when, after a long absence of extensive forest fires, the cleaning-up and replanting process of the CCC camps, Spring and Summer, in appreciation, brought out all the contrasting colors of wildflowers almost as forgotten as the old towns.

So many persons have assisted in the making of this book that it is impossible to thank them adequately—let the appearance and reappearance of some of them in these pages prove how great my debt is to them. There must be a word of appreciation, however, to Mr. J. Gearhart Crate, who loves the wilds and yet goes deer-stalking; Mr. Willis J. Buzby, still "King of the Pineys" and a devoted friend at Chatsworth; Mr. Southard Norcross, who told us, first, of old Spring Mills and then led the way to Georgia, N. J.; the late Squire Hargrove, whose dog, "Tip," still lives to reflect on our many journeys together; Mr. A. T. Cottrell, Assistant State Forester, who was just as excited by the old pictures of ships and shipbuilding at Dennisville as we; Isabel Ellis Beck, who aided in the arrangement of material and the cumulative index, and finally to Mr. Jack Sperry, Mr. William Augustine, Mr. William Connor, Mr. Emerson Penrose, and Mr. Donald Corvelli, the photographers responsible for the pictures that illustrate the text and in many cases prove our tallest stories.

It is my sincere hope that as the task continues, the reclamation of Forgotten Towns of New Jersey may be something of a contribution to Americana.

HENRY CHARLTON BECK

Haddonfield, N. J.

CONTENTS

13

Contents

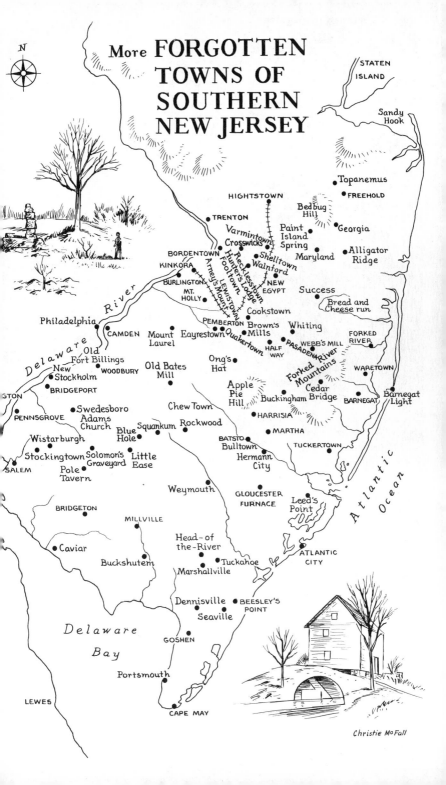

More FORGOTTEN TOWNS OF SOUTHERN NEW JERSEY

N

STATEN ISLAND

Sandy Hook

Topanemus
FREEHOLD
HIGHTSTOWN
Bedbug Hill
TRENTON
Georgia
Varmintown
Crosswicks
Paint Island Spring
BORDENTOWN
Shelltown
Maryland
KINKORA
Recklesstown
Walnford
Alligator Ridge
BURLINGTON
Hunter's Lodge
Foottown
NEW EGYPT
MT. HOLLY
LEWISTOWN
Success
Arney's Mount
Cookstown
Bread and Cheese run
PEMBERTON
Brown's Mills
Whiting
Philadelphia
CAMDEN
Mount Laurel
Eayrestown
Quakertown
WEBB'S MILL
FORKED RIVER
Old Fort Billings
HALF WAY
PASADENA
New Stockholm
WOODBURY
Old Bates Mill
Ong's Hat
Forked River Mountains
WARETOWN
BRIDGEPORT
Apple Pie Hill
Buckingham Bridge
Cedar
BARNEGAT
Barnegat Light
GTON
Swedesboro
Chew Town
PENNSGROVE
Adams Church
Blue Hole
Squankum
Rockwood
HARRISIA
Wistarburgh
BATSTO
Bulltown
MARTHA
TUCKERTOWN
Stockingtown
Solomon's Graveyard
Little Ease
Hermann City
SALEM
Pole Tavern
Weymouth
GLOUCESTER FURNACE
Leed's Point
BRIDGETON
MILLVILLE
Head-of-the-River
ATLANTIC CITY
Caviar
Tuckahoe
Buckshutem
Marshallville

Delaware Bay

Dennisville
BEESLEY'S POINT
Seaville
GOSHEN
LEWES
Portsmouth
CAPE MAY

Atlantic Ocean

Delaware River

Christie McFall

Yesterday, today, and forever are all one in Walnford, once Waln's Mill, by
means forgotten but, rather, once a thriving hamlet that centered around
mill of Nicholas Waln (right). The mansion (left), set off by venerable
wood and shaded in summer by buttonwood trees, goes back at least to
Nicholas Waln was preceded by millers named Weightman and Meirs. Not
away are Shelltown and Arneytown, where a Friends meeting-house once gua
forgotten graves.

WALNFORD AND SHELLTOWN

We stoop and look in through the gate,
  See the little porch and rustic door,
Read duly the dead builder's date,
  Then cross the bridge we crossed before,
Take the path again—but wait!
  Oh, moment, one and infinite!
The water slips o'er stock and stone;
  The West is tender, hardly bright:
How grey at once is the evening grown—
  One star—the chrysolite!
                —ROBERT BROWNING: "By the Fireside"

There is an area in the rolling hills of upper Burlington County and at the edge of lower Monmouth in which almost every house is an inspiration. But, tucked away beyond Stony Hill from which an interested observer may look down on the loveliness of the whole countryside, with Ellisdale at the foot of the steep like a tiny New England village, there are few to be compared with the mansion and its setting at Walnford, once Waln's Mill.

It had been down at Cedar Bridge, while we were looking through the ancient hotel left to itself on an abandoned strip of the old stage road to Barnegat, that a gentleman who said he was Isaac Harrison mentioned Waln's Mill. His reference was a kind of challenge. "If you are any good," said he, "you'll go to Waln's Mill and then, if you don't get enough inspiration to write something unusual, there's something the matter with you."

Although there was doubt in his tone, it was for our capabilities and not the inspiration. Mr. Harrison knew what he was talking about. If anything, there was too much for inspiration and now, when opportunity affords to describe Waln's Mill, even as the Walnford of today, a strange emotion slows the fingers and the mind. The muse is upon us and poetry charges the atmosphere.

The old mansion, burnished in its whiteness, the boxwood hedges lining the walks down to the mill stream, the mill itself, built by Nicholas Waln in 1822, present a picture from another world. The hurly-burly is far away. The purple crocuses, in a regimental line that heralds the coming Spring, seem infinitely more important than anything the present counts as precious. To live here in the old house with its memories, to watch the return of green to the fields, and to imagine the people who found contentment in more casual life, these are the inspirations.

What is the magic of a house that reaches back through the years? Isn't it a mingling of the hours passed by those who called it home, with the imagined pleasures of those who would like to continue those old traditions? In the dining-room are heard the whispered humility of graces said before a thousand cheering meals. Beside the fire there lingers the warmth of long comfortable evenings. All around, there is an air of security, the feeling of protective interest of hands unseen, faces that seem to smile, forgotten folk who reassure us that so little can be made so much, trivialities intimate and worth while.

Waln's Mill, like every mill everywhere, has its history, its names and its dates. In its background are linked together the Weightmans, the Meirs and the Walns. They tell a story of Aunt Sally Waln who kept post office there and who, tiring of an impatient government's complaints, sat down and wrote such a letter that Washington ever after held its peace concerning her affairs. The owner when we were there was Mrs. R. W. Meirs, of 2048 Locust Street, in Philadelphia, who naturally spent all the time she could away from the city.

It is quite wrong to think of Waln's Mill as a lost town. Naturally a gay and industrious life clustered about the mill, the houses across the sandy road where the mill workers lived, the tiny bridges over the creeks and brooks and the murmuring sluiceway. But the town was Shelltown and Shelltown is now Ellisdale, a crossroads village near by with old houses of its own. Close by, too, is Arneytown, sinking among memories of the past, its Quaker meeting-house taken down and its red brick smithy closed. But Waln's Mill was apart from even these.

The winding, dipping roadway from Ellisdale into Walnford is, according to Thomas W. Ridgeway, of Chesterfield, once Recklesstown, a part of the old York Road, the oldest highway in New Jersey. The York Road was built when settlers, establishing themselves in Burlington and at Bergen, about the same time, discovered each other. Led by the Indians, they made visits to one another's settlements and later, in order to continue the friendship and business relations thus begun, the road was laid out. This was long before William Penn established himself in real estate.

The mansion at Waln's Mill, rising majestically above the lake, was built in 1722 and has seven bedrooms. Until recently, it was furnished throughout with priceless antiques, appropriate to the period of its construction. Any venerable old house seems a friend but it was another friend whom we met in the person of the mansion's caretaker. This was Alec Yarr, who, many years ago, used to pilot a Haddon Avenue trolley from Camden to Haddonfield. Now there are no cars. Buses have answered demands for speed, at the cost of fuming the air and filling it with squeals and droning sounds.

Mr. Yarr took us down to the mill. It is unquestionably one of the best preserved in this area. Although many years have passed since it was in use, the solid interior is as if it left off service yesterday. Stored inside when we were there was an automobile of early design, a carriage of old-time vintage, and a sleigh whose lines reminded us at once of the illustrations from books of fairy tales. How nice it would be, we thought, to have some magic power that would restore everything in a twinkling as it once was, to start the mill wheel turning again and to have those who rode happily in sleigh and carryall return.

And yet, would it be the same? There is something of the old peace, to be sure—something, as well, of the old certainty and stability, despite all the world outside has thrust upon the scene. But there is a vague uneasiness, too, new roads coming over the hills, curious people like us who ask if they may tramp through the house. So many, Mr. Yarr said, come to Waln's Mill on the pretext that their relatives once lived in the mansion.

Taking a back road across the ridges, we arrived eventually in New Egypt. From there we rode back to Hockamick and then pressed on to Taylor's Mountain. This elevation, although it isn't as high as Stony Hill, is given greater prominence on most maps. Taylor's Mountain is a dismal place, marked, like Stony Hill, with an Army survey stone.

At the foot is the Poke Hill farmhouse, occupied by two families whose members, none of them, recall anything important about the mountain. Through the years there seem to have been mysterious diggings on its summit. There are deep scars, littered with Jersey stone. Near the topmost rise, we found the skeleton of a horse.

All this is a far cry from the cheer retained by the old house at Walnford. But this is a country of contrasts, both as to the panorama of the countryside and any appreciation of the past. Some folk reverence memories and see forgotten figures and scenes through time-honored doorways and in the shadows of long-silent mills. Others follow humdrum lives near such shrines without caring or remembering.

We returned to Waln's Mill later when the budding trees had burst into leaf and it proved even more impressive. There was green atop the old buttonwoods and peonies were in bloom among the boxwood. There was an even deeper feeling of an intangible presence, as if Nicholas, the miller, were somewhere near, or Aunt Sally might be sputtering over that letter she wrote to postal nitwits.

Waln's millpond as it appeared in the mid-1930's.

CAVIAR

ONCE there were sturgeon in Delaware Bay. Once there was a town called Caviar on the Delaware Bay shore. No sturgeon—no Caviar.

Modern maps of New Jersey boast no town named Caviar but its location hides behind a more deceptive monicker, Bayside. As for road, until one of Caviar's citizens—there's but one who lives there now all year—built his own, there were none to the village. To reach the place today you will have to drive over the rails and ties of an abandoned railroad line.

Once there were 360 houses, some of them shacks. Two large wharves reached out into Delaware Bay above the shore of Bacon's Neck in Cumberland County. Freight trains were numerous and long lines of passenger coaches went out to the terminus on the beach, with its stores and barber shop and other commercial enterprises. In those days there was a post office boldly identifying the spot as Caviar.

But the sturgeon went away and all that's over and done with.

Now there are a bare two dozen shanties and a pier, lost among the ugly pilings which once supported wharves in the caviar-making days. Then sturgeon roe was brought in, boned and shipped up the Central Railroad of New Jersey. Today crabbing and fishing of a different sort are all the industry left to recall the time when ships plied from the Delaware and Maryland shores with peaches and other fruit. Now we have Bayside.

It was Billy Gray who said that queer people who like to hunt forgotten towns might like to know about Captain Charles Roberts, last captain on the *Thomas Clyde*, a side-wheeler that used to run up and down the Delaware to the tune of Sabbath merrymaking and frequent holiday brawls. Captain Roberts, Billy said, lived in Bayside. In looking up Bayside, we discovered that older maps called it Caviar Post Office. That started us off in earnest.

We set out toward Greenwich and after making some unnecessary turns, found the road that Captain Wyatt Miller has built for the fishermen who go down to enjoy the sport from his boat. Miller's a waterman of the first water; he's forty-nine, looks much younger, and has been up and down that particular bit of bay shore almost from the time he was born a mile or two from Caviar.

There are scattered directional signs to Bayside and most of them send the wandering angler to Captain Miller's place, as well. He has a fine house, safely removed from a shore that's dangerous in stormy weather. Then, down at the end of the private road he has stretched across the marshes, one will find a refreshment stand, a tiny pier, a scattering of boats and the handful of makeshift cabins. Minnows swim in all the puddles. Fiddler crabs crawl in and out of their holes in the spongy mud.

Mrs. Miller and some of her friends had driven down to the pier just as we got there. The Captain, they said, was "up at the other pier." Wyatt himself was coming in aboard a small motorboat, with a barrel jammed full of big blue crabs.

"Wyatt's been down here all his life," Mrs. Miller said.

"He knows every inch of this shore. When the Government men came to put out those beacons on the shoals, they took him along to point out where the lights were most needed." Proceeds of his fishing parties have enabled Captain Miller to buy in most of the flats in the vicinity and he's quite content to stay just where he is, out of touch with things mostly, for the rest of his life.

The Millers remember the caviar days well. They remember when there was a town worth talking about, when sturgeon still swam the bay and when shipments of fruit were transferred to waiting trains there. It was years and years, they said, since the last sturgeon was caught. Previous to that time twelve and fifteen carloads of caviar, in the raw, was a daily event.

We set out to find Captain Roberts to gain more details.

That road across the meadows to the older section of the village has been made by the automobiles whose drivers have braved a straddling of one of the rails of the two tracks now hidden in marsh grass and reeds. Further up, back of the Miller house, we saw at least a hundred freight cars stranded on the spur. The last marginal road down-shore had been built so as to cover the tracks and we wonder, now, what the ultimate fate of those cars was.

Captain Roberts was coming in on his own boat with his own catch of crabs. He had stored most of his haul in what fishermen call "a live-car" offshore. Roberts proved to be a heavy-set man with ruddy cheeks. He wore tortoise-shell glasses, broken, and mended with odd materials. His mouth was stained at the corners with tobacco.

His greeting was accompanied by the assertion: "Don't know what I'd do without my chew."

Captain Roberts at once disclaimed being the last master of the *Thomas Clyde*. The last skipper, he said, was Captain Benjamin Denn—Ben Denn, they call him, at Bayside-Caviar. Captain Ben is the only all-year resident of the village and though he's an old man, sometimes no one sees him or inquires about him for weeks on end in wintertime.

Introductions to Ben Denn were difficult. He is stone deaf. We fell to using Captain Roberts as a sort of interpreter because his voice—well, it seemed to us that it ought to carry to the other side of the bay. It was a curious interlude. Old Ben Denn, among his fishnets, trying to be courteous, watching our mouths in vain and then listening to Captain Roberts' booming repetitions between tugs at pants that lacked appropriate buttons and braces adjusted with safety pins.

Ben Denn is ninety now but he climbs up and down to and from boats like an agile monkey. He goes out crabbing every day in season and makes a living from his catches, content on the isolated bay shore he knew when he was much younger. He's a smaller man than Captain Roberts, boasting the remnants of an old-fashioned walrus moustache and clothing himself as is appropriate only to the boats and piers and marsh mud.

Captain Denn was an officer on the old *Delaware*, the *Peary*, the *Major Reybold* and the *Thomas Clyde*.

"I was mate on the *Thomas Clyde*," he said, "when a cyclone came up the river during the Spanish-American War, striking us amidships and ripping off the pilot-house. The superstructure was torn away down to the main deck. Many passengers were injured and the pilot and captain, a man named Townsend, went overboard. They picked up his body some days after that, down at New Castle— the captain was picked up by a tug."

Ben Denn is a little hazy on dates. All the excitement of

the days of pleasure boats on the Delaware, runs to Woodland Beach, Reedy Island, and Augustine Pier is far away.

"He's used to storms," Mrs. Roberts told us, from the
doorway of their little nondescript shack. "He's the only
one who'll stay out here all Winter long. And although
he's deaf as a post, he ain't dumb and his eyesight's as good
as mine."

"Why when I get up at four in the morning," Captain
Roberts put in a hurried interruption, "I can look across to
Uncle Ben's cabin and see him reading last week's paper
by the light of a lamp. He does his reading late—and early
at the same time. He's a grand old guy. I'd rather sell a
dozen of his crabs than a dozen of mine."

The shad business is over, in the Delaware. Sturgeon that
gave Bayside its first name, Caviar, are no longer in the
bay. These hangers-on, recalling thriving days, are quite
happy in their remoteness from the world, catering to
fishermen's pleasure, one day at a time. Here where the
ends of two railroad tracks protrude over mossy rocks,
where the grass of the flats covers rotting foundations of
houses battered by storms, was an industry that many have
forgotten all about.

Caviar in the 1930's, after sturgeon stopped running in Delaware Bay,
and fishermen turned to crabbing.

III

LOST AND FOUND TOWN:
BROWN'S MILLS

BROWN'S MILLS, once Biddle's Mills, has been a "lost and found" town through the years. Lost time and again, it is rediscovered through the medium of some boom, some circumstance of the world outside that makes it a hub, some romantic memory. Time and again a murder has brought it into the limelight.

Newspapermen sometimes reflect that no sensation of great importance has been able to get along without what is called "a South Jersey angle." Almost as soon as the hue and cry starts, it is revealed that a principal of the story has or has had some connection in the southern end of the State. Then newspapers of the area pounce and the "angle" is magnified beyond proportions of the event itself.

It was thus with Brown's Mills upwards of fifty-five years ago. On January 6, 1872, two well-known men confronted each other on the stairway of a New York Hotel. There was the sound of a shot and one of them rolled, dead or dying, to the foot of the steps. The victim was Colonel Jim Fisk. The man they arrested for murder was Edward S. Stokes.

Before the last day of his life on earth, Colonel Fisk had spent many others in Brown's Mills—and he had not been alone. Permitted to furnish his cell in Murderers' Row in luxury, Stokes probably reflected at length on the charms of Josephine Mansfield, well-known actress of the day, in whose company Fisk was said to have spent many happy hours in Brown's Mills. Miss Mansfield and her association with Fisk were said to have caused the fatal meeting.

Brown's Mills was a recreation center even in those days. Reputed to have been the site of one of the first boarding-houses in the country, it served many who wanted to get away for a secluded weekend or longer in company they preferred not to have disclosed.

To digress for just a moment—the first towns founded in New Jersey were naturally along the Atlantic coast and the Delaware River. Clamtown, later Tuckerton, be-came the "capital" for shore settlers. Burlington and Toms River gained in importance, one with a saltworks and the other an inland seaport. A junction was necessary some-where between them all, and this was first Biddle's Mills.

The woodland beauty of the place was first discovered by Biddle who established a mill. Although there is no record to show that he did more than live there, it is probable that a Biddle's Mills Hotel was established, for such a hostelry and one at Mount Misery were great competitors.

Among the ships that brought British pioneers to Bur-lington were *The Shield* and *The Willing Wind*. Among their families were some Browns and Scattergoods. The Scattergoods went to a point near Columbus, establishing their first home in a kind of cave on what is now the Atkinson farm. The spot used to be pointed out where Thomas Scattergood raised a family of nine children despite great privations for those used to the warm fire-sides of the mother country. Two of the nine, Thomas and Thomasine, had much to do with the history of Brown's Mills in later years.

From the fragmentary information that has been discovered, it is evident that Thomas Scattergood was beloved
of the Indians who roamed the country where he had built
his log home. It is certain that his funeral was attended by
a host of warriors in ceremonial dress.

Meanwhile Abram Brown, who had remained in Burlington, took horse one day in the direction of Biddle's
Mills. Liking the spot, he remained there for an interval,
at the end of which he made Biddle an offer. Biddle may
have been a little tired of pioneering at the edge of known
territory—he accepted. Brown bought the Biddle tract,
together with the lumber and grist mills, changing the
name at once to Brown's Mills.

Brown was a man of enterprise. He soon had established
a friendship with Stephen Girard and began supplying
lumber for Girard's many undertakings. Brown met Girard
when he was a New Jersey resident, living in the village
of Mount Holly and planning quietly the career in which
shipping played a considerable part.

Those were days when lumber was cluttering the roads
between Brown's Mills and Philadelphia, hauled in cara-
vans, long lines of teams of all descriptions. Lumber from
Brown's Mills was usually in the charge of ox drivers and
other men who were heavy-set, muscular, in homespun
breeches and leather jackets. Girard had become something
of a marked man. Realizing that teamsters, making bids
at public sales, would arouse little comparative attention,
he often had such men act as his agents.

One such sale was held in Brown's Mills with a whole
shipload of molasses the coveted item. A teamster bid in a
cask. Little heed was paid. Courtesy demanded further
privilege. "I'll take it all then," said the man in the leather

coat, to the surprise of everybody, "and Stephen Girard's my backer."

It was in later years that the Browns and Scattergoods intermarried. Thomas Scattergood married Elizabeth Brown. Grandma Scattergood was born in 1809 and died in 1889. She remembered the Hessians well. One company that landed in Great Egg Harbor Bay marched cross-country to Trenton and camped near Brown's Mills, she said. A pig and a calf were taken from the Scattergood barn and a gold watch disappeared.

It was Grandma Scattergood who said that Brown's Mills had the first boarding-house in the United States. Old printed notices exist which point out that boats on Brown's Mills lake were for the use of boarders without extra charge. Fish were so numerous in the lake and nearby millpond spillway that it wasn't any fun to catch them.

Despite records 'elsewhere to the contrary, ice cream goes far back into the history of those romantic days in Brown's Mills. The boarding houses, vying for business, began advertising the new dish as a feature every Sunday. The boarding rate was five dollars per week. Sometimes that included a transportation ticket, by wagon from Philadelphia, or by boat to Bordentown and from there by carriage. Years later, in one of the many rediscovery eras, Brown's Mills provided special transportation by stage-coach from Lumberton, to which point boats plied up the Delaware River and Rancocas Creek. This trip required eleven hours.

Still later the Camden & Amboy Railroad was put through with "John Bull," one of the first of the historic engines, burning wood to Bordentown and return. Later came a line to Pemberton and its extension to Wrights-

...rgeon used to spawn far up in the uncontaminated waters of the lower Dela-...re River. Picture taken in 1901 shows skinning of fish prior to shipment of roe...be processed in Russia. Russians inspected the sturgeon roe put aboard trains...Caviar, now Bayside.

In days when railroads sprang up everywhere, the Columbus and Kinkora R
road Company, incorporated in 1866, gave birth to the Columbus, Kinkora
Springfield, and then the Kinkora and New Lisbon. Here the author, in the 193
found all that remained—one rail, ties, and a mound of cinders. Below, Ja
Longstreet of Monmouth County testing water in Paint Island Spring.

town, as well as the spur of the Kinkora Railroad, now lost in the woods near New Lisbon. In 1873 another branch, from Pemberton Junction to Toms River, made Brown's Mills the most outstanding boarding-house center of the day.

The Scattergood boarding-houses operated on the original site. Here many notables came for weekend retreat from "bustle" in the city. Here, officially incognito, came Colonel Fisk and Miss Mansfield for their last rendezvous, later exposed with the rest of the scandal. Squire Warner Hargrove, grandson of Grandma Scattergood, used to delight in telling his hearers how he later used the room the couple occupied, as a snake den—which may or may not be appropriate.

The Scattergoods did not look with favor upon the "encroachment" of the railroads. They feared them. They fought them. As a result the nearest roadbed was kept two miles out of town. John Horner was the hotel proprietor at the time and, it seemed to follow, the political leader of the district. He ruled with an iron hand. When he said the railroads, dangerous and impractical experiments, must stay out, they stayed. Thus Horner put a pall over his town and its future without knowing it.

Scattergood's boarding-houses were succeeded by the Newell House, operated from 1880 by Timothy P. Newell and Charles S. Ridgway, whose sign, "Wines and Liquors" at 16 North Front Street in Philadelphia, was a relic when Prohibition came along. Among other famous minehosts were W. Hulling Pennock, who directed things when every available room in the village was taken. In 1889 a large five-story building was erected by a syndicate consisting of prominent Camden gentry headed by E. H.

Cohn and backed by Dr. J. E. White, Senator E. J.
Cattell, Judge Armstrong, and Senator Pfeiffer. The idea
was to make the place a second Lakewood, with politico-
sequesterish trimmings but a fire in 1895 ended the hopes
that had dragged through several years.

Next came a chap named Reilly who established an inn.
Bertram C. Mayo added to the inn and made it "The Pig'n
Whistle," much of which remains today as it was then,
serving however as a sanitorium. Bertram and his son employed a whole army of proprietors through balmy and
bumpy days. Until 1900 the village owned the only building in South Jersey exclusively devoted to dancing. Warner Hargrove used to tell of a New Year's Day Leap Year
party to which the girls did the inviting—the night was
snowy and cold, he said, and the town full of sleighs.

"There was a jingle of bells and then the knockers would
clatter," he said, reminiscently. "Bashful swains told the
girls they weren't going but the girls said they were and
in some cases fond mothers pushed their backward sons
out-of-doors."

The quaint, backwoods atmosphere of cordiality hung
on through many years. City folk liked the quiet and far-
away for all sorts of reasons. Some came to see the Pineys
perform. At one time there was a twenty-passenger carryall, drawn by four fine horses, bringing holiday-seekers to
Brown's Mills. In 1889, through the efforts of James B.
Reilly, local feeling against railroads was overcome and a
spur was built to Brown's Mills over the two-mile wilderness barrier. A timetable shown us on one of our journeys
there indicated that at one time there was a through-car
to New York and another through Lakewood, to Brown's
Mills, and then on to Philadelphia, Pittsburgh, and Chicago.

Nowadays, when the wind is right, you may hear the Blue Comet, crack train on the Jersey Central, from far away.

Brown's Mills lost its popularity as a center of jollity and found it again repeatedly. The lakes, seven miles in a chain, were improved many times. The first forgotten town hunters went on trips to the ruins of Mary Ann Forge, Hanover Furnace, Union Forge, Lisbon, and the other near-by hotel stops on long-lost stage roads. Honeymooners came. Politicians gathered and mapped campaigns. Notable sportsmen stayed for the hunting, with seasonal restrictions, and found deer, rabbits, foxes, and pheasants in abundance. Nature lovers and writers came to discover for themselves the 175 species of bird life then to be found near by.

Booms have come and gone since then. A million-dollar poultry farm, a big bottling establishment and various small factory enterprises started up and gave up with an aggregate spending estimated at more than four millions of dollars. A real estate boom resulted in the selling of 30,000 lots in and around the village. On a comparatively small number, bungalows were erected. More recently many have built summer homes in the vicinity but those who live in them know almost nothing of Brown's Mills-in-the-Pines.

A wayfarer, returning after even fifty years, would find few of the old landmarks today. The old saw mill site is replaced by a tumbling dam. The mill that replaced Brown's original structure has since seen service as a novelty factory and recently was the headquarters of an electric light sub-station. A water-pumping plant marks the grist mill location.

Around the old mill-race are refreshment stands. A dance-hall is operated where sheep once waited for the wash. A miniature golf course was erected and since has disappeared where the mule stables were. Along the old ice-house water edge is a bathing beach. Iron and clearwater springs are gone with the old wooden bridge that led to them.

So far we have found no one can tell us with authority where the "sulphur spring" was—this and other features made Brown's Mills a health resort in forgotten advertisements. The railroad station that stood at the end of the spur, so bitterly fought for years on end, has been torn down to make room for a bowling alley—if that hasn't been closed by now. Picnic grounds are grown over by scrub oak and brambles.

Brown's Mills, in the original, is surely a forgotten town.

It is more than that, just as they say—a "lost and found" town which, for a remaining few is lost forever, and to newcomers is being found all over again.

Beards and moustaches distinguished glass blowers at Winslow.

IV

OLD SQUANKUM AND LITTLE EASE

MUCH has been written, from time to time, concerning the earliest glass-making establishment in North America, the Wistar works near Salem. Although we were to find the site of the plant and hear many of its legends later on, we preferred to approach it through the smaller glass establishments, founded and operated, for the most part, by men who had worked for Wistar and later had removed elsewhere.

It was while wandering about in the white-sand country near Williamstown on a mucky day that we had the surprising good fortune to find the location of the old Isabella Glass Factory at what is now New Brooklyn. If we had been much later it would have been impossible to talk with the very Isabella for whom the factory was named.

In searching out the little-known background of some of the smaller glass towns, trailing the founders to Glassboro and beyond, we found that the workers came from Germany to Wistar's plant and, after varying periods of service there, set up businesses of their own.

Williamstown, in earlier days, was known by the unlovely name of Squankum. Further down was Little Ease, now Franklinville, the old name being retained by a small stream that passes through it. Little Ease Run is still there as is the Squankum Branch which, eventually, gets down to the Great Egg Harbor River.

The road to New Brooklyn, out of Williamstown, is

easily found. We had been told by Harry Marvin, of
Woodlynne, a State Highway engineer, that if we turned
on a road that later twisted back toward the Black Horse
Pike, we would find a row of houses which obviously had
been constructed for tenants of some industrial operation
long forgotten.

We took the wrong way in, of course, becoming mud-
dled and muddied in a particularly forsaken sector an old
darkey told us was "practically nowhere." Finally we came
to the houses, small, unpainted, and weather-beaten. The
row stretched along the road for a distance of possibly half
a mile—there were six of them, not counting a little ramshackle building that may have served as a warehouse. Sheltering them were tall, stately oaks, trees that unquestionably remembered the glass-making days.

Edward Snelbaker and his wife, who appeared in response to our knocking at one of the doors, said that although they had lived there some time, they weren't sure
about the name of the glass works. It might have been New
Brooklyn, they said, but we immediately expressed our
doubts of that. Snelbaker said his uncle had worked in the
plant but when we began asking for dates, he replied that
he was but sixteen at the time "and was seventy and more
now." We were left, thus characteristically, to figure it out
for ourselves.

Snelbaker directed us, however, to the home of a Miss
Stanger, up the road. "She owns all the land around here,"
he said, "and ought to remember something."

How unprepared we were for the episode that followed!
Locating the modest little farmhouse and tramping around
to the kitchen door—sometimes the front doors of such
houses haven't been opened since the last funeral, years

ago—we explained our rather curious task and were bidden to come in.

It was a typical farmhouse kitchen, begonias filling the windows, sweet potatoes in a large bin beside the old-fashioned stove, a work basket and some sewing on the table. The lady who asked us in was not Miss Stanger—she explained that very quickly when she introduced us to a venerable and wrinkled companion at the table.

"This is Miss Stanger," she said. "She's ninety-four. I'm her niece, Mary Newkirk."

Miss Stanger, daughter of Thomas W. Stanger who died in 1894, told us she had lived a long while. We agreed that ninety-four years was a very long time. Her recollections of the early days were a bit clouded but she referred us for answers to many questions to the family Bible, quickly produced with its painstaking record of births and marriages and deaths.

We learned that the section where we had gone off the trail had been known as Broad Lane. The glass plant, when it was in operation, had had two distinct locations. The main branch was somewhere in the now much-plowed field directly across from those bleak tenant houses; the other was down across the cranberry bog around the bend of the road. We trudged through the woods now grown up on this second tract where the trail is brambled and overgrown and soon found a hidden clearing of white sand speckled with bits of glass.

Across the road from the bog was once an old manor house where Miss Stanger was born. The house burned down some years ago and the sawmill that stood near by has vanished altogether. A small bungalow has been erected on the site of the old house, on a rise in front of the woodsy patch dotted with holly trees on which the berries were already a burnished pink. There was a storm-blackened untenanted house down the trail and a few yards from it a small and uninviting relic of a building that once served for town meetings. Occupants there today are scurrying squirrels and chipmunks.

"There's a bottle from the old factory up there in the cupboard," Miss Stanger said. Her niece, who had lived in the West for sixteen years and who looked upon the changes she found on her return with resentful surprise, reached up and found it. It was more than an ordinary bottle of Jersey Glass—molded on it was an anchor and the inscription, "Isabella Glass Works."

Then we knew the name we had been looking for as we journeyed along.

"Isabella," murmured Miss Stanger, with a deep-throated chuckle. "That's my name! They called the plant after me! It was in full operation when I was a girl."

Thomas Stanger had three children, Frances, whose daughter was then taking care of her aunt; Elizabeth, who died as a child, and Miss Isabella.

In the *New Jersey Historical Collections* we found added information as we sought to attach added importance to Miss Stanger's assertion that her father came from Glassboro. A buried paragraph read:

"Glassboro is about 10 miles SE from Woodbury, in the NW corner of Franklin township, in the pine country. This village was settled during the American Revolution by Stangeer and Co., seven brothers."

The brothers "built some log dwellings and established a glass factory, which stood about 50 rods E. of the present tavern. They were originally from Germany, and had just previously been employed in Wistar's glass-house in Salem co., the first of the kind established in North America. Glassboro is an improving place, and land has trebled in value within a few years by the use of marl, lime and ashes."

It is doubtful if residents of Glassboro today would find such a description accurate or complimentary. It is bewildering, of course, to think of such towns, now in the heart of an agricultural area, grown up with hundreds of imposing houses, churches, and schools—a State Normal School, in Glassboro's case—in connection with industries that have gone forever, log houses so much dust, and folk who think only of the present. Very often the scene of chief activity is off on some hidden path, quite apart from any modern settlement, like Isabella Glass Works, you see.

Thus when you refer to New Brooklyn you are liable to be corrected, as we were by Miss Newkirk, who said we meant "Old Brooklyn." And when you refer to elusive Jersey glass and the folk who recall early glass-making days, you are likely to assume that both are extinct, while in reality, they are tucked away in dusty cupboards and old houses, just off highways of concrete and macadam.

The first mention of Squankum as a town was in 1758 when it was definitely located on the road to White Hall Mill. The name prominently linked with the village as it was then is Brockden, again giving evidence of the German background. The first evidence of definite settlement near Squankum, the Williamstown of today, probably a name first bestowed on the near-by stream by Indians, was the Cheesman location.

The corner of a road leading to White Hall Mill was

outside the present Williamstown, that is certain. The
second location was the Brockden place which may, according to deeds dated 1737, have had an earlier beginning
—and failure. Charles Brockden, according to old real
estate records, conveyed 1200 surveyed acres to his daughter, Mary Patterson, and her husband, Thomas, in February, 1769, the property later passing to Johannes Hoffsey,
in 1774. There is a record showing that the Pattersons
mortgaged their holdings, and the place, at the time of the
transaction, is given as Hospitality, Gloucester County,
when Gloucester County included all that is Camden and
Atlantic Counties today.

John F. Bodine, Esq., writing in 1878, said that he first
went to Squankum thirty-nine years before and that at the
time there was an old log house standing on what was
mostly referred to as the Sykes place there. This dwelling
was said to have been palatial in former times, being constructed of cedar logs hewn square and dovetailed at the
corners. It was two stories high, wainscoted inside with
planed cedar boards, and with a famous open stairway—
unquestionably the manor house of a "patroon."

The Charles Brockden who lived there seems to have
come from Philadelphia. After he and his daughter occupied the premises, records show a German family named
Craver were in residence. One of the Cravers, said to have
been born in the old house, long since a memory, of course,
is buried in the Williamstown cemetery. Near the site of the
house, until a few years ago, was a beaver dam, below the
knoll. Beavers refuse to live where humans come and the
dam remained long years after their departure.

In the records of early days at Squankum, and further
down at Little Ease, there are many unusual names equally

as challenging. To match the Hazletts, VanScivers, Butlers, and Youngs, there are the Cawns and Turks. The Hoffsey place gains added fame by claims of some that it was the site of the first Methodist preaching, with Methodism going back to 1796 in this particular area.

In many deeds there is mention of a road known then as the Old Cape Road. We have concluded that this is the road which today goes through Cross Keys and is said by many who have traveled it to be the shortest route to Cape May. Where a little-used railroad spur crosses the road today is an unused station, Robanna, and that's another stop few save those who live close by have located. In a similar fix is Radix, a depot on the Williamstown branch, on the trail to New Brooklyn. These stations will tumble apart some day, if they haven't even now, in spite of salty inscriptions inside, common to such wayside stops.

The Old Cape Road was in existence in 1743. The Tuckahoe Road was not laid out until February, 1784, long after the trails to White Hall Mill, the Hoffsey and Sennor place had been beaten down by time. The tract on which the village of Squankum grew up was first the Penn place and later the Williams location. The Penns deeded the land to the Williamses, through Israel Williams, remembered in the town's new name.

One of the earliest houses, standing near where the railroad crosses the pike, became a barn. This was the first frame house in Squankum and it was owned by Major John Tice, who moved there from Tansboro, the tannery center, in 1798. Uncle Porty Tice, one of the Major's sons, was our authority for the statement, leaving considerable writing behind him at his death. In 1800 the house was linked with the name of Davenport, and for many years after it knew the small talk of the times, fox and bear hunting, property values, log-hauling and political squabbles of Federals and Democrats.

John Williams deeded the plot for church and school but neglected to make his terms formal enough, so that a long legal skirmish ensued. Records of the Methodist Church say "they did not continue their meetings here (the Hoffsey house) but in 1800 preaching was transferred to Squankum and the first society organized, consisting of about twelve members who were formed into a class with Joseph B. Smallwood as leader. Thomas Everhardt, another German, was the first preacher."

This band of Methodist insurgents were not suffered long. The use of the log schoolhouse for services was ended when they encountered the sudden opposition of the owner. The meetings removed to a hotel, known as Sears Tavern. Beset by hecklers and strong-arm men at the tavern, they moved again. Opposition bred fortitude, however, and the purchase of a property as well as the building of a church. An acre tract was procured from Williams Strong in 1804.

This large meeting-house, scene of quarterly meetings of the Gloucester Circuit for a time, later became a school, the headquarters of a Presbyterian congregation and finally, the barn.

A glass works in Squankum, known as the Washington Glass Company, was established in 1804. The town then boasted thirty-five houses and two taverns. The glass-house, church, three stores, and two blacksmith shops kept things humming for years but, until 1842, there was no post office, the mail coming in from Cross Keys three times a week. The change of name came suddenly when it was discovered that a place called Squankum in Monmouth County had priority and was causing confusion of the mails. In 1842 a public meeting was held and Squankum disappeared for the less picturesque Williamstown.

Of the names that were familiar to Squankum—Brockden, Hart, Stangeer or Stanger, Patterson, Hazlett, Hoffsey, Burch, Smallwood and Craver, only a few remain in their descendants. The early Germans were a restless, roving people and many, long before the name of the town had been changed, had gone further West, to Ohio and Indiana, where many Old Brooklyn and Squankum names will be found today.

All is memory—days when Winslow Junction was Winslow Glass Works, when even Clementon had its glass factory, when Good Intent was a town with a woolen factory, when Seven Causeways had a meeting-house, glass plant and store and finally, when the Gloucester Fox Hunting Club helped the farmers of Blackwoodtown, Heston's Glass Works, and the Horseheads, rid Franklin Township of poultry marauders.

Miss Isabella's face seemed to brighten up when we spoke of these places but even she could not tell us where to find Seven Causeways and Good Intent. "My father and his brothers worked hard," she said. "Yes, they worked hard." Perhaps Little Ease, the old name of Franklinville, will testify forever to those days of hard work. But much must remain, like Miss Stanger's bottle, gathering dust on a forgotten shelf.

V

PAINT ISLAND SPRING

A CHALLENGE in a name, Ong's Hat, began this business of finding forgotten towns and determining, wherever possible, what their past had been, as remembered by those who might be found lingering somewhere near.

So the name, Paint Island Spring, culled from an ancient gazetteer, jumped from the yellowing page to demand investigation.

In Thomas F. Gordon's *History and Gazetteer of the State of New Jersey*, published by Daniel Fenton in Trenton in 1832, you will find the paragraph that launched this particular excursion:

PAINT ISLAND SPRING, on the boundary between Upper and Lower Freehold t-ships, Monmouth co., 5 miles E. of Wrightsville and near the source of Toms' river. This is a large chalybeate spring whose waters hold so great a quantity of the supercarbonate of iron, blended with the black oxyde of iron in solution, that they leave a very extensive deposit of this mineral. By exposure to the air an atom of carbonic acid escapes, the oxyde takes another atom of air from the atmosphere, and is precipitated in the form of oxy-carbonate, an insoluble powder of yellow colour.

The colour may be converted into a beautiful brown by heating the yellow ochre sufficiently to expel its carbonic acid, leaving behind the second oxide of iron. The heat of boiling water is sufficient for this purpose; and the ore so changed has most of the properties of umber. A manufacture of this paint has given name to the spring. It is esteemed by the neighbors for medicinal qualities, and picnic parties are made here frequently in the Summer. It was also formerly known as Lawrence's spring, but is now, we believe, the property of Samuel G. Wright, Esq.

It had been some time since we had traveled through this particular neighborhood. We had rooted about in that vicinity when we were relocating Prospertown, Collier's Mill,and La-Ha-Way, with their stories of oil-drilling, race tracks, and hermits. Until recently improved, the direct road from Mount Holly to Freehold, passing through a number of little-frequented towns, was impassable although, as the Court House Road, it follows the present County line and is obviously the shortest distance between the two points.

When the Redcoats retreated from Philadelphia, prior to the Battle of Monmouth, the majority of them traveled along this road, one of the earliest laid out. Some improvement today has made Jobstown, Sykesville, Prospertown, Burksville, and Smithburg more accessible than when we were first there. Then the wagon-track had cut deep into the rolling country, deep between the hills, with a long ridge, topped by leafless trees, in the background.

With gazetteer paragraphs as guide, we set out along this trail, inasmuch as Wrightsville still appeared on modern maps and since the source of the Toms River could be located by patient wanderers. The road indicated its historic import plainly enough. All along it were tumbling houses, gnarled desolate orchards, broken barns and rusted, disused farm implements .The old mill at Prospertown had fallen in ruin since our last inquisition and just beyond, within sight of a church obviously no longer used, was a dwelling that could never more know habitation.

Our actual inquiries began at Burksville, where there is a cluster of dwellings and a corner store. At this point, the hard-topped road to Cassville and Jackson's Mills crosses the sandy track and makes a stopping point. Across from the store there is a Methodist Church. We went into the store, stocked with a variety of wares and filled with the pungent aroma of wood smoke.

The proprietor was a woman who stared at us in a strange way when we asked her if she had ever heard of Paint Island Spring. It was obvious that even the name had never come to her ears before.

She was kind enough to direct us, however, to one of four men who, in a clearing behind the shop, were piling up firewood with a motor-saw. This gentleman, she said, was Sam VanHise, a native who had been thereabouts "a long, long time."

Sam reluctantly looked up from his task. A man who was straight and tall, whose head was crowned with a shock of thick, gray hair matching a full moustache, he readily admitted to knowing where Paint Island Spring could be found although he "couldn't see what anybody would want in going there." He directed us, by means of indicating "the road with poles" since the telephone and power companies still use the old Freehold—Mount Holly Road for wires and conduits.

In passing, we noted the name on the Methodist Church: DeBow. Mention of it here is necessary because of our first mispronunciation, for in this strip of Monmouth County it is called "Deboo." The original DeBow, or one of them, is recorded as being one of the Refugees, who wouldn't fight on either side in the War for Independence but who had their own wartime fun terrorizing those left unprotected at home. Here the name now graces a church!

Mr. VanHise's sketchy directions brought us to a ridge and a broken-down mill. We accosted a youngster in the yard of a farmhouse further on but he knew nothing of

Paint Island Spring, nor anything about the mill. The child's father appeared a moment later, however, calling his dogs and producing a business-like shotgun. When he heard our questions, he concluded that we were harmless and revealed that the mill had been a saw mill, that it had been owned by Josie DeBow and that after it had ceased operation for lack of good material, it "had just fallen apart all by itself" in a tangle of timbers and rusted machinery.

Pressing on, we came upon a group of men repairing the road, their shoes and overalls colored by the red clay that distinguishes this part of the State. The foreman was Irving Eldredge and it was he who directed us to the farm of James Longstreet, present site of Paint Island Spring.

As we passed through the woods where Eldredge and his men were at work, we saw an array of huge stumps, remains of trees which must have fed the DeBow Mill until there were no more.

The Longstreet Farm sits high on the brow of a hill, with a rounded promontory in the foreground as one approaches across the bridge that spans the stream below. Twenty feet from the bridge is the famous spring itself but you would not notice it in passing. In fact, we did not find it until Mr. Longstreet came down into the meadow to show it to us. Should you care to seek it out some time you'll find it at the foot of a maple tree with roots that have woven a protecting lattice around its brink.

The spring is not impressive now. It has the appearance of a small volcano, in more ways than one. The water at the top of its crater-like formation has an oily hue. The surrounding marsh is tinctured with the rich ochre that is mentioned in the description of long ago. The outlet is subterranean and flows free and clear from a small hole beside the stream closer to the bridge. The rise, contrasted with the brush-grown meadow that once bore cranberries, is scattered with bricks—once there was a wall around the spring.

Mr. and Mrs. Longstreet readily recalled the days when waters of the spring were considered curative and when the spot was of such scenic loveliness as to attract pleasure-seeking excursionists.

"Up there on the hill beside the house were the 'flying horses'—that's what they called merry-go-rounds in those days here," Mr. Longstreet explained. "The spring was all walled in and doctors used to send their patients here to drink the water. I remember a Dr. Thomas, and a Dr. Woodward, as well, who used to send them down in droves as a part of the prescription."

There was a dance hall, too, and on Saturday nights, Paint Island Spring was a merry place, with buggies tied up as far as one could see, down the road. The meadow's yield of cranberries, following the days when a man re-called only as Kirby presided over the picnics and outings, dwindled to nothing when help was at a premium in war-time and "groundhogs gnawed the dam away."

"The meadow all grew up on me," said Mr. Longstreet sadly. "The spring doesn't look much any more. And that DeBow Mill you were asking about was left alone long ago. Funny how things go down, ain't it?"

It was the farmer's idea that the name, Paint Island Spring, came from the fact that the spring itself was in the middle of the marsh, and thus a spring that was truly an island. Mrs. Longstreet said that occasionally an octogenarian came along the road and asked directions to the spring, not to imbibe its magic waters but to look upon it, apparently, for old time's sake.

Perhaps, for all we were able to find out, they tasted of this New Jersey fountain of youth and, long years after, returned to see the source of a renewal of life. It may be, in spite of Mrs. Longstreet's version, that they returned to see if it would be possible to taste of the fountain once again.

The Longstreets remember stories of when the soil from the meadow, in the area around the spring, was dug up and shipped to Imlaystown where there was a paint concern. Traces of these diggings are still to be discerned. After Sam Wright went away, Noah Hunt owned the farm and John Dawes came along still later, as the Longstreets' predecessor. Mr. Longstreet's father was a tenant on the farm, preceding his son's ownership.

So there you have it: paint from the oxydes and whatnot; island from the crater in the meadow and spring from that cold-in-Summer boiling-in-Winter water. Paint Island Spring, never sipped by its owner and even unknown to folk three miles away, for all its past.

Connecting Mount Holly and Freehold, the Monmouth Road of the 1930's was a trail of sand and little bridges.

VI

SHIPS AT DENNISVILLE

A HUNDRED YEARS or so ago there was no Dennisville. Nor was there a South Dennis, its next-door neighbor of today. Dennisville was Dennis's Creek and South Dennis was the important end of town.

This historian of a century back described Dennis's Creek as a post-town of Dennis's Creek Township, Cape May County, at the head of the navigation of Dennis's Creek, six or seven miles from Delaware Bay and seven miles north of Cape May Court House. Dennis's Creek was further described as "containing from 30 to 40 dwellings, 2 taverns, 5 stores and a tide grist mill."

"The town," it was written, "is built on both sides of the creek, extending each way, about half a mile." The conclusion that caught our attention was "Ship building and trade in lumber are carried on extensively here."

Unless the modern driver slows down with some intention of seeing things, he will miss Dennisville, the Dennis's Creek of present days, altogether. The new concrete highway cuts around it and, while its main street rejoins the modern road to lower county resorts, too few travelers are attracted by the pointed steeple and the cluster of old houses half hidden by the trees.

The same newer road passes through, however, the site of the old town's chief activity, crossing a concrete span over the narrowing Dennis, or Dennis's Creek. But the same traveler in hurried observation will most likely pass unaware of anything but wide reaches of marsh on the left, with a small boat or two under construction on the bank of the creek, and a gasoline station, with a couple of clam stands beside it, on the right.

After reading that line in the ancient history and after receiving an admonition from a friend that we ought to make the acquaintance of an old sailor before it was too late, we went down in search of the ships of Dennisville, once Dennis's Creek.

The season was prematurely warm. Taking an old back trail which once held its own importance, we approached the town from the back way. Weatherbeaten houses, many of them unpainted and in contrast to those that glisten in their whiteness like the houses of New England, are lined up along half a dozen unpaved streets. There may be forty, as there were on the occasion of Gordon's record, but there are no more; probably there are less.

We started by invading the largest of two village stores. A buxom gray-haired woman sat just inside the door. A man with white hair was stretched out comfortably in a chair beside the counter; he wore his hat and must have been a patron, resting until such time as the storekeeper came back to wait on him.

"You'll have to wait for I'm ahead of you," he greeted us, as if we came to make a purchase. "They'll be back in a minute, or maybe an hour."

They laughed and we joined them. We asked about ships and were assured that big ones once were built there. But the man with the white hair was so concerned with bemoaning the fact that Dennisville of the present was nothing like the Dennisville of the past that he wasn't much help.

We asked for Captain Ogden Gandy and were assured that he could tell us all we wanted to know and more. "He's been here longer than anybody else," said the woman. "Lives up next to the church. He's eighty-nine or close by it—and he's got a sister up there who's ninety-one."

We postponed our call on Captain Gandy, however, until we could fix in our minds the picture of the neighborhood as it was so that we could make comparisons with what we might be told of the vicinity as it had been. They told us in the store that the shipbuilding operations were "down the road to the side of the creek," so we wandered off to what is now South Dennis.

It was low tide. The marshes seemed dry enough but we knew that under the surface, beneath the scattering of dry and broken reeds and marsh grass, there was deep oozy mud, as we proved quite unintentionally a few moments later. A man with a clam stand came forward to see if we wanted some of his delicacies, raw and on the half shell—in spite of many Summers on one cape or another we have been unable to down them. The shipbuilding days were before his time, he said, returning to his wares with something resembling disgust.

First we went along the lower bank of the creek. Anchored in the mud was an oyster boat which, they said, hadn't been out in several years. A contractor who owned it had had reverses and had been unable to operate it. Two anchors, with their heavy chains, had been carried high in the brush and muck. A group of boys and men who knew nothing whatsoever of the vicinity were attempting to calk an old skiff.

In the oozy flats along the creek at the edge of the water were hundreds of black crabs, horrible little creatures that crawled hurriedly into squishy holes as we approached. Clouds of gnats and mosquitoes, disturbed in their languor in the heat that rose from the marshes, attacked from every side. In the distance, on the banks of mud on the other shore, we saw the rotting hulks of two small schooners.

Returning and crossing the bridge, we made our way along the other bank. Here on skimpy ways were two motorboats in process of construction. Tied up not far from the span were two small boats, one recently completed and being painted by a woman clad in white ducks. We hurried beyond—no, it was impossible to hurry. The path, such as it was, might have been easy for those wearing boots, but we were not so equipped. Slipping from a rotting log put in place for those without necessary footgear, we slid into the muck and emerged with elbows blackened in preventing a bad spill.

We reached the nearest of the two hulks, its decaying boom pointing at nothing, its deck strewn with bits of refuse, spars, chains, and useless nets. The crabs crawled in and out. The gnats brought up reserves. The mosquitoes staged a counter-attack which, when we had obtained the photographs we sought, drove us back for keeps. Here, among the mementoes of yesterday, with the red-winged blackbirds deriding such attempts at digging up the past, we were walking over the graves of ships and shipyards that once gave Dennis's Creek an importance it never can reclaim.

It was high time that we sought out Captain Gandy for proof. We found him, as we had been told we would, on the porch of the old house across the lane from the Dennisville Methodist Church. Active, agile, and loquacious, with an odd squint of his right eye, he introduced his sister and took us into the cool living room. The name of "Gandy" on the iron gate out front indicated that the family has been there since the first shipbuilding days— and that is almost true.

"Sure, they built ships here," said the Captain. "Didn't I help my father build them? And didn't I sail one of them for seven years until she sank in a storm off Monomoy Point, up Cape Cod way, with a cargo of paving blocks from New Bedford?"

We told the Captain that we had explored along the creek as far as we could go. "It must have been bigger in the days when real ships were built there," we suggested.

"Not much bigger," Captain Gandy replied. "Not much bigger."

"How big were the ships, then?" we inquired.

"From two hundred to a thousand tons," he startled us by replying. "Although there were few of the thousand-tonners. Most of them were between five hundred and eight hundred."

It was hard to understand how such ships could be built beside a narrow Dennis Creek and then taken to the sea, and so we asked about that. "How far were the ship-yards from the open water of Delaware Bay? How did they get the ships to the bay shore?"

"We had to wait for the tides," said the Captain. "The ships were moved with every high tide. We used winches and anchors and dragged them down by the capstans some-times. Sometimes we'd make half a mile and sometimes we'd make only a few feet."

"How far are you from the bay?" we asked again.

"Six miles as the crow flies—ten down the creek."

...e of Dennis Creek, Cape May County, in earlier days, is shown by this launch-... of a large schooner, to be hauled bayward on each high tide. Below, early ...otograph shows progress of work on a deck. Dennis Creek is on left, salt ...adows all around.

That big ships were launched sideways in Dennis Creek is proved by the posi⟨tion⟩ of this half-finished hull. Below, inside view of ship in yard which is now swa⟨mp⟩

"Why did you build boats here so far from the shore?"

"Well, it was a question of using the wood here, where it could be cut in those days, and taking the ships down when they were finished, or toting the lumber down the creek. And tides were too uncertain along the bay for yards on the shore. You might get a ship half done down there and then have it carried away by a crazy tide."

And tides were probably different years ago, too. In describing Dennis Creek Township, Gordon says, under the date of 1833, "the tide rushes in over the marshes and lagunes which border the eastern boundary."

In spite of the lack of anything indicative of shipbuilding days in the neighborhood, it is probable that the construction of big schooners wasn't given up until the late '80s or early '90s. We asked Captain Gandy for the names of some of the largest ships built in Dennis's Creek, or Dennisville, and he rewarded us with a colorful sea captain's story that we have been unable to duplicate elsewhere.

"Well, there was the *J. G. Fell*, the *Harry Diverty*, the *James Diverty*, the *Eva Diverty*, the *Deborah Diverty*, the *Emma Jean Diverty* and the *Jennie R. Diverty*," he began. "Everybody in the Diverty family down here had a ship named for 'em," he went on. "And there was the *Marcus Edwards*, the *Ella Matthews*, the *Gregory Matthews* and the *Mary C. Carrow*, as well as a lot more.

"Those were the days when the captain took his family with him if he wanted. There was a whole family lived across the street here who went off on one of the ships built up the road. She brought down some paving blocks from New England and was on her way back from Richmond, Va., to Troy, with cannel coal. Off Manasquan they struck a gale and went down off Sea Isle City, with all hands. There was the Captain, and his wife, and their baby—lived over the street here then—their son, an older boy, was the mate, and he was drowned, too. That ship was the *Deborah Carrow*, I think. She went down in shallow water but though a diver located her and tried to get to any bodies that might have been in the wreck, he came up with word that there wasn't a soul aboard.

"My father was better at boat building than I was. I didn't have much of a hand for it at all. I remember one day when I was trying to tap a band around a new boom straight, the hatchet head came off and I threw the handle in the water after it. 'That's like the Gandys,' sang out one of the Nickersons, who was the mate. 'Always contrary—won't row with the tide.' I didn't know the family was like that but I know I wasn't much good with ships, on the building side.

"But I had to find out, just as I had to find out what smoking was like with a snitched cigar. A pig never knows better than to eat hot swill until he burns his snout."

Asked what kind of wood Dennisville afforded to the construction of ships, Captain Gandy amazed us by saying that he still operated the saw mill where much of the wood was cut—and later, we saw the mill. "We used pine and oak and gum and hickory in the old days," he said. "We're doing a lot of shingles, now, that's all. But we're getting some logs from a swamp back of Port Norris, seven or eight feet down, that *I* say have been there since the Big Flood. It's lumber from Bible times, that's what it is."

Captain Gandy's father, Isaac W. B. Gandy, died from a fall from the mast of the schooner, *Henry W. Edmunds*, when he was sixty-four. His brother, William S. Gandy, broke his back in a fall from another ship while it was under construction, and died.

"I had no knack of tools while my brother, well, he was a-whittlin' all the time. I had to make up my mind whether to build or sail and so I sailed."

It was the sailing of a Dennis's Creek ship that almost put an end to Captain Gandy's career, thus making these recollections impossible.

"That was the *Edith T. Gandy* when I was forty-five," said the Captain. "She was a good ship—I'd been skipperin' her for nigh onto eight years. We had been up to New Bedford for paving blocks when we pitched into a nasty piece of weather.

"I wasn't afraid of those waters—I knew 'em well enough. When the sky came down and a heavy sea started, I kept the lines goin'. I knew where I was. I sometimes think that Tarpaulin Cove and Nantucket Shoals and Gay Head and the lightship off Monomoy were as familiar to me as the Delaware Bay down here.

"Those were the days of wire riggin'—and you should have heard the wind a-whistling up aloft. When darkness came we were worse off than ever. The topsail sheet parted and part of the mizzen came clattering down on the deck. Then I heard some of the blocks get loose and start banging away at the bottom. I knew we were in for it then.

"I wish I could get over to you the sickening feeling a captain has when he realizes that the ship that's been with him for a long time is going down. I knew that feeling then. I gave the order to lash the wheel and climb aloft. I remember seeing one of the men take a chance after that; he must have had some money in his bunk, for watching his chance, he dashed from the quarter deck, into the cabin and quickly slammed the door. 'All right, Mr. Man,' I said, 'now you've got to get back!' Pretty soon I saw the door a-moving, and then after the sea passed over, he made a dash for it. But a mountain-like wave came over the other side and would have got him except that he jumped straight up, caught a rope and swung himself like a monkey to the quarter safe enough.

"When the *Edith T.* went down, we found the water wasn't quite as deep as we expected. She heeled over a little and then righted up. The masts were well out of the sea but my hands were bloody from holding so tight to the riggin'. Well, sir, we were there for twenty-four hours. As the storm passed a yacht came out and sighted us, before the Coast Guards came. They took us aboard and dried us out in a sumptuously furnished cabin. Listen, if heaven's anything like that warmth and food of the cabin, then I'll have been to heaven twice, that's all.

"We were taken to Wood's Hole. There they wouldn't take a cent for food and lodging. What's more they gave us a paper that took us down to New York. On the boat the captain called me aside and gave me another paper that took us free down to Trenton. And the conductor brought us another 'passport' that got us all the way back to Dennisville. Things like that don't happen any more. We had a bit of money and we could have promised more but everybody was just as glad we were saved as we were ourselves."

Thus Captain Gandy is ending his days down in Dennisville, ready to talk to anyone who is interested about the years when big ships went down to the bay from Dennis's

Creek. With a squint and a laugh and a slap of his thigh, he'll go back over days before Dennisville was off the road and before "everybody dyin' off like" closed the Knights of Pythias Hall. The Gandy house was there in Civil War days and the Gandys, brother and sister, the last of their generation in town, expect to linger for some time.

"You remind me," said the Captain, as we were leaving, reluctantly, "of the man who came to an old town, looking for the oldest man. When he found him he asked the old fellow how old his father was when he died. 'Why,' declared the old codger, 'Father didn't die. He's here yet!' 'Well, then,' spoke up the other, 'if that's the case, I'd like to see *him*.' The supposed oldest man in town said: 'I'm sorry, sir, but Pop's busy now. He's putting Grandpop to bed.' Pretty good, eh?"

The village of Georgia, named for George III, has vanished, but the old school is still there, near Adelphia.

VII

GEORGIA AND MARYLAND

WE THOUGHT it would be fun to go marching through Georgia.

On the way, we planned to pause long enough to see what Maryland was like, without going beyond the edge of what is mostly referred to as Southern New Jersey.

The result was the saga of one John Lucky, who drilled for oil at Jackson's Mills; the Burls and Lemmings who twice changed the name of a town in Ocean County, and finally, a school named for old George III, who granted the land and established it.

This excursion was into the Refugee country, the war-torn territory south of Freehold where deserters from Washington's army and fighters who decided to stage their own kind of war, pillaged farmhouses, confiscated livestock, were hunted, and were sometimes hanged.

Georgia is a locality which remains on State Highway maps, across the Monmouth County border. Maryland we found on older charts of routes and towns, though its name had vanished from rumination as well as from the memories of those who live there now.

We traveled up to Pemberton and thence through Wrightstown, Cookstown and New Egypt. Instead of pressing on to Archer's Corner, where we turned off for Collier's Mill and Success, we tried an improved route of red clay that cuts across the piney plains of the Pinehurst Estates. Although this stretch, possibly ten miles across the scrub-covered toboggan hills of Route 40, was round-about, we wanted to be sure there was nothing in that little-traveled section that we ought to see or know about. From here we went to Lakehurst, past the hangars to Cassville, and then up the road to Maryland.

Our maps led us through Francis Mills but it was beyond, at Maryland, that we heard about the ruin of another old mill at the bend of the road. Two millstones lie in the weeds there and the mill dam is hidden by a low thick growth of trees. On the promontory overlooking the hollow and its rickety bridges left from yesterday is one lone dwelling, built but a few years ago.

The mill site was the property of Charles Allen, we were told—Allen was proprietor of a little corner store in Cassville. The framework of the mill itself was burned out seven years ago in a forest fire.

Several miles further on we paused beside a clearing, in the midst of which were two large buttonwood trees and a rise that looked as if a manor house had once stood there. A man and woman were carrying pails of water toward a little house at the side of the road and we asked them if they had ever heard of Maryland, New Jersey. They gave us a puzzled look.

Then the man said: "That's funny. They was somebody up this way last year, asking that very same question. We told him that Maryland was a new one on us."

This was Edson Patterson, who came to live there only recently from Smithburg. Mrs. Patterson was a Lemming, she said, daughter of Joseph Lemming and granddaughter of Ephraim Leming—somebody had added an extra "m"—whose house had stood under those buttonwoods. The house, like so many in this section, burned to the ground many years ago. When it stood in the clearing, boasting only a makeshift gun club now, days were different.

"They was a pile of people around here then," said Mr. Patterson. "Down there at Francis Mills was quite a town. Why, only fifty years ago the old mill was goin' every day with its up-and-down saw.

"They was a hotel and quite a pile of houses. Then along came a lot of city people who thought they could make a million dollars over night and they didn't know how to run things no how. They thought they'd do some big farming but that March, when the high wind blew away the topsoil, all they had was the sand underneath and that wasn't good for nothing. Maybe them people came from Maryland, I don't know.

"The days before that was days. The women stayed home and raised the families and the men went down to the hotels to drink and fight."

Mr. Patterson scratched his head in vain for any recollection of Maryland.

Further down the road we stopped at a house in the doorway of which Mrs. Mary Thompson, another of the Lemmings before her marriage, recalled definitely that the first name of the town was Maryland, but since then the area thereabouts has had three names.

A number of families by the name of Burk settled in the section and so the village became Burkstown. Later, when most of the houses were owned by Lemmings, or Lemings, it became Lemingsville. Now, because the school district is known as Leesville, that also is the name of the town. In the scattering of small farms, a curious little one-room house perched atop a woody hill, a new saw mill or two and a criss-cross of trails through the thickets, Maryland is forgotten.

The way to Georgia led on through Jackson's Mills, a pleasant cross-roads village in Ocean County. Here we found a lake, coated with thin ice, the Lakeside Inn, a small hotel beside it. There was a store and gas station, and twelve or fifteen scattered dwellings. On the plateau above the pond we came upon a conglomeration of abandoned machinery, piles of cable, huge wheels and miscellaneous equipment, black and broken. The presence of such materials in an old mill town brought surprising revelations.

They drilled for oil intermittently through eight or ten years on this plateau, giving up the venture as a bad job little more than ten years ago!

Many persons were skeptical when we said that there had been a search for oil at Prospertown, the town that expected to prosper and never did. Here was the concrete evidence of another such enterprise, obscure because it was carried on in an out-of-the-way village and not because it was so long ago.

John Bennett, the storekeeper, said he "had been away a little while" and so knew nothing of historical importance about Jackson's Mills. But there wandered into the store a rugged countryman, one Conover Reynolds, who said that important things had happened and had been forgotten in the neighborhood "by nearly everybody else but me."

Jackson's Mills, Mr. Reynolds said, took its name from the Jackson family, pioneers in the section. The old saw mill, on the brink of the lake, has disappeared. There's more doing in Summer than in Winter there, Mr. Reynolds told us, but in cold weather it's just another village on the

Lakewood-Trenton road, seven miles east of Lakewood.

Cassville, our informant said, had also boasted a previous name. Once, he said, it was called Goshen. The name was dropped because of several other Goshens in New Jersey. The present VanHiseville was formerly Irish Mills. Lakewood, once Bergen Forge, was the center of a section that was once a power to itself. "Why, they even coined Bergen money there," declared Mr. Reynolds, "for trading among employes of the bogs, the mills and forges around here."

Such "money" was probably akin to the "shin-plasters" and thin metal disks used as money by cranberry workers for purchases at the store operated by bog owners.

Then we heard about the oil prospecting. "It failed," Conover Reynolds declared, "but not for any lack of trying or persevering. John Lucky, the driller, lives up the road yonder. They brought him from Texas, with the drill and other stuff, but he didn't go back after the best they got was a couple of trickles, 'three thousand' feet down."

The drilling began and continued, when there was money enough to finance it, on the Zimmerman farm, up the Lakewood road, not far from all that machinery. The prospector was a man named Westerhouse. John Lucky may have lived up to his name, without any dependence on the oil diggings, although there are other explanations.

"What made him stay on, after they gave up the oil hunt?" we inquired. It seemed rather tragic that John had to live in sight of a dream that had promised much and yielded nothing but debts.

"Best reason in the world," Mr. Reynolds answered with a smile. "He married the farmer's daughter—one of the Zimmerman girls. He lives up there with her family."

We wanted John Lucky's version of all that but he has never been at home when we got that far to look him up.

However, still intent on locating Georgia and learning where its name came from, we hurried on. At the Jackson's Mills cross-roads there is a sign pointing the way, stating that there are regular services at the Georgia Mission, four miles north. Proceeding as directed, we had gone about half that distance when we spied another sign, pointing the opposite way and informing us that the same mission services were held somewhere behind us. Pondering a moment, we discovered that some playful wanderer had carried the sign to the wrong side of the road. We put it back where it belonged before hurrying on.

The road changes from hard surface to gravel before it attains a clearing. Here we found a picturesque one-room school in the midst. On the front of the building, painted white, was the name, Georgia, and it is here, on Sundays, that preaching services take place.

The teacher, Miss Laura Barklow, told us that she presided over forty-one pupils in grades from first to seventh—eighth-grade students go to Freehold. The school goes back almost a century. Before that there was another building, made of logs, on the other side of the road.

The name had come down through the years naturally enough: the land was granted for the first school by King George III, in the middle 1700s. In the Gazetteer of 1832 Georgia is described as "a small hamlet of Freehold t-ship, Monmouth co., 5 miles S. from Freehold town."

"I'm very proud of this old school," Miss Barklow told us. "My mother and my grandmother studied their lessons here."

She pointed to one of her charges, staying after hours to pore over an encyclopedia. "This boy's great-grandfather's name is on the original deed," she said. "His great-grandmother is still living."

This remarkable old lady, we learned, boasted a great accomplishment in writing four letters every day, addressed to friends in all sections of the country. The Rev. George Southard, a Methodist minister in Waretown, was once a pupil in the school, John Joseph Hulsart, Miss Barklow's prize pupil, pointed out. Nathan Koenig, a senator's secretary in Washington, also studied there, the boy said, adding that he had looked up such historic matters all by himself.

Thus do the personalities of the present link with scenes of the past, even when memories fail and when the names of obscure villages change in the surges of time. So do towns like Maryland vanish with no one to say who named them or why, and Georgia, which many would assume to be the namesake of another State, remains to recall a king's liberal mood.

Cassville, old Goshen, now has become Jackson P.O.

VIII

THE MURDER AT POLE TAVERN

CAN A MURDER committed in the Spring of 1824 find a possible solution more than a hundred years after the body of the victim has been committed to the grave?

Does the repetition of a name, first in Upper Freehold Township, Monmouth County, later in connection with a skirmish involving John Bacon and his Refugees at Cedar Bridge, still later when Bacon was ambushed and slain in Egg Harbor and finally, when an unknown assassin struck at Pole Tavern, down Salem way, offer a significant theory?

In the quiet dusk of a day in April, 1824, Joseph Cook, of Pole Tavern, was shot down as he sat with his wife, Mary, by the open fire. Scattershot from a flintlock muzzle-loader crashed through the window, struck Cook full in the chest and peppered the face of Mrs. Cook so that she was blinded and lived in darkness until her death in 1840.

Cook was the son of William Cooke, of the Monmouth County township. He was a man of prominence and considerable wealth, holding the office of deputy postmaster of Pittsgrove from 1808 to 1824, under patronage of Gideon Granger, then postmaster-general. He was a justice of the peace from 1813 to 1818 and some of his old papers, now in possession of his descendants, show that creditors often brought even their friends who were debtors into his court to settle debts of fifty cents. The practice seems to have been friendly enough, for even intimates and relatives indulged the legality.

Joseph Cook, who had somehow dropped the "e" from his father's name, owned a tannery which did a large and important business and was situated at the rear of his residence in Pole Tavern. It is recalled that he was a genial businessman and upright official. Just before he died of the wounds that cut his life short beside the hearth he loved so well, he said:

"I did not know I had an enemy in the world!"

The mystery was never solved. It was ascertained that the murderer rode horseback and that he fired from the shadow of a buttonwood tree, the wheeling hoofprints being immediately discovered in the soft clay of the road. The Cook house was still standing when we were there, together with the tree from behind which the assassin discharged his weapon.

Many solutions were suggested. Each was investigated and nothing of value definitely determined. However, through the years a weird chain of sinister circumstances trailed those connected, even remotely, with the crime.

One man who was attending a hog-killing, always a great social as well as practical function, had imbibed freely of liquid cheer. He boasted of knowing who killed Joseph Cook. As an interested crowd gathered around him, he suddenly pitched forward, stone dead.

Shortly after that, another man confessed to the murder. He promised to take authorities to where the ungainly weapon was buried. The search was made but no weapon was found. The prisoner, finally adjudged a lunatic, died a few weeks later.

Mary, daughter of the victim, immediately refused to live any longer with her husband, Dr. Richard Parker, a country practitioner, and the gossips of the day got busy explaining why, intimating that there was some link between the separation and the murder. Dr. Parker signed separation papers, accepted a sum of money and took leave for a village on the coast, accompanied by one of his wife's former maids.

Still the unrelenting chain of tragedy followed. While out in a boat, fishing with two small sons by an earlier marriage, Dr. Parker and his offspring were drowned in a squall.

The scandal mongers of Salem County are said to have explained all this as a sort of judgment on Mary who, it was suddenly recalled, had jilted a fiancé, Judah Foster, to marry Dr. Parker. It seems that Mary's trousseau was in readiness and the date of the wedding had been announced. Then it was that the dashing widower, Dr. Parker, appeared on the scene. Mary married him, to her own lasting unhappiness. She lived a lonely and secluded life, dying when she was seventy-four.

Judah Foster's heart was not broken beyond repair, however. It was apparent that he had no intention of allowing the tragic shadow to envelop him. He was a dashing fellow, as his cocked hat, still a proud possession of Mrs. Trueman H. Clayton, of Salem, proves. He married four times.

Foster was a Major General in the War of 1812. J. B. Fox, writing of him from Chicago in 1913, said:

"In 1846 and a few years following, there were great doings at the Pole on the Fourth of July, when my boyish heart would be gladdened by the sight of Major General Foster, dressed in full uniform with sword at his side and mounted on an old gray horse as he led a remnant of the Jersey Militia up and down the roads—and there are seven roads leading to the Pole."

"The Pole," a shorter name for Pole Tavern, derived its name from the Liberty Flagpole erected in front of the tavern in early days. An earlier name for the place was Champney's Corner, Pittsgrove being the name of the post office, taking its name from the township which, some say, was so called in honor of William Pitt. The tavern burned down long ago. However, although there is a new pole, rising in the middle of a modern traffic circle, it is graced by the ball from the old.

The house in which the murder was committed was purchased by Joseph Cook from Champney Rambo, who inherited it from his grandfather, Joseph Champney, son-in-law of John Fenwick, who settled Salem in the years after his arrival aboard *The Griffin* in 1675. Corner fireplaces, a quaint partition on the second floor with wide boards scrolled in pleasing pattern, and other architectural details were proudly shown us by Joseph Leary, occupant at the time we were there. Of late, however, the old house has appeared the worse for wear.

Mrs. Clayton, of "Penny Hill," 314 East Broadway, Salem, is a great-granddaughter of Joseph Cook, and it was she who showed us Cook's tombstone in the Baptist churchyard at Daretown. There is nothing in the inscription on the slab to indicate that Cook did not die a natural death.

Ever since the days of Judah Foster, the celebration of July 4 has been a gala occasion at Pole Tavern. On the program of festivities there is always the discharge of the handsome bronze cannon now beside the pole in the circle.

This old field piece, according to John Shade, who operates a filling station near by, has an uncertain history. Everybody says it has been at The Pole as long as can be remembered but no one recalls where it came from.

The inscription on the cannon offers the second mystery of Pole Tavern. Said to be identical with two other pieces, one at Salem and a third at Pennsgrove, the unusual "acrostic" is as follows:

Dn Hie vs Castronov
R. F. F. Neapol 1763
Il Lucano

Once, about fifty years ago, according to Mr. Shade, Caspar Richards got too close to the cannon one Independence Day and his arm was shot off.

But to get back to the murder of Joseph Cook and a plausible solution, these long years after. In our quests for information concerning the Refugees, we have learned, through sources of unquestionably authentic information, that one of those killed in the skirmish with John Bacon at Cedar Bridge was named Cooke and that he was a militiaman from Freehold. The man who later tracked down and killed Bacon at Egg Harbor was another Cook, and this time the "e" had been dropped.

Isn't it possible that the feud went on, that one of the Bacons, or one of Bacon's confederates, or one of the descendants of either, decided that an eye for an eye, a tooth for a tooth and a Cook for a Bacon was the only kind of justice in such a day?

It is worth considering and mulling over, anyway. When we suggested such an explanation, there was a curious silence from authorities of Salem County who should have had something to say, one way or the other. Even Mrs. Clayton was non-committal. But as we pass the new pole at Pole Tavern from time to time, we look curiously at the old house where murder was done, where a woman was blinded for life, and where her daughter figured in a romance that was blighted by suspicions, connected, perhaps, with the death of her father.

Mrs. Trueman H. Clayton, of Salem, recalled Pole Tavern as Champney's Corner. Here she exhibited cocked hat of Major General Judah Foster, jilted 1812 veteran who later married four times.

IX

AND ALL WAY STATIONS:
THE LOST "U. T."

ONCE UPON a time there was a railroad known as the Union Transportation Company. It operated through the last twenty-five years of the last century and kept up its courage through at least as many of the 1900s. Pausing at Lewistown, Wrightstown, Cookstown, New Egypt, Hornerstown, Cream Ridge, Davis, Red Valley, and Imlaystown, it opened up some of the richest farming country in Burlington and Monmouth Counties.

Today there is no "U. T." In some places even the rails have been removed. In others, stations are sheds, filling stations or nothing at all. The motor truck era changed everything for the farmers and the railroad, which had opened up a whole section of New Jersey, closed much of it down, as effectively as by the closing of a door. From Pemberton to Hightstown, terminals of the line, little is as it used to be.

Lewistown probably would never have had more distinction than that of a crossroads if it had not been for the U. T., constructed in 1868. With the laying of the tracks, it was dignified with a station, long ago a ramshackle building on the Wrightstown Road, with windows broken, posters tacked on its walls and, apparently, no use to anybody.

Lewistown once had its crossroads store, a combination post office, hotel and dance hall. Two houses constituted the remaining real estate even in 1930. The post office-hotel-dance hall have gone altogether. A garage, established in wartime, is vacant now. The hotel's last-known proprietor was Samuel Stackhouse, minehost for many years that began in 1872. Previously Tom Horner held the job. When the building was deserted, mail was delivered by a rural carrier and has been ever since.

Once Lewistown had a prosperous farm supply business. Later, the Lewistown Poultry Farm was a thriving enterprise. But these are memories now.

Stories of Cookstown and New Egypt have been told already. Hornerstown, although it has many of the aspects of a forgotten town, must not be treated unkindly. In it and around it are those who have seen better days, natives who, in spite of change, still call Hornerstown "up town." In former days a country store, a post office and a tavern stood at the crossroads. On the elevation near by, graded gracefully down to the creek, was the church, a structure of much ornamentation. On the other side of the dusty road, beyond the "mill-tail," was the village blacksmith shop, surrounded by its litter of broken wagons, sleighs, and bobsleds awaiting repair.

Across the road, desolated and in disrepair when we were there, was the mill. No one in the vicinity seemed to know how old it was or just when and why it ceased operation. Beyond the mill, across the dam, its sagging monkey-walk slung across a stream no longer needed, the Hornerstown station is as lonely. Behind it were, until recently, two old passenger cars of the U. T., long out of style. In one, somebody kept chickens. In its shade we found violets in bloom, in strange contrast to the frosty ground and the cold winds that swept the vicinity that day we were first there.

John Harker, formerly of Hornerstown, was a kindly old gentleman whom we ran to earth in Hightstown. When we saw him, his good health was obvious, his eye was keen, and his memories went vividly back to the early days of Hornerstown. He told us he often went back and looked things over. Born in 1844, he said he had lived all his life in the country served by the old U. T.

"I remember the building of the railroad," he said. "The work was started at Hightstown and Pemberton at the same time. The workers who laid the tracks met in Hornerstown. Everybody was on hand to see the last of the grading, all of it accomplished by horse and cart. Cattle-droving was at its peak in those days. Dealers would come to town with motley herds of cattle, cows, sheep, and hogs which they exchanged for cash or traded for other livestock. Butchers were on hand to make the best deals they could.

"The day of the opening of the old U. T. was a big occasion," said Mr. Harker, who was a woodworker on arches for the railroad bridges. "There were twenty-two cars of guests and officials with plenty of refreshments. By refreshments—well, nobody had thought of Prohibition then and nobody paid any attention to local option regulations on the train. I remember one fellow named William Moore, who had been a teetotaler until then— he was so overjoyed at the coming of the road that he went up the street in Hornerstown shouting the merits and expectations of the line until, from sheer exhaustion, he fell flat on his face, much to the amusement of the entire company."

The first engines on the road were wood-burners. As traffic increased, and as the public realized the advantages of the U. T., produce began moving in huge shipments.

Nicholas Waln, owning one of the best farms near Hornerstown, established a large dairy. Hotels, dance halls, and stations were built and put in operation.

Powell Evans and Samuel Giberson were the musicians of the day in that locality. Both played violin and banjo. Giberson was celebrated in the pine area as "the left-handed banjo player." He could play a fiddle behind his back and dance the hornpipe at the same time. Evans and Giberson were often in demand at Hornerstown.

Stump Tavern wasn't far away and this, we have been assured, was the real "social center." At the hotel, travelers found room and board, billiards, quoit-pitching, all-night dancing and other entertainment. On special occasions there was horse-racing, sometimes at Prospertown, sometimes nearer at hand.

"Sometimes the crowds were five hundred strong to witness the races and tests of skill," Mr. Harker told us.

There were all kinds of gambling gadgets, everything from the "sweatcloth" to the roulette wheel. Thousands of dollars changed hands every day. George Clift used to come over from Bordentown to supervise the gambling enterprises. Clift fared well except on one occasion, Mr. Harker said.

"That was when a swanky gambler came to town with the declared intention of cleaning up," he told us. "The arrival of Clift behind his flashy team of horses made no impression on him. He dared George with heavy stakes and bet time and again at long odds. After the stranger had gone, it was discovered that he had used notes on a Pennsylvania bank that were worthless. Needless to say, he never came back."

"Nucky" Bills was another hanger-on at the tavern,

of oil rig left behind in a venture that left many legends behind in Jackson's
s: one that oil was earlier secreted where it might be found. Below, Collier's
mansion as it appeared long before the lake became a happy fishing preserve.
e say "colliers" were Jersey charcoal burners.

The winding street in Imlaystown blames its twists and turns on Doctor's Cr
and the Indian path that once followed its shores. The Imlays, not to be confu
with the Emleys of the same lower Monmouth County area, knew the celebra
mill long before it closed. Name of the Doctor of Doctor's Creek never has b
ascertained, although some say it was Dr. Daniel Coxe, of Coxe Hall, who bou
land all over New Jersey.

well recalled by many but he, with the tavern, passed out of existence long ago. The hotel site is marked by a refreshment stand today.

Mr. Harker remembered many trips he made to the swamps in quest of white cedar. On those rides through Brown's Mills, he recalled seeing Indian Ann, Indian Peter, and their children, generally conceded to have been the last Indians in Southern New Jersey.

Shreve was another station of the old U. T. Its importance is forgotten with the heydays of such places as Burnt House, Smalley's, Day's, Sharp's, Pine Lane, Allen's, Wood Lane and Deacon's, many of them named for proprietors of near-by taverns. If these crossings are all that remain of a railroad company's struggle to obtain rights of way through farms it aimed to serve, progress must bring its own decadence.

In 1886, it is recorded, the Shreve Station School cost $400 to operate. Miss Mattie Antrim, the teacher, had long since retired, when we were there, although we talked with her later in Pemberton. Teachers in those days were paid $35 a month and taught all the children who cared to be educated—there was nothing compulsory about it. Books were purchased by the pupils themselves. By a previous law, students contributed two cents a day for their schooling and the only big expense was for wood—about $25 a year.

Miss Florence Deacon, who is now Mrs. Thomas Shreeve, told us she succeeded Miss Antrim as the teacher at Shreve. She kept the fire going and the room swept out. It was she who supplied the bucket for the "drinking fountain" with the occasional addition of a wash basin. Under such operation, the schools of Pemberton Town-

ship, of which there were six, cost $2200 a year. It was in
1930 that some officials expressed surprise as to why edu-
cation should demand $30,000 in the school budget when
the population of the township had shown no marked
increase over the old days.

Today the Shreve school is a tenant house and the station is a discarded and unlovely shed.

Imlaystown is one of the discarded station stops of the
U. T. A journey to Upper Freehold Township, Monmouth County, in which it is located, is interesting at any
time of the year. Near Imlaystown is a quaint, plain building known as Ye Old Yellow Meeting-House. Although
frequent repairs give it an up-to-date appearance, it is an
historic place. Tradition says that the Reverend John
Coward joined the carpenters in building it and then
preached its first sermon in 1720.

Tucked away and almost forgotten up a winding clay
road, the meeting-house is to be found under sheltering
oaks, close by a farmhouse and surrounded by tall grass
which almost hides the burial ground. Here is one of the
few places in the area adjacent to Southern New Jersey
where tombstones may be found with those most
ungodly-looking angels carved at their crest.

One of these stones is that of John Saltar, of whom
more is told in the story of Abraham Lincoln's forebears
who lived not far away. Saltar gave the land for the meeting house and died in 1723. The meeting-house stands on
the site of the first Baptist Church which was a tiny affair
erected some years before. Services are held here on the
last Sunday of each July. In addition to the one annual
service, there is a reunion of members and descendants of
members in May or June. The proceeds from the service

and a dinner served at the reunion go for the upkeep of the shrine.

Cream Ridge is further down the road. Once its prosperity knew no bounds and its name was chosen to show that here, in rich dairying country, farmers could attain the cream of everything. Warner Hargrove used to say that he remembered Cream Ridge in the late 1800s and that in those days it was alive with commerce, farming, and all sorts of activity. There was a general store, operated by the genial Bob Woodward, who was postmaster and an authority on agriculture. There was always something doing at the hay and straw press and livestock was sold here by the carload. Cars of produce and milk went swinging along the old U. T. every night.

Cream Ridge served as the hub of a cluster of hamlets, most of which are seldom if ever referred to now. There was Fillmore, which we never found. There was Walnford, Ellisdale, Extonville, and Prospertown. Rural mail and daily papers became everyday commodities for the first time.

The blacksmith shop was the first to go. As trucks appeared to take out the farm products, milk and cattle, the U. T., still operated by a stock company of farmers ignoring the subsidy offers of railroad corporations, cut its schedule. With the curtailment of trains, Cream Ridge and the other stations quickly lost their individuality and importance.

Bob Woodward is still in the neighborhood—or was, when we were there. He rents out the store. His five sons and daughters have married and have their own homes near by. Bob says he doesn't feel much different but he admits that the former glories of this sorry-looking railroad line can never come back. "Not even with soldiers to haul from Camp Dix and Wrightstown," he said.

Barclay Malsbury, who still operates the store in Imlaystown, is one of Bob Woodward's closest friends. He was also postmaster when we were there. "Who started Imlaystown?" he repeated our question. "Why, the Imlays, of course, and that's more than a hundred years ago—for the name's on old, old maps. This was and is cider country—a man named Dawes made Red Valley a real apple center. Davis? Well, it had a threshing and baling plant, a big creamery and lots more houses. Look at it now!"

By this time even the last rotting timbers have been taken down. Even today the old U. T. means little except to oldtimers in the immediate vicinity.

Joseph Cook of Pole Tavern was mysteriously murdered here in 1824.

X

REFUGEES AT CEDAR BRIDGE

ON A MAP of New Jersey, issued in 1834, the principal route to Barnegat was shown through Bordentown, Recklesstown, Fooltown or Georgetown, Penny Hill, Mary Ann Forge, Mount Misery, and Old Half Way.

At Cedar Bridge this highway, built by order of the Crown, converged with another approaching from Burlington, through Mount Holly and Ong's Hat. Today Recklesstown is Chesterfield, Penny Hill is Wrightstown, Mary Ann is remembered only in a broken water gate and Old Half Way is a series of holes in the ground. Even Ong's Hat's last lone resident has departed.

The road itself has suffered in the intervening years, years in which motor transportation has demanded hard-surface paving to replace the twists and ruts of yesteryear. Although the concrete of the Ocean County half of the route, completed before Burlington County improved its half, follows in part the old stage line, many points have been stranded on half-moon curves eliminated by modern road engineers. Cedar Bridge is one of these points.

The impression may be gained that there is little connection between this section and the country that lies around Imlaystown, south of Freehold. This is not true. The connection of that road, as well as many family names that remain in the countryside close by, provides many a link that has held fast through the centuries.

One very obvious link tieing the present with the past

is the Cedar Bridge Hotel, still standing intact and serving as a very comfortable home when we went down to see it. Because the old road was orphaned by the newer highway, as can be seen so well from the vantage point of the Cedar Bridge forest fire lookout tower, it is now a bit difficult to find the hotel. The best way is down the Barnegat Road, turning to the right on the gravel highway to Warren Grove.

Perhaps two miles beyond the old stagecoach route which, incidentally, passed by the site of the fire tower, there is a wide clearing, overgrown by Indian grass. It stretches far off toward the woods on both sides in a panorama that is pleasing except for the reflection that this land once was cultivated, that the cavity in the foreground is all that recalls a burned farmhouse, and that the scattered white objects, viewed through the dark grove of pines, is a cemetery. Here repose, under plain, uninitialed field stones and more pretentious monuments, two hundred pioneers of Cedar Bridge, Warren Grove, and their descendants.

The burial ground, known as the Warren Grove cemetery despite the new tendency to mix the names of the towns so that Cedar Grove is one as often heard, is a lonely place. Completely screened by pines and attained by a close-grown drive that enters from the wooded side on the West, it is a favorite resting-place for deer, whose tracks indicated, when we were there, that they feed on moss under the trees and browse among the tombstones. To prove the assumption, three does and a fine buck went leaping from the place as our car approached it.

Names on the stones include those of Stackhouse, Corliss, Brown, Cranmer, Kerner, Reeves, Walton, Kilpatrick, Leary, Collins, Parker, Gray, Holloway, Brewer, Mick, Bowers, Morris and Couch. Among them are many whose forebears were one with the days and scenes of the old Barnegat Road. George Cranmer, whose brother lives in Burlington, is still in the neighborhood, as are many other kin of the first inhabitants.

The road that leads to the cemetery at the edge of the clearing goes on back to the Cedar Bridge Hotel. Our directions for finding it, as well as locating the little schoolhouse to be encountered on the way, came from Norman Rogers, watchman in the fire tower, and Mrs. William Holloway, whose husband learned his three R's in this very school. The school is intact, although it isn't used as such any more—now, in season, it is a gun club.

It is a small frame building with a pointed roof, its weatherboards blackened by the weather. Inside were several bunks filled with straw, but the places on the wall, from which slateboards were removed, are proof of what was there.

It was one of the Cranmers—Lizzie, they all called her—who taught at the school. There were from eight to ten pupils, according to Tom Sweeney, one of them, whom we met at the erstwhile hotel. Mr. Sweeney was in his late fifties when we met him.

Close by the school are the remains of a saw mill and a cluster of dwellings, some of which may have been the homes from which children went to the school. Trees have grown for at least half a century from a thick carpet of rotting sawdust, some of which has been taken away, from time to time, by those who find it serviceable now as fertilizer.

Back of the school the road—it is hardly more than a

pathway here—turns sharply and then forks. Either branch will bring the inquisitive traveler to the hotel, but the trail to the left is best, even though the car one uses must ford a small stream.

The hotel looks just what it was. The clearing around it has protected it from forest fires that came dangerously near. Across the way, at the other side of the yard and close by the bridge, is a garage and chicken house which served as bowling alleys and game rooms when stage-coaches brought guests to the hotel. The hotel property is now part of the holdings of the Penn Producing Company, operating a chain of blueberry and cranberry plantations throughout the bog country.

First consider the hotel in its historic aspect. According to the *New Jersey Gazette* of January 8, 1783, John Bacon, perhaps the most notorious of the Refugees operating in this section, caused a skirmish there when an attempt was made to capture him. Bacon had several murders to his discredit but somehow gained the sympathy of folk who lived in the vicinity of Cedar Bridge.

The action was at a time when legal forces were stamping out the last of the Pine Robbers. They had murdered a woman at Crosswicks. In Toms River they had a part in the hanging of Captain Huddy. Here at Cedar Bridge on December 27, 1782, John Bacon was compelled to put up a barricade at the bridge in order to defend himself and his men against the forces of Captain Richard Shreeve and Captain Edward Thomas. Shreeve, a member of the Burlington County Light Horse, and Thomas, a member of the Mansfield Militia, had been sent down with a corps to capture the marauders, dead or alive.

The outlaws knew that there were so many counts against them that they could expect no mercy. So, having put up a barricade, they concealed themselves. The militia-men arrived and opened fire. The battle began. It seems that the posse was getting the best of the quarry when, for some reason, perhaps Tory sympathy, the inhabitants of the area opened fire on the would-be captors. In the confusion that followed, Bacon and his men escaped.

William Cook, a militiaman, was killed in the affray, and Robert Reckless, unquestionably a forebear of the founder of Recklesstown, was wounded. Ichabod Johnson, a Refugee on whose head there was a bounty of twenty-five pounds, was slain. Bacon was wounded as were three of his company. Seven of the inhabitants of Cedar Bridge were taken prisoner and lodged in the Burlington County gaol, then in Burlington.

Bacon was killed a short time later at Egg Harbor by a young man named Cornet Cook, perhaps a relative who had vowed to avenge the death of the militiaman at the Bridge.

The hotel was standing then, in sight of all that took place. Today it remains an interesting structure, inside as well as outside, and, as is the usual thing with houses near which blood has been spilled, it has the reputation of being haunted. Perhaps, if they were standing, the other wayside inns at Butler Place, Ong's Hat, Old Half Way, and Eagle, would have ghost stories, too.

"I ain't never seen the ghost," Sweeney told us, when we asked him. "But old Sam Truax used to tell me about it." Mr. Sweeney took the discolored pipe from his mouth. "He used to say that no matter how many times he made sure to put the light out, he would wake up and find it lit—bright and early, some mornings. He just had to get used to sleeping with the lamp going.

"And he told me once that he could lock the door of the old place and hide the key and find the door open when he got up of a morning. Sam used to see things, he did, and hear 'em, too, but I guess there's somethin' wrong with my ears and eyesight."

Although the ghost has never been positively identified, he could be one of many who figured in sudden death at the Cedar Bridge Hotel.

John Wildermith fell downstairs and died of a broken neck. "Shorty" Loveless came in one night, complained of not feeling well, and died within the hour. And it was to the hotel that they brought a renowned country auctioneer when he died of wounds suffered when somebody's gun was mysteriously discharged on a gunning trip, Mr. Sweeney disclosed.

No matter how Mr. Rogers feels about it, as he has looked out across the plains from his fire tower for more than ten years, Cedar Bridge is a forgotten town, on a forgotten road, in country laden with legends and folk tales, as well as stories of more Refugee caves than ever have been found.

There is an enigma about the place, however, as much of eerie bafflement as confronts one from a stone in the Warren Grove cemetery:

"Babies

"For we must wait and not forget. . . ."

XI

BUCKINGHAM AND WHITING

NEXT TIME one of your too inquisitive friends asks you where you are going, tell him:

"Buckingham!"

"Buckingham?" he will ask. "Where on earth is that?"

"Near Van Note Camp," you can reply, with a smile.

"And where is Van Note Camp?" he may persist.

"Not far from Gravel Switch," you can say, and that should end the matter, especially if he knows Upton, the home of Rattlesnake Ace Pitman.

None of these places is imaginary. Buckingham is a deserted station along the Tuckerton Railroad which, now, they tell us, has been all but abandoned, too. Buckingham is between Mount Misery and Whiting. Van Note Camp and Gravel Switch are between Buckingham and Upton Station where the road winds toward the old hotel, Aunt Sally Pitman's house.

The way to Buckingham is dismal even on a sunny day. You can find it, at last, from either direction, Whiting or Upton—at least, you could when we first went there, although new roads have made the trip much easier. The only way to Upton used to be out through Pemberton to Brown's Mills and then out to Whitesbog Crossing. Here, before New Jersey built a ribbon of concrete directly through the pines, the traveler had to turn over a narrow trail that led past deserted hunting cabins.

To get to Buckingham, new roads, even today, are of

little avail. One must turn sharply to the left before reaching the rusted tracks. The trail snakes through the brush, blackened by many fires, and then, twisting suddenly and with customary bumps, goes down along the single track elevation.

When we were there, Buckingham was a cluster of weather-beaten dwellings strung along the track across from the station. There was a shanty which was used for telegraph emergencies, beside the shed in which passengers, when there were any, shivered as they waited for winter trains.

But Buckingham wasn't always a forgotten town. Back in 1880 it was founded by a gaunt and homely man with a beard, recalled as John Buckingham. Buckingham and his wife came to this section from Eastern Pennsylvania to found a lumber camp.

Throughout the New Jersey pinelands are large tracts of cedar timber. In those days white cedar from the swamps was used in the construction of ships. With the completion of the railroad in 1873, an opportunity came to market the product from Buckingham and the man who came there made arrangements for a siding. A modern saw mill was erected, as were a number of houses for mill workers, teamsters and foremen. In those days there were no trucks, of course, and no power except that generated by water or steam.

Horses and mules were used everywhere in this area, as well as a few teams of oxen in scattered villages. Stables were built everywhere to house them. At the center of the new village a store was put up so that the mill hands could make purchases and have them chalked up against their pay. For the "cedar-swamping," as Buckingham's venture was called, broad and narrow tread wagons,

olster-tongues, log chains, "off and near" mules, cant
hooks, poles and slabs and other equipment began to arrive. In those days "heart cedar" shingles sold at eight dollars a thousand—compare such a price to what is paid
today. Pine frame "stuff" sold then for twelve dollars in
quantities now bringing five times that.

Buckingham was a man of spirit. He insisted on good
order and as many comforts of home as he could bring
down to the woods. He personally supervised construction
of the homes. He provided for the erection of a school.
Things began to hum. The camp grew to a village and the
village to a town that wasn't as elusive as it is now. Buckingham's career as a thriving lumber center continued fifteen years.

Buckingham, the proprietor, was happy. He had created a town, a town that was prosperous. In the evenings
he returned to his wife and little daughter to relate the
experiences of the day and the hopes for the day to come.
A luxury Buckingham had given his little family ended all
that, bringing the tragedy that ruined the village and
brought its founder to the end of his days.

Milk came to the lumber camps in cans. But Buckingham was different—John Buckingham insisted on fresh
milk for his little girl. He bought a cow and fresh milk,
every day, added a delicacy to his far-away table. But the
bad came with the good and the cow, driven mad by mosquitoes that swarmed from the swamps, ran amok and
plunging around the field, espied Buckingham's little girl.
The child ran screaming before the animal's frenzied
charge. Her flight was short and her death a horrible one.

From that day on, Buckingham began to fail. Its
founder, hale and hearty up to the day of his daughter's
tragic death, became erratic, haunted by that awful scene.

The mill, after running a month like a ship with no one at the wheel, closed down. Shortly after, John Buckingham died and his wife moved away.

Three or four houses remained of all that was Buckingham when we went there—by now these are probably gone. No one seems to have remained at Buckingham very long after the mill failed. Even Sam Bailey, a veteran woodsman, could not subsist there.

During the war a man remembered as Max Voight, a German, came to live at Buckingham with his family. There were the usual suspicions which accompanied the arrival of such people at such a time. A daughter, Gertrude, remembered by the people in near-by hamlets as highly intelligent and good-looking, obtained a position with the railroad company and because she seemed to do more traveling than was usual, caused further talk. When the war ended, the Voights moved away and were soon forgotten.

Forgotten? We have wondered. Now and then there has come to us the story of a "wild man," a German who is said to live somewhere in this dismal area. We have never caught up with him but we have wondered, too, if he knew the Voights, or if he is one of them.

Around the houses at Buckingham were erected high, rustic fences—although these are one with the ruin of everything else. They were to keep the deer from enjoying fine fare in the village gardens. The last laughter, if deer laugh, belongs to these graceful creatures of the pine, for they are now in possession. Members of a section gang to whom we talked on the day we broke through, told of seeing many a fine buck in Buckingham's "streets." And when, in a particularly desolate spot, we had to change a tire, we saw two of them watching us from a distance.

Gravel Switch gained its name from its business. Much of the sand used in the Eastern States used to come from New Jersey. Gravel and sand for building and filtration purposes is found in the pine barrens. For instance, there was a time when six thousand cars carrying 300,000 tons of sand for a filtration plant at Holmesburg, Pennsylvania, were shipped from a pit near Pemberton. Gravel Switch, a point from which shipping of sand was carried on for years, has long been abandoned.

When Buckingham passed out of the picture, another camp was established, apparently in the hope that it could live down the tragic pall that had fallen on the other lumber town. This place, Van Note Camp, seems to have been started about 1900, down toward Upton, where additional cutting rights had been obtained. But when the timber here was worked off, the workers were released and today only a rusted boiler remains to show the camp existed.

The road to Whiting—carelessly called Whitings on present road signs—winds through all sorts of country from the backwoods. These trails are seldom traveled now that the new State highway cuts by just out of town. One road, to Forked River, passes directly through and is used by those who know the short-cut to Barnegat Bay. But on the old trails there are forgotten crossings where fallen chimneys, bits of masonry and stumps of trees recall brief dreams of prosperity.

Whiting, named for a man who thought to found a lively town there, used to have numerous signs directing the traveler to Roosevelt City. This abandoned development, named for an earlier President, is a maze of broken concrete walks and street lights, weed-grown and depressing. Once, when we were in Whiting, there was a sign in the post office advertising for girls to work in the Roosevelt City shirt factory. When we came upon the factory building we found the wind had been blowing through for years on end.

Whiting, still on the Central Railroad of New Jersey, has served as the junction of three railroads. Here the Pennsylvania, the Central, and the nearly defunct Tuckerton Railroad met. As a town, it boasts about two score houses, the usual combined post office and general store, a church, a school, and a gasoline station.

Peter Christafsen was postmaster when we were there. A Dane, he has been in Whiting more than thirty-five years and can tell you tall stories about the many who have lived there and have moved away. One saw mill was still operating not so long ago, working cedar timber into shingles, and a residue called dog-hair and baled for packing concerns and firms making automobile upholstery.

Pine Tavern wasn't far from these forgotten places. The original inn, the center of a tract that once looked forward to streets and modern appurtenances, was kept by Debby Platt. Debby's fate was as tragic as that of the little girl at Buckingham. Living alone and selling liquor to natives and such travelers as came her way, she is remembered for the "Jersey Lightning" provided in stone jugs in help-yourself quantities at six cents a drink. She served a meal and provided a room in the hotel for a quarter.

Debby kept Pine Tavern going until about 1875. Then she retired and went to live in a tiny cabin not far removed. The tavern, which afterwards served hunters in deer season, burned down one night. Not long after, Debby's cabin burned, too.

For years the story had been heard that Debby Platt had plenty of money. A lone woman, off in the middle of nowhere, can hardly give up a tavern and move off to idleness in a pine hovel on nothing at all. As the story grew, the detail was added that somewhere hidden in Debby's cabin were her life savings. At last, when a glow in the sky summoned natives of Whiting to the scene, the cabin was a crumbling mass of embers and in the midst was Debby's body. In Whiting, some will tell you that years after that a man made a death-bed confession that he murdered Debby, robbed her, and set fire to the hut.

For a time it appeared that the name of Whiting was to disappear. Interested parties from Wilkes-Barre, Pennsylvania, built a mansion they said they would set up as a sanitorium, calling the place Lancewood. Shortly after that another structure went up for bowling and billiards, with a bar in the front room. A long line of stables was erected for the renting of ponies and horses. All the ventures failed, the bar was removed, the horses never arrived and carpenters from the section are still said to be whistling for plenty of their money.

Legal matters used to be attended through the Whiting area by Andrew M. Battles, a colored justice of the peace. Battles got his job by virtue of a few ballots cast in an election when few persons on the back trails were paying much attention. We saw Squire Battles. He resembled a Southern preacher, a gaunt, smiling, dignified man, with dark clothes and a stringy tie. He said he held hearings on his front porch as he would miss a sale of gasoline from one of his pumps out along the road, if he didn't.

Depression years have revived some of the smaller lumber camps, in Burlington County especially, but Buckingham, Van Note Camp, and Whiting were pioneers, however forgotten they may be today.

XII

TOPANEMUS: SCOTCH QUAKERS OF 1685

WE HAD been reading Browning, warm, mellow Browning. Browning of the snug, curtained window seat. Browning of the fireside, recollective of Summer, hopeful for another Spring:

> "Where the quiet-coloured end of evening smiles,
>   Miles and miles,
> On the solitary pastures where the sheep,
>   Half asleep,
> Tinkle homeward thro' the twilight, stray or stop,
>   As they crop. . . ."

And then we went into Monmouth County, climbed that lonely hill crested by brambles and locust trees and tombstones two centuries old. The chill north wind swept across the solitary pastures, swirling flurries of snow into the tufts of haggard grass. The ridges of furrows in the fields that had been plowed too soon were stiffened in the killing cold.

There was nothing of poetry here, nothing presaging Spring, nothing of lost "quiet-coloured" ends of evenings in Summer. And yet, high on that bleak promontory was once a town, "Topanemus," and under those rugged stones, brought from England as ballast no doubt, slept pioneers who had come to East and West Jersey, contented colonists of a King's domain.

Topanemus seems a strange name for a town and so,

through the years, there have been strange ways of spelling it. In the will of Thomas Boell, dated March 20, 1709, it was thus designated when the estimable Mr. Boell devised one and a half acres of land to the Church of England and, at the same time, gave six pounds toward the building of a church.

In 1930 the Monmouth County map gave the town site no distinction whatsoever but still named the near-by brook "Tepehemus." On a map in the history of the Old Scots Church, by the Rev. Henry Goodwin Smith, written in 1895, the brook is called "the Topenhemus" so that today the commonly accepted variation is "Topanemus."

As to location, you will have to do some twisting and turning to find it, as we did, unless you head directly for Freehold, swing out to Tennent and go on to where the name of the old town appears on the sign at a farm entrance, with that of the farmer, Ernest Voorhees. In all the stories of Tennent and its restored meeting-house, as well as data concerning the Battle of Monmouth, the forgotten and traditional past of Topanemus seems to have been completely overshadowed.

We have naturally inquired as to the meaning of these names that cling to ghost villages and what may be found remaining of them. But Col. William C. Richardson, of Haddonfield, journalist and owner of the farm on which the site of Topanemus may be found, can offer no solution. He has delved into Indian books, dictionaries that deal with such terminology and consulted with renowned authorities. The best conclusion to which all of these have come is that the town, settled by Scotch Quakers in 1685, was called for a friendly Indian chief.

The weather played us false the day we went there. A

quick change in temperature brought a bitter gloom upon the Monmouth hills. The snow, occasional flurries further south, had all but covered the fields near Clarksburg and Perrineville. Once the cold was so intense that the car stopped dead. Pushing up-hill and down-dale to a little store to accomplish necessary repairs and adjustments, we found the temperature at six.

Northwest of Freehold, in the open country, it seemed to grow even colder. The car sneezed and choked. The road became corrugated and narrowed down after it turned past the Tennent church and cemetery. Then we came to the Richardson-Voorhees farm.

The farmhouse itself is believed to be the last dwelling of Topanemus and if so, is at least 200 years old. But when we arrived there, atop the drive, cordially greeted by Mr. Voorhees, we confess that we were more interested in the warmth of the place.

There have been alterations in the house, in which the beams have been harshly covered and the general alignment of the building changed. Colonel Richardson discussed repairs, however, by which much of the interior was to be restored.

To reach the site of the town proper, which clustered about a meeting-house which became one of the first, if not the first outposts of the Church of England in the State, or colony, one must go downhill toward an old apple orchard and thence to the right, toward the property line. Then one can see the gravestones, similar to those brown markers, topped with carved skulls, crossbones, and fantastic angel faces, recalled from Kingston and other ancient cemeteries of New York State.

The meeting-house which stood here, surrounded by

k Claverkamp of Lower
taps rust from pig of Jer-
iron retrieved from bottom
Iullica River. Below, the late
re Hargrove, of Pemberton,
his dog, "Tip," explore slag
Ianover Furnace, long ago
lowed up in Fort Dix.

This ancient graveyard at Topanemus, lost in the woods and blanketed in myr
and mayflowers, is the legendary site of a church that was moved, its timb
used in historic St. Peter's Church, Freehold, a temporary hospital in the Bat
of Monmouth. Stones are topped by the characteristic skull and bones, remind
that "man is but dust, to dust returneth."

the little graveyard of long ago, was built in 1692 through the influence of George Keith, who returned to England after a fuss with his associate Quakers, was converted to the Church of England and was sent back to the colonies as a missionary. Keith led many of his Quaker followers to Confirmation but here at Topanemus he persuaded the whole meeting of Friends to become Episcopalians. Keith's name is written large in the records of many early New Jersey parishes, especially that of Old St. Mary's, in Burlington.

Here is a strange detail, worth remembering. The church was not abandoned after the town began to disintegrate and its people to move toward Freehold. It was torn apart in 1708 and removed to Freehold for the construction of St. Peter's, one of the most picturesque and historical church buildings in Central New Jersey today. So, by reason of the record of St. Peter's, and the background of its career at Topanemus, the parish is the oldest in continuous service in the State.

St. Peter's was used as a hospital for British soldiers in the Battle of Monmouth, June 28, 1778, as a tablet on its façade indicates, but that is quite an old and well-known story. Another tale, too, is the recollection that if Washington's underlings had stuck to their orders and had refused to waver, the Revolution would have ended then and there.

The cemetery at Topanemus is believed to be the oldest in the section, apart from some sequestered family burial plots. It is the resting place of hundreds of residents whose descendants are still in Monmouth County. The inscriptions on the stones are more legible today than those to be found in many cemeteries that are comparatively new.

Surely the most notable grave is that of Lieut. Col. John Anderson, once president of the Provincial Council and at the time of his death royal governor of the Province of New Jersey. The inscription on the tomb, cracked across the middle, reads:

"Under here lyes interred the body of Col'l John Anderson, once pres. of His Majesty's Counsil for the Province of N.J., who departed this life March the 28th, 1736, aged 71 years.

"His country's friend, obliging to neighbors,
  Gave no man offense, paid each for their labours,
  Was easie at home or abroad dare appear,
  Gave each man his due and no man did fear,
  The same in all stations, from flattery far."

Colonel Anderson's wife and daughter are buried beside him and the grave of one of the first, probably the first, sheriffs of that section of New Jersey, is near by. It was a common thing to disclose the cause of death on the tombstone, after the manner of a death certificate, as one stone points out:

"Here lyes interred the body
  Of Mr. Allexander Clark
  Who was born in New Jersey
  Who Departed this Life August
  the 7th 1730 Aged 37 years
  Who died with the Cancer."

Atop this stone are first the crossed bones, then a grinning skull and finally, an hour-glass.

The cemetery is believed to be the property of St. Peter's Church, Freehold, as the deed for the surrounding farm excepts an undescribed plot of land "belonging to the church." It is assumed, according to Colonel Richardson, that the land was taken over by the Church of England along with the Quakers and their meeting-house and that later, after the Revolution, title automatically passed to the Bishop of New Jersey.

The burial plot and the forgotten town it recalls do not in any sense resemble a shrine. Except for the stones themselves no recognition would be given the place. Little by little, members of an American Legion Post in Freehold have been restoring the grounds, cleaning away the brush and felling the diseased trees. The owner and tenant have given a right of way from the road to the enclosure, but historical groups move slowly and little response had been given to opportunities offered at Topanemus.

So this was the village that had vanished, long before the first war days!

The little lumbering town of Buckingham failed when the daughter of its founder was killed, gored by a cow.

XIII

SUCCESS: THE STEAM-SHOVEL THAT DUG FOR CARP

SUCCESS, in the world, lies at the end of a winding road, cluttered with stumbling blocks and pitfalls.

Success, the forgotten town in Southern New Jersey, was somewhere at the end of a bumpy, log-strewn trail plainly posted with signs still bearing such unmistakable injunctions as "Road Closed"—"Don't Drive In"—"Private Property"—"Keep Out."

On the day we went hunting for Success, the town, we had to choose between searching for elusive Wrangleboro, once Clark's Mill down on the Nacote Creek, or running down two other challenging names, Georgia and Maryland, on the border of Ocean and Monmouth Counties. Success won the toss and because it did we discovered the doctor who took a steam-shovel deep into the pine woods in order to dig a deep hole in which to raise carp.

As was the case with so many of the expeditions, the day proved dull and overcast, with a penetrating chill reaching through the scrub of Ocean County. The barren hummocks east and southeast of Collier's Mill are similar to the fireswept wastes of near-by localities. However, with the deer season over and the clearings strewn with papers and cans left behind by hunters who these days gorge themselves while awaiting the approach of their quarry, the mystery of the far-away near-at-home seemed more ominous, the unearthly whispering stillness more oppressive.

The stories of Prospertown, where nobody became prosperous although they drilled for oil, and of Collier's Mill, where a horse-fancier built two race-tracks on one of which he was killed by a favorite mount, are familiar to those who know this particular area. Success seemed the next logical invitation to accept.

The road through Collier's Mill and on toward the tangles of burned and broken pines joins up with an old route known as the Gun Road. According to tradition, it was along this road that cannon and shot were taken by oxcart from Hanover Furnace. The folk to whom one may talk in this vicinity will refer to the familiar Gun Road but will express doubts when you ask them if this was not the direct way to Sandy Hook in the old days.

The trail from Archer's Corner strikes out well enough and for a time, beyond Collier's Mill and a dilapidated house at the end of the bogs where the land steeps sharply to a small black stream, the way is smooth. Then the road narrows to a path, rutted and full of hacked stumps. We had gone perhaps six or seven miles along this road, as carefully as we could, when we veered to the left because, according to our maps, this was the direction of Success.

On the oldest maps no passable way is indicated to Success. However, because many of these backwoods trails which see no human being between the days of deer-stalking each year have been cleaned out by WPA crews as fire-stops, the way seemed navigable, by comparison to what we had expected. We had gone perhaps another five miles between sandy ridges and dense cedar swamps when the signs, nailed to several pine trees, halted us temporarily.

The warning injunctions were backed up by a number of logs, obviously hurled across the trail to prevent progress by any kind of an automobile. We were compelled to abandon the car and, piqued by renewed curiosity, proceed on foot. We counted twenty-seven logs across the path before we grew tired of such diversion.

This trip was one with several others in which we disregarded warnings of some forgotten landowner. With those signs and logs on the trail we began to wonder if there would be dogs or if somebody was running a still back there in the middle of nowhere. We reconnoitered through one clearing where we found a hardened bag of cement, more tin-cans, and skeletons of a number of large fish.

Those skeletons were to figure importantly in our discoveries of the day but we didn't know it then. It was surprising and most unnatural, of course, to come upon traces of large fish so seemingly far from civilization, there in the midst of the fire-swept and water-sponged woods. Reconstructing the find, we thought that some intrepid woodsman might have caught the fish off-shore and paused here, for some reason, to enjoy a meal. But the backbones were so large and long and the heads so full and bull-like that we decided they had been carp and had not been eaten at all, not by a human anyway.

All was explained satisfactorily, or perhaps too glibly, after we had pressed on to where the roof of a house, a large steam-shovel and the white sand of a deep excavation came to view around the next bend. We had been wondering, as we came along, about the strange track we saw, now and again, at the side of the log-crossed trail and the sight of the steam-shovel explained it. Caterpillar wheels, bearing the huge apparatus, as out of place here as anything could be, had made its painful way into the barrens the way we had come!

Who would want a steam-shovel back in here? What could anybody in his right mind be digging for in the white sand under the cedar-water swamps? Was this Success?

Approaching gingerly, listening for the bark of a dog and ready for the unheralded appearance of a bearded man with a shotgun, we stopped suddenly. A tree had fallen across the path not fifty yards ahead, perhaps to join the other barriers already felled behind us. Then we saw a man, a chap in a cap and sweater, with the stubble of a two-weeks' beard around a grin marred by broken teeth.

"What you 'fraid of?" the man wanted to know. "You make no noise. I didn't know you was there. When you chop you chop."

We moved forward then and said we were looking for Success.

"No Success—no Success anywhere," the woodchopper replied. After a moment we knew he was talking of the town that had failed and not of any pinnacle of attainment.

But the quest for a forgotten town was put aside until we heard the tale of the steam-shovel and the deep pool, hemmed around with the white sand and clay it had lifted from the depths.

The man told us he was Joseph Palonncak, a Czech. A couple of years before, he had been a gas station attendant in Lakewood, earning $12 a week. One day Dr. Edward Smith, of Lakewood, came along with a proposition. The physician, Joseph said, owned some property here on the site of an abandoned cranberry settlement once known as

Charlesville, a tract of some 600 acres. Dr. Smith asked
Palonncak if he would like to go there as caretaker.

Joseph jumped at the chance. He packed up his belong-
ings, told his wife what he had decided to do, and then,
with his children, took up his abode in the little unpainted
house, the only one left on the site of Charlesville, not far
from where Success had been.

Dr. Smith, the caretaker said, had many ideas. First they
had tried strawberries but the ground was too wet. They
planned to try raspberries. Just now, Joseph said, the carp
venture was taking most of his time. Dr. Smith had always
wanted to raise carp, it seems. There might be money in
it, with Lakewood, mostly a Jewish resort, near by. But
there was no lake, no pool, no pond. One had to be provided.

A hundred diggers working several months would have
made little headway in the spongy ground. They would
have been engulfed, probably, as quickly as their shovels
pried downward. Dr. Smith thought of the steam-shovel.
But few contractors would handle the job because the site
of the undertaking was so far back in the woods. Finally
a firm from Perth Amboy signed a contract and the tor-
tuous journey was begun, far back there where the road,
uncertain as it was, became almost a deer run.

It took more than a week to get the steam-shovel from
the Gun Road to Charlesville. Trees had to be cut down.
They had to make sure of the ground over which even the
caterpillar treads passed. Boards were carried and put
across muggy places time and again. The journey seemed
so slow and painful, Palonncak told us, that the trees
seemed to grow up again behind them. They almost gave
up.

The shovel was finally mounted in place and the digging began. When the pool was hollowed out, filling immediately with water that wells from subterranean sources all through this area, the shovel was put to one side. That had been some time before our arrival and we have always surmised that Dr. Smith bought the steam-shovel outright rather than bring it back for the digging that has to be done all over again from time to time.

The first spawn were released. The first crop of carp was doomed to death, for an acid from the swamps seeped up and left the finny expatriates on the surface one morning. But mistakes were corrected and that day we were there three tons of carp were swimming in the pool—or so Palonncak said. Some, he told us, weighed fifty pounds, thriving now because the pond is chemically treated every week.

Joseph declared that Dr. Smith had already invested $22,000 in his carp farm. We told him of the fishy skeletons we saw. He frowned. "What you call—poachers," he said. "They steal the carp now and then." But we think he was wrong, that few poachers would venture so deep in the pines as Charlesville. It is more likely that some creature of the woods fished out a few of Dr. Smith's prize specimens and then went off into the scrub to enjoy them.

We bid Palonncak good-bye and looked back to see his wife and one or two small children with noses pressed to the windows, snatching furtive observations of our departure. Joseph said he went to Lakehurst now and then for provisions but that only once or twice a year, apart from deer season, did they see anybody to talk to. Schooling, perhaps, is forgotten altogether.

We were told we might learn something of Success in

Lakehurst but it was at Cassville that we obtained such information as there is. District Warden Burk, of the New Jersey Forest Fire Service, was our informant. Success was a failure, long, long ago, he said.

All that ever distinguished it was a sawmill and one or two houses. When the serviceable cedars in the surrounding woods were all cut, Success went to pieces, its houses were deserted and its mill tumbled apart. Nowadays, if you are a good walker and care to carry boots for emergencies, you may get to it. Even so you'll have to figure your own means to ford two streams where old bridges burned down or fell apart some years ago.

Perhaps we saw no definite evidences of the town itself, but with carp, a steam-shovel miles from any sizeable hamlet, strawberries, raspberries, and falling trees all considered, we returned homeward feeling that at least some measure of success had been attained.

Although Success was something less than that for raising strawberries, raspberries, and carp, Joseph Palonncak laughed about it all.

XIV

STOCKINGTOWN

Down in the neighborhood of Alloway and Remsterville, in Salem County, there is an old cabin of oak logs which goes back beyond the memories of stories told by parents and grandparents. It is one of the few houses left to identify the location of old Stockingtown where a weaver, more than two hundred years ago, classified his business and named the village with one move:

He built a yard-arm and hung a stocking at the end of it.

Who the weaver was is as much mystery as why the white oak tree died down the road after the farmer was murdered beneath it and why, until Civil War days, there was a hallowed patch of grass there that kept perpetually green.

Our search for Stockingtown was a cold one, too. There had been more snow in Salem County than nearer home. Deep drifts lined the roads and a temperature far below freezing kept us clinging to our coats and robes.

We had been directed to the farmhouse of Joseph and Sally Emmel and it was in their warm kitchen that we heard all that is known of Stockingtown, snatches of stories Miss Emmel remembered her mother and grand-mother recounting from time to time. The Emmels are brother and sister.

It seems that all the lands in and about Stockingtown were and still are owned by one of the Emmels. John

Harding Emmel held title even before the Revolution. An old map in the Salem Library shows several houses in the neighborhood owned by various Emmels. But the age of the Stockingtown cabin cannot be accurately determined.

"My grandmother was born there," Miss Emmel said. "She told us she couldn't remember a time when the cabin didn't look just as she saw it in her childhood days. My mother, who was ninety when she died, used to say that the stocking 'factory' was about two or three hundred yards from the cabin."

The cabin itself is an interesting building. Its original lines have been somewhat marred by additions at either end but the main structure itself is stalwart enough. There is a large field of Indian grass stretching behind the place to the tangle of woods—the old stocking plant may have been there.

It is interesting to think of a stocking establishment as it would have been in those days when men wore knee breeches, and hosiery as we know it was unheard of. The hosier decided, simply, that it would cost less and take much less time to hang out one of his samples than paint a sign. But the name of Stockingtown remained from that day until quite recently on maps of the vicinity.

The Emmels have seen the old houses disappear, one by one. There were three more near the cabin of which not a trace remains. Another stood on the Friesburg Road. One dwelling Miss Emmel particularly remembered because of its queer architecture, with deep overhanging eaves. Locked in Winter, none of this country is impressive except for its consistent bleakness, its drab fields, and the general gloom that gets into the tempers of the countryfolk as we were soon to find out.

There is one other outstanding house, off another road but in sight of the cabin and the barn across the way, beyond untilled fields. It was in this house that the Emmels' father was born. His grandfather used to say that the dwelling, constructed of field stones, was old when he first knew it. The date, 1798, has been scratched in one of the stones but that is probably someone's guess-work. The date of building is without a doubt much earlier.

The good folk of Stockingtown and Remsterville went to Friesburg to church. One of the early Lutheran churches was established there.

"Remsterville used to be quite a town, too," said Miss Emmel, "even though you wouldn't think so now. There was a saw mill, a grist mill, a woolen mill, a wheelwright shop, a shoemaker's shop and a brick kiln." Whatever might have been found remaining of these early industries has been lost in a Boy Scout colony, "Camp Lodge."

We spoke to only one other pioneer of the vicinity and he was exceedingly taciturn. We learned that his name was Charley Hogbin, that he lived alone and that he had a lot of wood to chop. Questioned as to his age and how long he had been in Stockingtown's neighborhood, he declared he was "seventy-five and as hale and hearty as they come."

The area is rich in tradition, however, no matter how little the people there like talking about it. One of the most interesting stories concerns a murder which, committed in 1775, left its mark until 1861. The scene of the crime was a farm, since owned by John Garrison, east of Friesburg and southeast of Aldine, the newer name given to old Watson's Corners.

Recompense and Boston Sherry, the records show, had

two slaves, Cesar and Kile. Recompense was a farmer, living in Alloways Creek Township, and was fairly well-to-do. In 1775 there appeared an advertisement in the *Pennsylvania Gazette* which may have been the motive for the crime itself. Recompense announced charitably that he was offering for sale a slave who had smallpox. Shortly after the date of the advertisement, Recompense sent Cesar back into the woods to chop. When the black man did not return in a reasonable time, Sherry set out to look for him, in the dying light.

Recompense Sherry met Cesar abruptly under a large white oak where the slave immediately set upon him with axe and club. Sherry died almost at once and Cesar, with the help of Kile, both "property" of Recompense, hid the body in a hollow log. That was May 31, 1775.

Almost immediately the murder was revealed and the slaves accused.

Cesar and Kile were charged with murder and petit treason and were arraigned in Salem Court June 14, Edmund Weatherby, last High Sheriff of Salem, presiding. The verdict is quaint and deserves quotation:

"The jurors of our sovereign Lord and King, upon the oath and affirmation of at least twelve honest and lawful men, do present that a negro man slave named Kile, the property of Boston Sherry . . . and his companion, Cesar, the property of Recompense . . . not having the fear of God in their eyes but being moved and seduced by the instigation of the devil . . ." and so on.

The instruments of murder were described as "a certain axe made of iron and steel and a certain wooden club of value of ten penny."

It was perhaps an early example of Jersey Justice that

the murder was committed May 31 and the murderers hanged June 20, less than a month later, on Gallows Hill, at Clayville.

The sequel of the crime is interesting, inasmuch as it is still a tradition in the neighborhood of Remsterville. The tree under which Sherry was so brutally killed never pushed forth its leaves after that Summer. And underneath, for a space of some twenty feet square, thick grass sprang up, remaining green in Summer and Winter alike. So remarkable was the sight of the gaunt dead tree and the plot of verdure that for almost a century the oak was not hewn down though all who lived near it vanished one by one.

Before we tell of our tour's strange conclusion, we ought to say that from time to time we have been properly scolded for inferring that colored folk chased anybody from a "Copperhead" meeting down in Alloways. However, that story is told time and again. There used to be a sign, those who deny the tale insist, warning darkies to be out of Alloways by sun-down and, it is suggested, feeling against Negroes, left over from the celebrated murder, found few of them in evidence until much later than the time of "Copperhead" demonstrations. But by Civil War times there must have been a change. For, after we had interpreted the "U.S.C.T." of many tombstones in the area as meaning "United States Confederate Troops" as a feeler, we were quickly corrected and informed that the initials mean "United States Colored Troops."

Somehow we prefer our own explanation best, especially for those lonely markers in the forgotten cemetery back of the Salem County Poorhouse.

Queer circumstances have often concluded our inquisitive excursions. Once it was examining tombstones and writing down epitaphs by the light of the moon. Another time it was walking through snow-laden pinewoods seven miles to a cranberry town after our car, moving gingerly over what appeared to be a smooth stretch of road, cracked through the ice into a small stream. This time we ran into difficulties when we asked permission to photograph a Colonial house at Stockingtown.

The wife of the tenant was in the barnyard, trying to use a buck saw on a thick log. Inasmuch as we have always had difficulty in some sections explaining what anybody in his right senses would see in forgotten towns, we realized that we would have a greater problem here.

"We are taking pictures of old historic houses," we began uncertainly. "May we take a picture of your house?"

"We want none," replied the woman, sullenly. She was obviously foreign and, we thought afterward, slightly tipsy.

"Perhaps you do not understand," we said. "We do not wish to trouble you. We are not asking you to buy anything. All we want to do is take a picture of your house and then we'll go away."

"We want none. Don't want no pictures here," came the ungracious reply, with a vulgar gesture to emphasize it.

We hesitated and as we did, the woman babbled on: "All you got to do, go around taking pictures?" Her English was poor and we cannot attempt to achieve more than the sense of what she said here. "You ought to do the real work. Chop wood. You think it's so easy, coming to this country like I did, working with my hands like I do? Freedom, where is she? You help me saw this wood!"

This was not a question. It was an order. And so, grasping one of the handles of the big saw, we assisted this ugly customer with the wood while our photographer scurried off and took the pictures we wanted. Our help and our sympathy made little headway, however. As we left the barnyard, only too happily, we heard hot words, colored with expletives, hurled after us:

"Women have to work while the likes of you go around taking pictures of houses. Who the hell cares about houses? You ought to be shot, that's it! You ought to be shot!"

We were glad that only the words were hurled and that the axe slashed deep into the end of the new log.

Who cares about houses? Who cares about forgotten towns? Who cares about legends and folk tales and tradition? We wonder, sometimes. A date, scratched into a stone, meant nothing in Stockingtown.

The old Mathis house of Jersey ironstone at Leeds Point marked Oyster Creek turn.

LEEDS POINT: AN ALMANAC OF 1687

CLOAKING its forgotten importance in a newer settlement along the Oyster Creek, Leeds Point is seldom remembered as the town founded by the author of what is probably the first American almanac.

Today there is an old house, dated 1814, all but hidden in an overgrowth of lilacs and shrubs beyond an empty tavern. It was to this site that Daniel Leeds, of Leeds, England, came with his family after landing at Burlington in the good ship *Shield* in December, 1678. The date, 1814, is probably that of a remodeling of the original construction.

The *Shield*, as nearly everybody knows, was the first ship to ascend the Delaware as far as Burlington. Daniel Leeds married Ann Stacy, daughter of a Burlington tanner, in 1681. Ann died in childbirth not long after and Leeds remarried. In 1683 Daniel and his second bride, Dorothy Young, lived near Jackson, now Jacksonville, not far from Burlington.

In 1682 Leeds became a member of the Assembly, and it is indicated by such records as remain that in 1703 he had become a member of Lord Cornbury's Council. Appointed one of the Councilors of New Jersey in 1704, he had already "located land" in Great Egg Harbor's lowlands, obtaining a long grant after completing the required survey.

Leeds holdings embraced "all the land from James B.

Smith's place, near Smithville, running north to Holly Swamp Creek, to Wigwam Creek, to Mott's Creek, to Duck Creek and thence to Lower Island." Lower Island was also known as Further Island and today is Atlantic City. When Leeds settled on the seashore property, he called it Leeds Point, a strip of land varied by high plateaus then declared among the highest land from the Atlantic Highlands to the Capes of Virginia.

Unquestionably the family had to put up with hardships in this sparsely settled locality. Leeds found time however to serve the colony, becoming the first Surveyor General of West Jersey, or West New Jersey, in which post he was assisted by his son, Bethanah.

In 1687, Leeds began the compilation of almanacs and continued yearly editions until 1716, when two other sons, Felix and Titan, carried on the work. The almanacs were printed by William Bradford in Philadelphia. The little books were subtitled "an almanac for the year of the Christian account 1687"—or whatever year was covered— "particularly respecting the meridian and latitude of Burlington." It seems logical to suppose, from such records as have been handed down, that the publication was Mr. Bradford's first, inasmuch as the copy of a 1687 edition sold for $500 to the New York Historical Society many years ago.

Benjamin Franklin, in his *Poor Richard's Almanac* of 1735 makes mention of Daniel Leeds and another famous figure, Allibone, calling him the first author south of New York. Leeds also wrote *The Book of Wisdom* of which there was but a lone copy a quarter of a century ago.

The Leeds Point of today reveals nothing of this colorful past.

Passing an old schoolhouse, now closed, on the shore road which runs parallel with the coast, we turned in on the Leeds Point Road, passing an old tavern and discovering a house of ancient Jersey stone at the elbow beyond. This was the old Leeds house, unquestionably, but we were interested in the ancient hotel as well.

There are two descriptions of interest in Thomas Gordon's *Gazetteer* of 1834 in this connection. Leeds Point is therein described as a post town of Galloway Township, Gloucester County, containing a tavern and store and some four or five houses. Smithville, a village a mile and a half away that grew up around the mansion of James B. Smith, is listed as another town of the same township and county, with a tavern, store, Methodist meeting-house and ten or twelve dwellings, surrounded by pines near the salt march.

In the passing of a century, Galloway Township has remained. But old Gloucester County, which once stretched from the Delaware River to the sea, has been cut up in subdivisions. Smithville and Leeds Point are now in Atlantic County, which came into existence in 1834.

We paused at the ironstone house, parting the thicket of lilacs to find our way by a small path to the broken porch at the rear. While we were knocking and demanding loudly if anybody was at home, we were hailed by a man in a blue jersey, trousers slung dangerously low on old-fashioned braces, heavy shoes and an ancient, battered hat. He carried a rake over his shoulder and walked with a cane, apparently from a near-by field.

This, we found out, was Jesse Mathis, a man of seventy-one years who had lived sixty-eight of them in the old

Point, as it used to be,
own best by Jesse Mathis,
-one in 1936, when this
raph was taken. A lineal
lant of Daniel Leeds,
of early American al-
and Great John Mathis,
shipbuilder on the Bass
Below, a building said to
en the Leeds Point Hotel.

Now buried in Fort Dix, Cranberry Hall is a village that few remember a[...]
Above, its main street as it never can be seen again. Below is Greenwood, v[...]
also has disappeared, broken mill and all. Warner Hargrove recalled a time v[...]
it was a convenient hideaway for convivial political rallies.

house. Mr. Mathis told us that we'd have to excuse the appearance of the old Leeds house and the yard surrounding it, inasmuch as he had decided long before to leave everything just as his mother left it.

Mr. Mathis knows the history of the old house and appreciates it. He lived there then with Dan Sooy who once owned the hotel at New Gretna and who now "sails and fishes" to his heart's content.

"I tried living alone for a time, after my wife died," Mr. Mathis said, with a tug at his breeches, "—let's see, that must be twenty-one years ago. Then I got Danny to come and live with me. Those are his nets over there, slung on the porch rail."

Mr. Mathis explained that there were two families of Leeds and that he was "someway connected." "That was with the other one," he said. "One side had William and Henry and Jesse. The other had David and Brazilla and Samuel. We're all Quakers—all the way back to Danny Leeds and the first settlers."

We couldn't pin the old chap down to details. He seemed to be one of those to whom one day is as good as another, nothing very interesting, everything in a kind of fog. So we took our leave and went down to the marshes at the edge of Great Bay.

This road, Mr. Mathis said, is an older one than that which leads in to what remains of the old towns today. Here beside a private oyster planting house he operates we were fortunate enough to meet one of the younger Leeds, still engaged in the business best known to his forebears and as proud of his lineage as he ought to be.

This was William Leeds, who now lives in Oceanville.

The Wharton Estate, he said, has title to a strip which reaches out to the shore. William Leeds plants oysters out in Hummock Cove.

"The old hotel," he said, "hasn't been occupied in years. Jess Mathis has had a job renting those houses even for ten dollars a month. There's plenty down here to do but there's plenty of time to do it in. And you've always got the sea and the salt tang of the air to make up for what you don't get."

Near the old Leeds house and on a rise of land dotted with cedar trees is the charred ruin of what was once the Robert Scott mansion. Behind it is a picturesque bungalow, occupied in Summer by Mr. Scott's widow. Mr. Scott, we were told, invented much of the early machinery used in knitting mills. He also dabbled in explosives. On the other side of the road is a rifle range and proving ground where he carried out his experiments close to the sea.

The old Leeds house once served as post office although the mail, when we were there, was delivered from a dwelling farther up the road. Pressing down the trail cut through, according to Mr. Mathis, when he was a boy, we looked over the habitations of the Leeds Point of a modern day. Houses and cabins are box-like, with motorboats playing up and down the creek or tying up at front doorsteps.

Visitors who enjoy raw clams and oysters have a good time at McClain's Store. Mr. McClain sells everything from staples and produce to fishing tackle. Over the boats and boathouses and a sign advertising shedder crabs loom the aerial masts of far-away Tuckerton. Overhead the gulls scream crazily.

In Smithville, the site of the old meeting-house is up the Moss Mill Road which, if you follow it through, will lead you to Amatol and Hammonton. The site itself is marked by a cemetery in which names prominently identified with the seashore settlements are found on the stones—Clarks, Doughtys, Conovers, Higbees, Smiths, and Leeds. Back on the shore road is the newer Emaus Methodist Church, dated 1869.

Jesse Mathis and his friend, Danny Sooy, with the cat they rescued as a kitten from a deep, forbidding well, are quite happy and content, with next to nothing of this world's goods. "The family's well known in Philadelphia and other places," Mr. Mathis said. "They sort of leave me here to myself—and maybe I like that as much as they do."

The whole drowsy humdrum is summed up in the inscription on the Smithville tombstone of Ann Clark, which reads:

"She has done what she could."

Should a respectful "Ho, hum!" be added, would you say?

This was Varmintown's blacksmith shop, operated by the Lincolns.

XVI

COOKSTOWN: COBWEBS AND
HALF-CASTES

Soon after these researches were begun, long before many of the lost backgrounds of other towns were hunted down, it was suggested that a somewhat garish story could be made if we rediscovered a strange colony of blond and red-haired people with dark, yellow and almost white skin, in an out-of-the-way corner of Burlington County.

We hesitated to write about them for a number of reasons. First, while the clan itself seemed to be well known to the folk of Cookstown, New Egypt, and that vicinity, we had never seen the people ourselves. Second, it was indicated that the "white niggers" had a perfectly natural origin with no reason for their comparison to the white Indians of South America, as the man who spoke to us about them chose to believe.

Yet these people, with straw-colored and carroty hair and peculiar color, have cropped up in the small court of the County in a variety of cases which have brought them time and again into undue prominence through the years of more than half a century. Although there has never been anything approximating an organized colony, this group of people has come from and clung to an unnamed settlement not far out of Cookstown.

Here, on the fringe of the pine belt, near the Camp Dix that has seen war-time, ruin, and reclamation in these latter days, they are reputed to be the result of a condition which once caused serious trouble and drawn-out investigations in the backwoods—intermarriages. In former years there were many mixed marriages of whites and blacks in Burlington County.

It is recalled that one of the late Warner Hargrove's favorite stories concerned the disconcerting experience of a traveler, trapped by a storm, who asked shelter at a piney shack, only to find that the owner was a negro and his wife a white woman. We often suspected that the traveler was Warner himself but he never admitted it. He used to give the story point by saying, as he quoted the wife of the anecdote:

"Of course, my people were low-down mad when I married this way but they admitted I done better than my sister. She married a man who wrote pieces for the paper."

Tracing the lineage of this coterie of "lost" souls, one runs across a story that sounds suspiciously like one which is an old chestnut in this and other sections of the State and of the country. It seems there was a certain captain who saw service in the Civil War. Mustered in Burlington County, the officer is said to have divided his attentions between his own people and those of an adopted negro shacktown. Squire Hargrove used to say that he knew the name of the captain and that his people were still prominent in the County.

When we were there, having had no difficulty in finding the shacktown but having more in keeping ourselves from staring at the mysterious combination of red hair, blond hair, brown skin and skin that was freckled and almost white, the majority were laborers. They were and still may be employed by farmers and bog owners. In season they pick blueberries and cranberries and at others they hark back to the habits of their forebears, hunting and fishing in primitive fashion. Most of these people live routine, humdrum lives. Only a few get beyond the neighboring villages or ever expect to. To venture far is to be conspicuous and the cause of trouble.

The fact that most of the families of the clan have been known by the names of either Greenwood or Minney proves the mixed marriage background. It may be that Greenwood was the name of one of shacktown's white visitors and again, it's possible that some of these folk came from Greenwood, a town of which not one brick or joist remains today.

Strange first names matched hair and skin, we found. Old Diademi Minney seems to have held considerable sway in her lifetime, although she is said to have complained that her large family was getting beyond her at the last. One of her daughters, Julia, was said to have married a Greenwood, and, according to the Squire, our guide, figured in a recent court case. Warner sat as judge so the story ought to have some weight.

It appeared from testimony given that Walter Green, a white man, had married Margaret Greenwood, a half caste, and that Margaret had complained to the State Police that Walter was at best an irregular provider for her and their two children. Green informed the Squire that he was perfectly willing to support his family with his $7 weekly wage but he objected to supporting her mother, old Diademi, and Julia, too.

It was brought out that the home of Diademi and Julia had burned down two years before at the climax of a strange rite, akin to voodoo. It was no mere wild party that is certain. Whatever was happening, some of the countrymen outside the shacktown's limits were not sorry to hear the place had gone up in smoke. Julia, called as a witness, said she was white—and she seemed to be, almost. When she said her husband was a Negro and that she had eighteen children "by last count," the poor Squire decided he had heard enough testimony and advised Diademi to find another roof under which to house Julia's brood.

We wondered if some of those we saw knew Julia as their mother. Their features were regular. A few noses were large and flat but most of them were not. Only here and there were there thick negroid lips. Hair that appeared to have been bleached, tresses that was of a beautiful auburn color and fine texture, mingled with the usual ink-black woolly tops.

So, against the background that is Cookstown, these people have moved from cradle to grave. Cookstown is located in North Hanover and New Hanover Townships on the eastern border of the County. Tradition has it that its earliest settler was Daniel Leeds, who located on a tract of 1000 acres on North or Tunis Run some time prior to 1704. Perhaps there is some connection between these black people and that name Tunis, with the stream an African namesake, but we have never been able to establish it. The Leeds farm was later divided into parcels and sold to John and Mary Mills, Richard Kirby and Jacob Andrews.

John, Warren and Jacob Platt, three Cliver brothers, and Jesse Lane were early settlers who left an indelible mark on the affairs of the community, and their names, borne by descendants, are still there. The township of Hanover was set off from Springfield and Chesterfield Townships by letters patent from the King in 1723.

Cookstown, as you will find it today, on the modern road that used to be the main artery to the seashore through Lakewood, before the building of Route 40 that cuts directly through the pinelands, is a peaceful little village going about its chores in much the same manner as it did more than fifty years ago. As you turn on Main Street, you will come upon the house that was occupied by the late General Edward S. Godfrey when we were there. General Godfrey was the man who placed a little white cross on the grave of General George A. Custer after the celebrated massacre.

The General was eighty-eight when we called on him. He had long since retired and had grown reticent about his Indian-fighting days. A stately old man with a flowing white moustache that recalled prairie times, his favorite pastime was debunking many of the stories told about Custer. It required many calls to make him talk, but once he started, one would have to spend the afternoon listening.

General Godfrey denied, with fire in his eyes, that Custer committed suicide rather than face death at the hands of the Sioux. The General said he was with the party that found Custer and his men where they fell. We met Mrs. Godfrey and their son, a physician, but at the sight of a camera, the old Indian campaigner belied his age and speedily retired indoors.

In spite of its name, Cookstown never seems to have been particularly annoyed by too many cooks. The name came to the town which apparently existed without one for the better part of a century. From Leeds, in 1703, the major holdings went to the Mills and Kirbys until 1727 when Richard Kirby established a sawmill. The frame of the original mill dated back to 1732 and, when we were there, served as the structure of the Hendrickson flour and feed mill, still in operation.

William Cook came to the vicinity after families of Andrews, Ivinses, and Middletons directed the village destinies. In 1776 the place became Cook's Mills. John Lane and Ben Rogers, Peter Nevins, Ben Rogers again, Charles Ivins, Joseph Hartshorn, Thomas English, the Keelers, and the Woodwards transferred the original tract to one after another until 1920, when the owner was Reuben Hendrickson.

Up to the time of the establishment of Camp Dix, Cookstown, as it later became known, supported two hotels, three stores, the mill, an impressive-looking railroad station, and a barber shop. Ben Huss kept the one store we visited and had part of the interior set aside as the post office. He said he had tried to quit several times but no one else would have the job. "So I still got it," he said.

A visit to the old mill proved more than interesting. The timbers are those of the old saw mill. From them hung cobwebs which, the miller pointed out, were perhaps a hundred years old themselves. Never had we seen such lacy decorations of time, flecked with the dust of the grinding grain. Dampness from the rush of cedar water over the wheel aided their formation. Whenever an errant breeze entered the dark caverns of the place, an unusual circumstance, odd portions of the clammy webs used to blow down on any inquiring caller.

Until recently, at least, the mill was going on with its ancient wheel and water power just as it always had. We saw the miller's cat which, we heard, was a descendant of several feline generations who called the mill home. Grain was the payment for the grinding more than cash ever was. When a farmer brought a hundred bushels of grain to be ground, or perhaps an even larger quantity, the miller took out ten bushels or a proportionate share. This was his pay and this he retailed to those who wanted flour and had no grain.

Cookstown's railroad station, no longer necessary when the railroad gave up the ghost, was moved to Main Street where it became a refreshment stand and pool parlor until it burned down. Among those who used to come to the village on Saturday nights were those yellow and red-haired dusky "suburbanites" to get what they called their "draw" of provisions from the stores.

Cookstown, with its proximity to these people, always brings to mind the newspaper rumpus of not so long ago when an Episcopal rector residing in Vincentown, recalled as the Rev. Alexander Bostwick, made an attempt to operate, in the manner of a hospital, a retreat for defectives in the pine country. He made money for the support of the project by lectures on the Pineys in New Jersey and parts of Pennsylvania.

About the same time, Squire Hargrove used to say, a woman known as Elizabeth Kite engaged in backwoods investigations and similar philanthropy. The activities of both provided believe-it-or-not stories for the front pages of newspapers over a period of many months. There were many exaggerations, many injustices, and today the barrens and plains have no counterpart in the lurid details the rector and his helpmeet inspired. There seems to have been some sort of a scandal relative to whatever happened to the charitable venture and the money given for the cause.

There are oddities of Piney parlance which once were common to Cookstown and which are heard no more. A supply of provisions for a week or more was always "a draw"—we heard an echo of this one day as we sought some information near the Forked River Mountains: the man we wanted to see was "down to Toms River, drawing his relief." Any kind of apparatus was "a duflicker."

Here a mule kicked "faster than a preacher kin shake hands." Speed was measured "quicker than Hell would scorch a feather." There was once a tasty dish served in the locality known as "fried snowballs" although we have never managed to find anyone who prepared it.

Nick Green—there's another Green for you, to embroider the mystery—was one of Cookstown's unforgettable characters. We looked for him later at Cranberry Hall, the "end of the world." Nick called frequently at the stores, sometimes in company with Indian Ann, the last native of a band once quartered at Indian Mills. In season they would make baskets, drink rum, chop wood, pick huckleberries and cranberries.

One of the stories of Nick Green, told in Cookstown, recalls the day a hotel barkeeper asked how old he was. "Seventy-two," Nick replied, soberly. "You must be older than that," the barman replied. "Look how black your feet are!" There was a general howl and everybody had another drink.

Nick still had the last laugh. "Would you take the last cent a man had, if he asked for a drink of rum?" he asked the man in the apron. "I sure would!" answered the barkeep, with much bravado. "Then give me one," cried Nick, slapping down a copper amid the shouts of the company. It was the old Piney's last cent, sure enough.

XVII

ABE LINCOLN'S KIN NEAR
VARMINTOWN

As WE progressed in our travels in quest of forgotten towns or at least villages whose former importance has been forgotten, it became certain that almost every important event and figure of American history had relation to or background in Southern New Jersey.

Reluctant to leave the borders of the section that comes, in any sense, under southern classification, the neighborhood of Allentown, Imlaystown, and Cream Ridge, we passed a few additional hours there on a new excursion and before long we were examining—

A Quaker Meeting-house attended by the ancestors of Abraham Lincoln.

A blacksmith shop operated for generations by Lincoln's kin.

The Willow Tree, a tavern on an old stage road, visited by General Washington, either just before or just after the Battle of Monmouth.

A memorial stone to relatives of James M. Cox, former Governor of Ohio and once Democratic presidential candidate, as a tribute to their record in the Revolutionary War.

These were the principal stops, of course. In between, traveling through the highest land in Upper Freehold and Millstone Townships, Monmouth County, in a comparatively confined area, we discovered, or rediscovered, many interesting things.

The road which passes through Allentown and Shrewsbury, joining main highways of today at Hightstown, is the Old York Road, a link of the well-known road that continues over in Pennsylvania. In this vicinity, in Colonial times and continuing through 150 years of operation, were several stage stops where passengers spent the night or at least appeased hunger and thirst.

There was the Eggleston, or Egglestown Tavern, the Willow Tree, Stone Tavern, and Burnt Tavern, as well as many others. Of these, the Willow Tree, located at Clarksburg, is perhaps the best preserved. Stone Tavern, still to be found as a crossroads name on modern maps of the State, is a mere pile of stones, having burned down more than six years ago.

Our first stop was in Imlaystown where William Hendrickson, for more than three decades principal of the public school there, became our guide for the day. We had not gone far, in the direction of the Old York Road, when Mr. Hendrickson told his first story, a modern one, with the stately old house of Harry H. Wright as a locale.

Mr. Wright, a Princeton man, lives in the old home of his ancestors. The Winter we were there, during extremely cold weather, a whole army of squirrels came out of the woods and decided to make their temporary home in a large commodious barn on the Wright farm. The chief element of their choice was, of course, the corn inside. When the corn supply had been considerably lowered, Mr. Wright decided to adopt stringent measures, Mr. Hendrickson told us.

The squirrels had taken to a hollow tree when it was decided that the quickest way to solve the whole situation would be to set a fire going at the foot of the tree, either destroying the creatures or smoking them out. There was a weird climax of retribution in the outcome. One of the squirrels, his tail aflame, scrambled out and ran directly to the barn and haymow. The barn was in flames almost at once and, before help could be summoned, burned down.

Mr. Wright's forebears were interested in the operations at Bergen Forge which came to an end when larger and better deposits of ore were found in the neighborhood of Jersey City.

On the way to Stone Tavern, we saw a tiny windswept cemetery, at the top of Covell's Hill, up a wagon lane from the Cox's Corner—Clarksburg Road. This burial ground was established, so the legend goes, when Richard Saltar, grandfather of Deborah Lincon—this is the spelling used in the earlier days—objected to the girl being interred in the graveyard of the Yellow Meeting-house over at Red Valley, in the direction of Cream Ridge.

The name of Lincoln had two distinct spellings before it assumed the one most generally known and associated with the martyr President. There were sections in which it was Linkhorn. In Upper Freehold Township, it had dropped, or had not yet acquired, the extra "l" and so was just plain Lincon. This was the spelling we found on the rough brown field stone on Covell's Hill. Deborah was three when she died in 1720, a great-aunt of Father Abraham, as far as such relationships can be worked out.

We visited the little East Branch Meeting-house, built in 1816, where some of the early Lincolns are said to have attended service. The land on which the meeting-house stands, in the foothills of Atlantic Highlands, with the

Willow Tree, an early tavern in lower Monmouth County, was said to have
there in Revolutionary days. Below, the East Branch meeting-house, near
ished Stone Tavern, not far from a field where Clinton's army camped. By
, it has fallen in ruin.

Tombstones of John Saltar, buried in 1723 behind the Yellow meeting-house, Red Valley, and Deborah Lincon, a niece, buried on the Saltar farm at Cove Hill in 1720.

ridge of the Backbone Hills just beyond, was once part of the land owned by Saltar, a tract of some 1600 acres. The countryside here presents a splendid panorama, far different from any to be seen farther south, with Timmons' Hill, from which messages were once sent by flags and sun-glasses to Ellisdale and on to Philadelphia, from mount to mount. Even the winners of horse races were announced to scattered devotees of the track by this pioneer tele-graph system.

Deborah Lincon's grave, that of a child, was placed at a far, high corner of the Saltar farm and so another ceme-tery came into being, with many of the earliest graves, engraved with the earliest 1700s, marked with field stones. On other stones, some decorated with the sinister skull and cross-bones, are names of pioneers well known all through this section, VanMartens, Clarks, DuBows (DeBows), and Imlays.

The Lincoln background is made up of solid facts. No less a student of the family than Ida M. Tarbell traced the relatives of the Great Emancipator here. The Saltars lived at Buck Horn Manor and it is suggested that the name, Buck Horn, became Buck Hole, when it was given to a tributary of the Doctor's Creek which winds through the valley. Up toward Timmons' Hill there is a spring in which the creek rises and natives of the vicinity will tell you that in the worst droughts the stream has never run dry.

The first Lincolns were established in Massachusetts. Samuel Lincoln, traced back to 1637, one of the many grandsons of Mordecai Lincoln, came from England to New Jersey, where he married Hannah Saltar, daughter of Richard, owner of Buck Horn Manor.

The Yellow Meeting-house, at Red Valley, is interesting and historic, but it has been mentioned in connection with the passing of an early farmer-financed railroad, the Union Transportation Company. The oldest grave there is that of John Saltar, one of old Richard's sons.

Although annual services and other festivities are held at the Yellow Meeting-house, the East Branch Meeting-house has no such activities. We found it easy to get inside, take note of the smell of musty cushions, and see the ancient and rotting woodwork which ought to have been preserved long ago. In the yard of the Yellow Meeting-house are interred General Elisha Lawrence, a Revolutionary notable, and Jonathan Cox, one of ex-Governor Cox's kin, who wrote to his father, as recorded in the stone's inscription: "I have this day joined the Light Horse." Presumably this was his last message home.

The road to the Lincoln blacksmith shop at a place called Varmintown, although we spied no "varmints" there, is easily found. The traveler may take the road to Cream Ridge, turn to the right at a gnarled apple orchard and then to the left at a deep gravel pit. The shop is at the crossroads of the next turn, constructed of huge Jersey ironstones. No one who sees it will doubt its age, close to three centuries.

Half the smithy caved in some years ago. William Oakerson, who lives in the adjacent dwelling, says that most of the stones in the damaged section were broken up to repair the road near by. One of these was said to have had a name and date scratched into it. "But," said Mr. Oakerson, disclaiming any responsibility for its destruction, "it wasn't so as you could read it and so it went along with the rest."

The shop is now a shed and a garage. The bellows and other marks of a smithy are gone. No horseshoeing business has been operated here since twenty years ago when Charley Haley was the last man in charge. Here, though there is nothing left to indicate it, is a Lincoln shrine worthy of the attention of enthusiasts who go about setting such places apart or at least making their history plain to the wanderer.

We will conclude with the story of "Black Diamond" as Mr. Hendrickson told it to us. At the Colonial Farm, not far from Imlaystown, there was, until a few years ago when some unthinking tenant chopped it up, what appeared to be an ordinary stall. It was down in the cellar of the barn, built especially for a stallion, famed around the countryside.

When news came that the British were on their way, the horse was considered a likely prey to the marauders and so was placed in this special stall in the barn. The British came and with them, their horses. "Black Diamond," hearing his English relatives outside, stomped and whinnied. His hiding place was revealed and he was taken prisoner a few moments later. "Black Diamond" went off to the war.

From the graveyard of the Yellow Meeting-house, we obtained this epitaph and placed it in our notes:

> "A mournful scene I here record—
> It was the dealings of the Lord:
> How thus in less than one month's space,
> The father and five of his race,
> One fully grown and 4 under age,
> Were called by Death from off the stage."

XVIII

FROM BREAD AND CHEESE RUN TO APPLE PIE HILL

AN OBSERVANT traveler, taking his way through the bleak woods in November, especially along the tangled and moss-carpeted trails among forgotten towns, must sooner or later acquire something of a philosophic viewpoint.

If he goes down to Retreat, four miles or so out of Vincentown, as we did, he will hear people recall how Charlotte Cushman, one of the most famous actresses of her time, spent vacations there.

If he presses on to South Park, on the trail that carries through miles and miles of desolation to Chatsworth, he may see a small truck marked "Fire Patrol" emblazoned with the red diamonds of the Fifth Division—the carryall of hard-working Albert B. LeDuc, who guards 80,000 acres from forest fires.

If he goes on down to Eagle, beyond Apple Pie Hill, along Bread and Cheese Run, he will find, forgotten among the trees, a line of charred wooden grave-markers, near a lone stone inscribed "Charles Wills—1839."

Weighing these considerations, the traveler will consider them in relation to the information that no one now remembers how Apple Pie Hill and Bread and Cheese Run got their names, still retained on modern maps; that Retreat was once a thriving little town with four mills and fourteen dwellings; that Fire Warden LeDuc remembers his artillery service in the World War and so goes every

Memorial Day to decorate the forgotten grave of a colored soldier; and finally, that nobody recalls much about that cemetery at Eagle except that it was and is consecrated ground.

Contemplating the transient values of so much that many of us hold to be worth while—identity, reputation, accomplishments and this mortal life itself, the lesson seems to be, if we take the traveler's viewpoint, that we put entirely too much emphasis on inconsequential things. Surely among all the weird surroundings that are to be found in villages that were scattered here and now are gone, as well as in the chilling penetration of snow-laden winds across the barrens, there is a mantle of peace and of freedom that one does not sense elsewhere. It is as if, in this very decadence, there is a special kind of release from care.

We heard about the "Lottie" Cushman story at Retreat in an unusual way. Since our journeys began, the study of forge towns and the background of lost New Jersey industries has been belatedly added to the curricula of some public schools. In that connection, John F. Wells, another fire warden, told us how his granddaughter had written an essay in her work at Pemberton High School. And Mr. Wells' recollections had provided material that made the essay an unusual one and Retreat a more important town than it is today or ever will be again.

Going out beyond Vincentown on a sandy road among snake-fences, one arrives in Retreat almost before he knows it. The Wells house is on a corner, at the cross of woods trails. The main one goes through White Horse and South Park, which now are little more than names. The one to the left joins the Buddtown road. If you take the opposite way, you find the going rough but you can struggle through to Chatsworth, in good weather.

We found Mr. Wells a bit shy at first but after a moment or two he agreed to take us across the road to a point opposite a three-story weather-beaten building which, he said, was once the Retreat Store. Now it's used for storage, with the long door at the top, once opened for loading provisions, all boarded up. In a field, a mere pile of pegged lumber, some of it bristling with nails made in the old Retreat blacksmith shop, and surrounded by bricks and Jerseystones, is what is left of the old Cushman house.

This pile of rubble, Mr. Wells said, was once a mansion of some twenty-two rooms, with a fireplace in each of them. It was the chief boarding-house in the village in those early hopeful manufacturing days.

Charlotte Cushman came there before she was famous and later, presumably, when she was managing the old Walnut Street Theatre, in Philadelphia, now given over exclusively to the presentation of Yiddish plays. She returned to Retreat for holidays with her grandparents and other kin. Mrs. Wells said her father and uncle knew Charlotte as Charlotte and "one of the girls."

Charlotte Cushman was born in 1816 and died in 1876. She was a native of Boston, the daughter of a West India merchant who left his family in straitened circumstances, so that Charlotte, who had an unusually fine contralto voice, went on the operatic stage. She made considerable success as the Countess Almaviva in *The Marriage of Figaro* and then, when her singing failed, was an equally memorable Lady Macbeth.

It was in 1842 that she took over the management of the Walnut Street Theatre, appearing in many of the plays she directed. In 1845, and again, ten years later, she appeared in London, winning unusual acclaim. The classic roles she played included Queen Katherine, Meg Merrilees in Scott's *Guy Mannering,* as well as the male roles of Romeo and Cardinal Wolsey. Her last stage appearance was on the boards of the Globe Theatre, in Boston, May 15, 1875.

The name of Lottie Cushman brings up instant associations with the theatre but her connections with little Retreat, in New Jersey, are little known. When she came there the Cushman House was in full operation. There were merry companions at every hand, going by stage from Philadelphia and elsewhere to mingle with the folk who worked in the thread mill, the saw mill and the smaller enterprises huddled about the blacksmith shop.

In the house where Charlotte stayed there was the atmosphere of an old manor. The dignified boardinghouse was amply surrounded by porticos and the rooms, large and with high ceilings, connected with broad halls. There was elegance and charm, despite the wilderness in which it was situated.

The water operating the mills came from a lake which, today, you'll have to look for: the water gates broke through years ago and have not been repaired. Here the amber cedar water comes through Southampton Township by the Friendship Creek, through Bread and Cheese Run, Burr's Mills Branch and Cedar Run to the south branch of the Rancocas.

The lake, when it was full, covered about one hundred acres. Back from the shore were two other large houses, surrounded by imported shrubs. In the present field of Indian grass were the houses of the villagers, larger and much different in appearance from the newer dwellings which have now been built further up the road to maintain a location for Retreat, closer to the cranberry bogs. All that remains of the older town are holes in the ground, grown over by underbrush and moss, or else are mere scatterings of foundation stones. One lone chimney and its fireplace stand like a sentinel in the midst.

The Shreeves operated the thread and hosiery mill, Mr. Wells told us, later moving their interests to Smithville, High Bicycle Town, and still later to Mount Holly when railroad facilities did not come in the direction of Retreat, as had been promised. Since those first hopeful days, the Forest Colony Corporation came to town with new ambitions, laying out streets and making surveys. But that venture failed, too, and until another boom comes along, the old forge once operated by the same owner who had charge at Birmingham, the mills and stoves and stove-lids made at Retreat of Jersey bog iron, sink deeper in the woodland ooze.

We went on to South Park where Mr. LeDuc was waiting for us, or rather, putting in his time by sawing wood. His fire district is certainly one of the most extensive and important in the pinelands. However, despite the breadth of his territory and the alert anxiety he must observe for the breaking out of fires somewhere in that vast stretch of 80,000 acres, he maintains a cheerful mien and a surprising agility for his fifty-seven years. What is more, he knows these back trails, lined with brambles and pine and cedar scrub, like a book—and so he told us why we missed that cemetery near Eagle on previous excursions.

Warden LeDuc did not take us to Eagle immediately. Recalling how well the late Warner Hargrove, our first guide, had spoken of him, we were only too glad to listen to his enthusiastic talk of everything. We had been up Apple Pie Hill before, of course, but his companionship made this journey like a first visit.

The hill is the highest point in Southern New Jersey, two hundred and ten feet above sea level. Mr. LeDuc said that if the woods were cleared and the hill surfaced in packed snow, the impetus given by the slope would carry a bobsled ten miles. The hill is scarred with sharp ravines and on its top is an emergency fire observation tower. From its lookout platform one can see far across the blue haze of the barrens, twenty miles in any direction. On a clear day, the masts of the radio station at Tuckerton are etched against the sky.

The late Dr. William A. White, a New York physician, always contemplated building a sanitarium on the rise of the hill. It is his modern white-painted dwelling in the midst of a cluster of small buildings on the promontory. Down the slope is a small bottling house where Dr. White obtained and circulated a health water under a State license, water Mr. LeDuc said was so pure that it is used in storage batteries of this vicinity—he gave us two dusty bottles of it but thus far we have lacked the courage to try it out. The water came from a well seventy feet deep.

The fate of the hospital, called Pine Crest on the labels of the health water bottles, has been uncertain since Dr. White's death. A key to the place was on Warden LeDuc's large jingling chain but he used it only for those interested in another broken dream of the pine country.

From Apple Pie Hill he led the way to Eagle, across the Jersey Central at Sandy Ridge. There is the evidence of one large dwelling here, on a surprisingly green rise, shuttered in by buttonwoods, trees that don't belong in this area at all and prove that many years ago they were planted there. This was the McCambridge house, the warden said, and it was built of logs. The McCambridges and a family called Wills were the only settlers in the vicinity.

The old fences leading down the hill into pine timber that was worth looking at until the fires choked it out stand forlornly askew. Then down where the fires have crackled through, time and again, Mr. LeDuc found the cemetery for us—you'd hardly call it that, even though a wandering priest came there and hallowed it for all time. Headstones and footstones were never stone at all but pine boards. Today the fires have eaten along the ground to leave them standing on mere spindles.

The one inscribed stone in the line half covered with muck of the years gives authenticity to the legends of habitation there:

"Charles Wills—1839."

XIX

CHIMNEY OF GLASS: HERMANN CITY

Down on the pebbly shore of the Mullica River, not very far from Crowleytown, there is a point designated on present-day maps as Herman. It is difficult to realize that here, but a short distance from where they buried the Revolutionary outlaw, Joe Mulliner, was a town that existed for a bare six months, Hermann City.

The "city" was not a facetious dubbing, for the New York capitalists who financed its founding fully expected a permanent community of impressive proportions. Even so, it was not until the town had gathered together at least sixty or seventy houses, a store and a hotel, clustered about a glass-making plant, that Hermann City came to a standstill in the panic of 1873.

From the road that winds from Hammonton to New Gretna, the site of Hermann City would be no more than a bend in the road, with a large unpainted dwelling off across a clearing on the river side. From the Mullica River, however, there is obvious evidence of an old landing, with the hulks of three ships rotting on the shore and visible when the tide is down.

Two of these were the *Frances* and the *Argo*, tied up and awaiting cargoes of New Jersey glass for shipment to New York. When the town went to pieces, the ships were abandoned to a similar fate.

Working on the principle that navigable rivers of Southern New Jersey were the first roads and that there might be ruins of villages along these streams, unattainable over land because old trails have been lost forever in dense thickets and swamps of pungent cedar water, we took to a boat to approach old settlements on the Mullica. Making a seven-mile "voyage" in *The Flying Dutchman* of Howard Dunphey, and later, in *Sunny of Sweetwater* of Harry Thurston, surprising information came to light.

One of the first buildings noted as we traveled up the carefully marked channel was the only one left to distinguish the site of Hermann City. We beached our boat a few feet from the wrecks of the glass ships and made inquiries at the house. This, we learned, was the old Hermann City Hotel, a structure of some eighteen rooms, now more than a century old. Living there was the Koster family, direct descendants of those who operated it in Hermann City's heyday.

The hotel is surrounded by venerable buttonwoods. Beside it is the ruin of an old spring house, constructed of Jersey stone. Augustus Koster and his family can look out from upstairs windows on a river which once saw much commerce and hoped forlornly for more. They look down on winding paths through a straggly truck patch leading to the bricked kilns and tunnels of the glass plant's furnaces. Of late, many have carried away the stone of the factory for building fireplaces in Summer bungalows.

The glass plant itself, from this angle of approach, proved easily found. A labyrinth of passageways and crumbling brick, it showed a blackened circular space which, according to Leon Koster, who acted as our well-informed schoolboy guide, was the base of the tall stack which fell in 1921, littering the roof of the hotel with bricks. The chimney was blown down for safety's sake

rmann City's glass plant, down the road beyond Batsto, failed in the panic of
73. This picture was taken in 1910, and a glass replica of the chimney remains
the Koster family. Below, the author, with the late Jack Sperry (center) and
e late J. Gearhardt Crate, who accompanied him on early Forgotten Town ex-
ditions, pause at a cemetery near Batsto.

Never having seen a camera before, little Dorothy Dixon was full of wonderm as she posed for us in her father's wagon at the Blue Hole, near Winslow.

Hollis Koster examined the timbers of one of the glass-laden ships abandoned the Mullica River beyond the Koster home at Hermann City.

but the men in charge were not experienced in their task. Sticks of dynamite are often found in the tangle, young Koster told us.

Hermann City was one of two establishments from which sponsors expected great things. The other village was Bulltown, a few miles back in the deer woods where, according to those who live in the neighborhood, a seven-blast furnace was built. Bulltown specialized in making jugs and demijohns.

The captain of the *Argo* died only a few years ago. When, as the ship lay idle off-shore, this gentleman, Otto Wobban, ordered his crew to stop bailing to check a leak, he had apparently viewed the future's store, insofar as Hermann City was concerned. "Cut her up for Gus Koster's icehouse," he ordered. The alternative legend says that Captain Wobban, apprised of a leak in midstream, told his steersman to try for the icehouse and, when the *Argo* sank gently in the mud, left her there.

The *Argo* and the *Frances*, it seems, had anchored in the Mullica for weeks on end, awaiting the glass that never materialized.

One of the principal streets of Hermann City was Skin Row, Leon Koster said. "Nobody knows where the name came from but my father used to say that a skinflint lived at the end of it. There was a family of Fords, too," Leon told us, "and all the Fords down this way go back to those who worked in the glass plant for that little while. They just stayed and stayed like those wrecks out there.

"The town only ran six months, or about that. It was all hopes and plans and preparation—and then, nothing. A railroad was pledged to come through this way from Tuckerton. The fellows who backed the new village knew that boats would not be practical for long. But the railroad went down by Egg Harbor instead and the whole scheme was given up."

Traces of the same tragedy of community-building were found, we remembered, when we visited Little Gloucester and pioneers there told of abandoned tracks in the woods and cars left to rot on the rails because the wrong end of a road that never came through was finished first.

Although it is difficult to believe, Hermann City was once as imposing a town as Hammonton in its first and last days. In 1873, the year of its rise and fall, there was every kind of community activity with everybody happily at work, dreaming of a future that was upheld by ships off shore, glass bottles being made and loaded aboard, and New York financiers itching their palms in expectation of big money.

Grandfather Koster was the only one of the stranded property owners who refused to sell his holdings to Joseph Wharton, once Mayor of Philadelphia, when Wharton was buying up so much of the pinelands for a projected water reservoir that the State has never approved. All that was Hermann City, with the exception of the hotel and adjoining fields, is now a part of the vast Wharton Estate. The present owner of the unpainted stagecoach stop is now employed in the new State Forest Preserve at Green Bank.

It was a somewhat gloomy trip. Those crumbling kilns, those rotting timbers in the mud, a pause in the marshes to examine an oyster boat, the *Freeman*, of Port Norris, that had been stranded high and dry in a storm—all these attested a forgotten Hermann City and the town as it was seemed fated to be known only in imagination.

Then Augusta Koster appeared, carrying a prized possession. This proved to be a glass bottle, molded so as to become a miniature of Hermann City's high point, the stack of the ruined glass factory.

"This was Grandma's," she said, "and she showed it to people who didn't believe there was a Hermann City. That's what I do now."

We told her that we believed everything they had told us, without the glass chimney. We urged her, too, to guard the relic well but we wonder if it has become a collector's item by now.

All along the river are old wharves and landings. From them in yesteryear, went tons of charcoal, as well as glass from Bulltown and Hermann. Now, with Bulltown marked by a clearing and "outlander" trees and Hermann City a bend in the road, glorified by maps without the second "n," it is difficult to understand how time, in such a short interval, can trample history so effectively.

These ruins of an old tavern where Joe Mulliner, Refugee or Revolutionary outlaw, is said to have been caught, have disappeared, and so has the name, Washington Field.

MAYBE A METEOR: THE BLUE HOLE

A STRANGER looked us up one day and asked if we had ever heard of "the Blue Hole." We replied that we had heard people talk of it but no more. He told us it was back of Winslow somewhere but he couldn't put his finger on the spot, exactly.

Not long after that two policemen from Audubon who had been spotting deer told us they had stumbled, quite by accident, on "a blue grotto," filled with clear water to a fathomless depth. But they, too, when they came back, didn't know exactly where they had been and were unable to help with maps or diagrams.

Then Bernard Anlage, of Cramer Hill, Camden, paid us a call. "Did you ever hear," he asked, "of a place called Inskips?" This was the way he spelled it for us when we asked for help. Our reply was in the negative. "I wondered," Mr. Anlage went on. "Well, then, have you ever heard of the mysterious Blue Hole?"

So we were back again, facing the same riddle. But it is a riddle no longer now, at least as far as location is concerned. Our informant was on vacation and offered to go along as a guide.

We set out by way of Berlin, taking the rise of the White Horse Pike overpass and then swinging off to the right through New Freedom. We turned left toward New Brooklyn. Our guide was well known in the neighborhood, having grown up there. We stopped at a farmhouse, asking detailed information.

At the first stop we drew a blank. Although the farmer's wife knew a lot had been said and heard of the Blue Hole, she didn't remember anything very specific except that small boys had been told ominously to stay away from it. It was a bogey of at least a hundred years, she said.

Our next stop was at the hermitage of Joe Dixon. Joe, a large, gaunt, and lumbering man, with a week's growth of beard on his chin, lived in a one-room miniature house, amazingly clean. He was eating his dinner when we put in our appearance. His meal seemed to consist chiefly of bread, which he crumbled nervously as we sought information.

"Joe will remember all about Inskips and the Blue Hole," Mr. Anlage had said, on the way. "He used to tell us boys to stay away from there when we longed to go swimming in the icy cold blue water."

But years had passed and Joe was an old man now. His memory had failed. His hearing was so poor that every question had to be shouted. He seemed to remember the Blue Hole vaguely but beyond that there was nothing. "Don't you remember me?" Mr. Anlage persisted. "Don't you recall how you used to tell us that there was no bottom in the Blue Hole, that the Devil hid there, and that once we touched the quicksand—"

Joe's expression did not change. If he heard, he did not understand, although we managed to persuade him to pose for a picture.

That was more than did his brother, Dave Dixon, who runs a little farm, further up the road. Something happened at Dave's that reminded us of the tale they tell in Chatsworth of the Rt. Rev. Paul Matthews, Episcopal Bishop of New Jersey. When Bishop Matthews, who had

worn only a cassock on previous visits to the Pines, came
down to confirm a class of backwoods children, they saw
him in pontifical vestments for the first time and fled into
the scrub, out of sight. Confirmation had to be set at a later
date. No word of persuasion from the late Father Twing,
missionary of the pines, who had prepared them, would
induce them to come back to the little chapel.

The appearance of our car, driven into the yard of the
Dixon farm, caused two little children, picturesquely
dressed in the mode of at least fifty years before, to hide
behind a chicken coop. Later they grew more courageous
but when their father, Dave, who was seventy-two, de-
clined vehemently to have his picture taken, even his
persuasion, and that of their mother, a much younger
woman, did not reassure them. The boy, when he saw
the camera, scuttled off through a cornfield and could not
be recaptured. The girl, Dorothy, was brought back, after
much persausion, by her mother. It was apparent that the
children, near as they were in miles to paved roads and
buzzing villages, had seen few automobiles and no cameras.

Dave Dixon remembered about the Blue Hole. He recalled that many of his boyhood friends were rescued and
revived after they had dared the hoodoo and sought to
swim across.

"Inskip," he said, "was the name of a sawmill, a rather
large brick house, and several other dwellings on the rise
of the Blue Hole. Inskip was the first name of the man
who lived in the largest house, Inskip Brick. They got to
calling the place Inskip's. The mill was before my time—
and that's a long while ago. They had farmed the land in
the vicinity when I was a boy and it had become quite
a center. Sometimes it was called Inskipsford.

"My father and others warned me and the boys I went around with not to hang around that bottomless pit. They used to say things about cramps but they meant more than that. It was as if there was something about that pool that had them scared, something they didn't want to understand, something that gave them the shakes.

"I remember John I. Brown—maybe it was John Inskips Brown, I don't know—he was a big, heavy-set man. He laughed at their warnings one day and swam out to the middle. Just as he got there he let out a shout. We thought he was fooling, at first—he was a great one to cut up. Then we saw that he was going down for the last time. They managed to fish him out and he came to after they rolled him all over the place and bounced him up and down. He said the devil reached up and got him from deep in the pool."

Thus armed with a few facts, we started off for Inskip, or Inskips, and the devil's puddle. We found it off a side road that cuts to the right through a second growth of oaks on a sandy trail that goes in from Winslow toward Berryland. We picked the wrong path first and then found another that allows the passage of a single car to a rise above the Great Egg Harbor River. Inskip was on the promontory.

For those who know about it, the cedar water here provides a sequestered bathing place. Several women and two children were there, as well as a genial Williamstown man, Charles Downs. Mr. Downs left off swimming for a time to go down to the Blue Hole with us and swim about in the crystal clear pool to prove that the middle, actually, seemed without bottom.

"The legends clinging to the hole have been handed

down for years," Mr. Downs said. "Some boy scouts came here a few years ago and cleaned it out—this bridge is new as are those concrete pipes under the sluice. They managed to give the pool a free outlet for a time but now, as you can see, the flow is sluggish and the Blue Hole as sinister as ever."

There is movement in the Blue Hole, however, as if from innumerable springs welling up through the white sand. Downs said that white sand and cedar water on the surface always provide a bluish color. Stones tossed from the bank seem to change several colors as they drift slowly down out of sight. The pool itself may have been larger years ago when tall pines surrounded it. The trees were cut long ago and there is nothing, after years of forest fires, to recall the old mill.

There are portions of the pool, as Mr. Downs demonstrated, that are icy cold even in Summer, water not to be lingered in on any day. Other spots are contrastingly warm.

"I've been here in Winter," Mr. Anlage said, "when all but those warm spots would be caked with ice. These places never froze over. From the gaps, on some cold days, clouds of steam would rise. Say, there used to be a big pike that hung around down there on the other side for many years. He would never even look at the bait on my hooks when I used to fish here. They tell me he got caught two years ago."

"How long does a pike live?" we asked.

"As long as a carp, sometimes," we were told quickly.

Mr. Anlage said that some years ago a party of scientists visited the Blue Hole, with the purpose of coming back with an explanation for it. They obtained a huge weight and a long line of cable. The weight was dropped in the middle of the pool and it kept going down until all the cable was paid out. More cable was obtained and the same thing happened again. There was no explanation, as far as we have been able to discover.

From the trees along the stream there appeared another delegate to this unofficial congress we were holding. This was George Brown, who told us that he always went fishing when he got tired of trying to sell automobiles in Williamstown. He had two beautiful pike in his basket, to prove that his luck wasn't mere boasting.

"I used to live around Weymouth," he said. "The Blue Hole always gave me the creeps so I usually go down stream toward Bates Mills."

So the mystery of the Blue Hole is still a mystery. Possibly the pool is fed by chalybeate springs, as was the case at Paint Island, near Clarksburg. Perhaps the cavity was caused by some falling meteor, as some folk in the vicinity maintain to this day. Perhaps half the legends are untrue, merely reinforced by half a century of repetition and trimmings. Nevertheless, we found Inskip and located the bottomless pit of Beelzebub.

XXI

WHALING DAYS OF PORTSMOUTH

IF YOU would stump some present-day traveler who thinks he knows his New Jersey, ask him to locate Portsmouth for you. And if you would confuse the boy who won all the geography prizes, ask him to tell you where Cape May's Middletown is located.

Long before the incorporation of Cape May County in 1710, Portsmouth is said to have had its beginnings near Town Bank, that promontory along Delaware Bay where North Cape May is located today, below Fishing Creek.

Middletown's case is easier. Its present name is Cape May Court House.

There are some quaint paragraphs in the *Gazetteer* of 1833 which, incidentally, does not mention Portsmouth at all. Thomas Gordon, writing more than a century ago, said:

This portion of the State has not generally been holden in due estimation. If its inhabitants be not numerous, they are generally as independent as any others in the State and enjoy as abundantly the comforts of life. They are hospitable, and respectable for the propriety of their manners and are blessed, usually, with excellent health. Until lately they have known little, practically, of those necessary evils of social life, the physician and the lawyer. Morse assures us that their women possessed the power not only of sweetening life, but of defending and prolonging it, being competent to cure most of the diseases which attack it. We learn, however, that their practice in the latter particular has lately been contested: that one or more physicians have crept in, but we rejoice to hear that they find little employment. We learn also that in the County, like Ireland, refusing nourishment to noxious animals, no lawyer can subsist in it.

The picture of doctors "creeping in" like thieves of the night, and the reference to lawyers, dismissing them as a sort of vermin, must have had some reflection in the experience of the historian. Such attitudes have no part in the Cape May of today. Physicians aid the curative benefits of salt air and legal experts wrestle with criminal complications and public scandals. Perhaps Gordon's experience, even so long ago, was similar to ours, in that he found experts of local history stern guardians of the legends of old, resentful of outsiders prying into locked cupboards of ancient lore.

Cape May County, described by the same Mr. Gordon, began "at the mouth of a small creek on the west side of Stipson's Island, called Jecak Creek, as high as the tide floweth; then along the bounds (of what was then Salem and is now Cumberland County) to the southernmost branch of the Great Egg Harbour River; thence down the same river to the sea; thence along the seacoast to Delaware Bay, and so up the same bay to a place of beginning." Stipson's Island was described as "a neck of fast land extending into the marshes" about three miles long—on this island came into being and, to some extent, has already disappeared, the fashionable seaside resort that was a favorite resting place of Presidents.

There are many old stories about Cape May County which have become so tattered in the telling that one is hard pressed to divide fact and fable. It has been, through the years, a favorite hunting ground for those collectors whose discerning eyes seize upon Indian relics, arrowheads, hatchets, stone pestles, and bits of pottery. King Nummy, potentate of Indians who roamed the vicinity before the early whaling days, has been the subject of schoolboy essays in the neighborhood for many years. Pictures have been drawn showing what the King's village, Nummytown, was supposed to have looked like.

It is well known, of course, that if the proper spelling had been retained, the county and resort would boast the name of "Mey," not "May." For it was Cornelius Jacobse Mey, a navigator of the Dutch West India Company, who visited Delaware Bay and the shores adjoining it in 1623, for purposes of colonization. But whatever settlements there were in these and later days went without record and vanished without trace.

It was in 1630 that a purchase of land extending along the bay for sixteen miles was made of King Nummy and his associates of the Lenni Lenapes. This purchase was made by the Dutch governor of New Amsterdam, Van Twiller, acting for the Sieurs Goodyn and Blomaert, directors of the West India Company. No colonists are supposed to have made permanent settlement as a result of the sale, however.

The first settlers to establish themselves at Town Bank were from Connecticut, coming down from New Haven, just as the good folk over at Fairfield, now Fairton, came riding horseback from the county of the same name there. The seat of justice was still known as Middletown 100 years ago, boasting a frame courthouse, brick fireproof offices, and a stone prison. The early colonial charm of Middletown has been preserved in Cape May Court House today, with many of the first buildings maintained intact . . . but this story concerns Town Bank, or old Portsmouth, of which there is neither stick nor stone.

The first inhabitants along the bay were engaged in a whale fishery, later on in cutting timber and cordwood. "At Cape Island," says Gordon, "a considerable revenue is derived from the company who visit the seashore during the hot weather." It may be that bathing in the sea, a practice received with much surprise by those who first witnessed and wrote about it, began at Cape May Island and on the upper coast in the vicinity of Point Pleasant, at about the same time.

Cape May Island is described as "a much frequented watering place, the season of which commences about the first of July and continues until the middle of August or first of September"—this was prior to 1832. "There are six boarding houses," the early chronicler says, "three of which are very large; the sea bathing is convenient and excellent, the beach affords pleasant drives, and there is excellent fishing in the adjacent waters." As an after-thought he concludes "There is a post-office here."

Town Bank is "marked" today by a growth of trees which have come up among the larger, or Paradise elms, as we were told to call them. These larger trees have been rudely hacked off or burned by shell-fire, for this was a proving ground for the Bethlehem Steel Company during the World War. High explosive projectiles were shot along the bay, northerly, toward Fishing Creek.

We had the good fortune to meet Nathan Sheppard, a deep-chested and weather-beaten native of the Cape, when we went down on one of several quests for information. For twenty-six years Nathan had been carrying the rural mail, angling for drumfish, watching the sea and remembering old times.

"Sure, they used to fish for whales," said Captain Sheppard, waxing loquacious. "Why, there used to be a couple of big whalebones around here in the bushes. There was another one down the beach a ways but I guess somebody must have picked it up."

Back of one of the bungalows Sheppard owns, we saw the ruins of a building which was once a mansion-like boarding-house, or hotel. Its chimney was the last to come down. The street beyond this building was an ancient racetrack which, even in these days, can be traced almost all the way around. "They were using that track all of two hundred years ago," declared Captain Sheppard, but perhaps he thought he was commenting on the size of a fish.

Captain Sheppard's prize possession proved to be a blueprint of a map made in 1726, showing the houses in Portsmouth or Town Bank, and naming their owners. The dwellings shown are those of Dr. Daniel Coxe, for whom Coxe Hall Creek is named; Elizabeth Newton, William Simpkins, Nathaniel Foster, Ebenezer Newton, and others. In the midst stood a Town Hall. Mill Island, with its mill plainly shown, is next to the name of Jeremiah Basse, whose property transfer is noted with the date, 1685, with the new owner, Abigail Pine. Ephraim Bancroft obtained title to a parcel in 1695, the map shows, plainly identifying such places of lost significance as the New England Town Bridge, the John Crawford Estate of 1699, and the New England Creek.

The names of settlers and places trace their origin to Connecticut and elsewhere in New England. In his years on the Cape, Captain Sheppard has picked up articles for a private museum in the manner of countless residents of the County. He has a frying pan with a ten-foot handle, an old-fashioned griddle, a teakettle, and a small boiler with legs. These remained buried in the sand after Portsmouth disappeared. Now there are stumps, charred and ugly, where Town Bank knew a stately grove. Tangles of honeysuckle have pushed their way everywhere and scores of land-turtles come wandering over the roads in such profusion as to provide a traffic menace for drivers who seek to avoid tortoiside.

Portsmouth bloomed and failed long before the first bathing resorts were thought of. Although real estate brokers have taken us to task for our observations, we must say that the passage of the years in these lower seaside settlements has taken such toll that unless a miracle happens, there will be new material for such interests as ours twenty years from now.

Cape May has ever been an old-fashioned resort. Its patronage has mainly been of a fashionable class that prefers quiet and segregated charm to crowds and modern excitement. Perhaps Summer makes up for Winter's appearances but Cape May seems to retain a lonely mien. The abandoned sand engine and half-sunken concrete boat, out at the Point, a boardwalk constantly battered and continually repaired, the huge Admiral Hotel in which navy officers were quartered during the War, and the Corinthian Yacht Club, now a boys' camp held together with jerry-built alterations, all give the vicinity a lost appearance.

The yacht club was designed by the architect who later created the Admiral Hotel. It was part of the E. C. Knight Estate, which also has in its charge historic Congress Hall, a pioneer hostelry, and Knight Park, in Collingswood. Parts of the track of the Pennsylvania Railroad have been torn up as a result of the Reading merger. Only the Reading track remains all the way through. If it were possible for the past of the Cape to move forward just a bit, those middle days of glory would sink back to meet them—days when shingles were "mined" from the submerged timberland of yesterday, days when great ships were built at Goshen and Dennis's Creek and Mays Landing, days when Dr. Coxe, of Coxe Hall, experimented with manorial government.

The seas sweep in on flood tides each year, putting layer upon layer of muck on the hidden timber in the marshes, carrying away whole sections of the beach. Drumfish slide up the bay where once were whales. Captain Sheppard continues to pore over his map, with a sly dig at historians who say that Portsmouth was here or there, that there wasn't any Portsmouth and that it was New England Town.

"They think they know a lot," he told us. "They think they're getting some place by locking up what they know, as if only Cape people cared for what the Cape used to be. They think they're smart, some of 'em, laughing at what I find on the beach and what I say about old pots and pans and the like. The laugh's on them, that's what it is.

"This bay shore didn't used to be like this. Lots of these here marshes used to be solid land. You want to know where Portsmouth is, see what's left of Town Bank? Well, my friends, get ready for a dive into the briny. Portsmouth, Old New England Town, Town Bank or whatever you want to call it, was out there in the bay. There was a cemetery between the town and here and that has gone, too. Maybe this was somewheres on the edge of it but what was the village has been crumbling off into the shoals these forty year, to my knowledge—and long ahead of that if them that were here were livin' to tell about it. Yes, sir!"

XXII

DOG CORNER, ALLIGATOR RIDGE
AND BEDBUG HILL

FORERUNNERS of American gangsters, terrorists of Revolution and post-Revolution days, the Refugees or Pine Robbers infested the hills and sandy wastes of Southern and Central New Jersey, leaving memories and mementoes behind them that remain in our midst today.

Although there are many who believe that the Refugees were stragglers whose depredations were magnified by time and tradition, we struck out one day in search of proof that all such nondescripts, glorified in some New Jersey folk lore, were not playboys or practical jokers, proof that some were actual desperadoes with more than legends to remember them by.

We have referred to some of the stories that have rise in the career of Joe Mulliner and proof in his grave. Joe was one of the least offensive of the hoodlums but he paid with his life for the nefarious conduct of his companions when the defenders of law and order had to make an example of somebody. But our rediscovery of Fagan's Cave comes under a different classification.

We had heard there was a cave and that Fagan, another of the Refugees, had been described as "a monster of wickedness." Any traveler, with time and patience to spare, can see the cave for himself, even now, and imagine how safe the pine robbers were when they retreated to such a hideaway. There can be no doubt of its history for, in this case, we had the good fortune to find the great-grandson of the farmer who, with his wife, were held up by the wild rovers of the plains.

The Pine Robber country included most of the barrens in Ocean County—then part of Monmouth County—down as far as Cedar Bridge or just beyond, and up through the rolling hills south of Freehold in Monmouth County itself. Nowadays the names of crossings and points of interest are as colorful as the exploits of those gangsters of long ago.

In reaching the vicinity of Farmingdale and Ardena, where, on the farm of George Patterson, the Fagan cave is located, we spanned the Alligator Ridge and turning at Dog Corner, continued beyond Rattlesnake Crossing, looking off toward Bedbug Hill.

It was customary for the robbers to carve caves out of the sandy slopes in secluded situations, covered by scrub and brush so as to be almost indiscernible. Fagan's cave is just so located, despite the passage of more than a century and a half, for when we had gone down the path leading to the retreat, we found that someone had stalked a deer with a bag of feed there, had skinned the creature and had taken most of the meat, along with the head. Mr. Patterson said he knew that there were poachers in the neighborhood and that wanderers were always to be seen on the cave mount—but the find was as much of a surprise to him as it was to us, although the Patterson farm is close at hand.

In olden times these miscreants used to steal out from their caves at dead of night, plundering, burning, and murdering in cold blood. Those who lived in this area of New Jersey in that day carried their muskets wherever they went. So numerous and so daring did the Refugees become that the State offered inviting rewards for them, dead or alive. Toward the closing years of the Revolution, they saw their heyday but with the return of patriots from army service, militias and volunteer posses were formed and the marauders were gradually stamped out.

The most notorious of the robbers were Fenton, Fagan, Burke, Williams, DuBow or DeBow, and West. Fenton was a blacksmith and learned his trade in the County seat. Once he robbed a tailor shop in Howell Township, through which our search for the cave led us, and word was sent to him that if he did not return the pilfered clothing, he would be hunted down and shot. He returned the loot, but also a note, reading:

"I have returned your damned rags. In a short time
I am coming to burn your barns and houses, and
roast you all like a pack of kittens."

It was in August, 1779, that Fenton and his gang attacked at midnight the dwelling of Thomas Farr, near Imlaystown. Farr and his wife were in their seventies. However, with the aid of a daughter who was with them, the couple barricaded the door. The robbers tried first to batter down the barrier with fence rails. Not succeeding at once, they fired a volley through the woodwork and one of the balls broke Mr. Farr's leg.

Then forcing an entrance, they murdered Mrs. Farr and despatched her husband as he lay helpless. The daughter, badly wounded, escaped to the swamps.

Fenton was finally hunted down and shot at Blue Ball, now Adelphia. He and Burke had robbed a young chap known as VanMater as he took some meal to what may have been the DeBow Mill. VanMater escaped, took the information to Lee's Legion, formed to fight the Refugees, and a party started off in pursuit, using a low wagon. VanMater drove the wagon, with a sergeant and two soldiers under a tarpaulin.

As the wagon passed a pine groggery, Fenton came out and told VanMater that he thought the beating already given him would have taught him a lesson to keep off the roads. VanMater replied that he had forgotten all about that and asked Fenton if he would like a drink. Just as Fenton placed a foot on the wheel hub to imbide from the proffered bottle, the two soldiers revealed themselves. The desperado was shot through the head at close range and his brains dashed all over the side of the wagon. There is no record of the part the sergeant played in the affray.

Burke, who had been awaiting a signal from Fenton, heard the shooting and thought the volley the sound he had been looking for. He discharged his own weapon in response. However, he escaped when he learned what had happened.

Back at Freehold Courthouse the body of Fenton was pulled from the wagon by its heels and tossed in a clearing "with the ferocious exclamation: Here is a cordial for your Tories and wood-robbers!"

Jonathan West was another of the colorful thieves. Once when caught in a skirmish with orderly house-holders of the area, he was wounded and taken as a prisoner to the Courthouse, his arm so badly mangled that it had to be amputated. Later West returned, on parole, and almost at once resumed his old pursuits, becoming adept in using a gun with that stump of an arm. He was pursued again and given a chance to surrender. Refusing, he was shot down.

Fagan, whose cave we found, was killed in Shrewsbury by a party of militiamen led by Major Benjamin Dennis. Fagan, Burke and Smith had gone to the home of Major Dennis, on the south side of the Manasquan River near Howell Mill, to steal plunder already captured from a British ship. Smith had joined in with the others for purposes of spying on them and arranging their capture.

Frustrated in an attempt to get eighty dollars concealed in a bedtick, the Refugees first declared that they would kill Mrs. Dennis and then, instead, strung her up to a young cedar with a bed-cord. The woman struggled and managed to get free just as a wagon's approach shifted the robbers' attention. The bandits fled and Major Dennis moved to Shrewsbury next day.

Advised of the fact, the robbers planned to rob his new place of abode. Smith informed the Dennises, there was an ambush arranged and Fagan was so badly wounded that he died after crawling into the woods.

Fagan's body was found by soldiers and decently buried. However, it did not remain in its grave. Just as in Joe Mulliner's case, feeling among residents of the section ran so high that they assembled, dug up the corpse, heaped indignities upon it and then, wrapping it in a tarred cloth, suspended it in chains from a chestnut tree about a mile from Colt's Neck. Rocked to and fro by the high winds, the cadaver finally fell prey to buzzards and tumbled, bone by bone, to the ground.

The skull was afterwards fastened to a tree, a pipe

jammed into its mouth and the exhibit left as a horrible warning to any surviving robbers who might come that way.

The fate of Burke seems doubtful. It is certain that one of the surviving robbers took vengeance on Major Dennis and killed him as he was traveling one day from Coryel's Ferry to Shrewsbury. The Major's widow was a sturdy sort for in addition to her harrowing adventures with the Refugees, she was knocked down and left for dead by a party of Hessians in a later encounter. She survived to marry a second husband, John Lambert, Acting Governor of New Jersey in 1802.

The open country used by the Pine Robbers is much the same today as it was then. Dense scrub covers the sand hills and conceals the pine trails that run through them. We found Fagan's cave after we had struck up a bargain with Miss Barklow, the school teacher at Georgia. When we were there, we wrote the last lines of a playlet about the Great Stone Face for Miss Barklow's motivation of the story and in return she sent us to a guide.

The guide admitted that although he had heard a great deal about the Refugee cave, he had never seen it himself. He took us on the road back of the Georgia School to another rural school building called Fort Plains, thence to Dog Corner and off on another overgrown trail. Asking the village blacksmith for added directions, we learned only that the cave was supposed to be on George Patterson's farm. The smith had heard of the cave all his life, he told us, but "never got around to finding time to see it."

We passed the farm with the windmill, somehow—the smith said we couldn't miss the windmill—and found the wrong George Patterson, in Ardena. It was the wrong Patterson who gave us specific directions on how to find the right one. Meanwhile we had seen a number of farms linked with Revolutionary days, we had passed the ancient "Our House" Tavern in Ardena, and had put the Harmony Methodist Church down in the overflowing notebook. Nearly every house in this area is a burnished white.

Farmer Patterson's barn is red, however. On it has been painted an eagle and two flags, with the inscription, "Fagan Cave Farm." Here it was that in Colonial war days, Patterson's great-grandmother dropped a silver dollar in a dye-pot she was using, to deceive the robbers of Fagan who raided the farm.

Mr. Patterson led us up a wood road along field fences to the rise around the cave. It is a dismal forbidding place. Down at the bottom, marked by stumps of huge trees which were part of a grove once shielding the place, is the site of the cave itself, the hideaway to which Refugee bands retired, time and again, with perfect safety and concealment.

The farmer's great-grandfather owned 3000 acres, of which the Patterson farm is a remnant.

"I'm bothered all the time by people who want to dig for the treasure they say Fagan buried up here," Mr. Patterson told us. "You can see that the place is all dug up—for lots of them sneak in without permission. If any treasure was ever found by any of them, nobody told me. I had a man up here a while ago with a contraption he said would find the hidden money. He tried the rig out but whatever happened, he never came back.

"Personally, I'd like to sell the place to some rich fellow

who wants to play around looking for the treasure. The place has been handed down for generations but I'm not going to be here much longer. I've got a son and a daughter —and they're good children, too!—but I'm seventy-seven now, and just a little tired."

Shaking his head as we put new questions concerning that raid of the Refugees on this very farmhouse down the hill, the farmer, chuckling to himself, turned his back and went off, limping in search of a milk pail. "Time for milking," he said, and that was his good-bye.

Near Winslow, or Winslow Junction, as it became in days when there were many excursion trains to resorts of the lower beaches, John Sampson showed the bell that summoned glass blowers and others to their varied tasks. Early Jersey bells were rung for fires, church services, work hours, seven days a week.

XXIII

CASPAR WISTAR AND WISTARBURGH

IN THE rolling country of Salem County, where barren fields of brown and yellow spread beneath the feeble warmth of a Winter sun, we paused beside a small, insignificant cross-roads. Far in the distance was the hazy blue of woodland patches on the horizon, with snake fences and lines of brambles wandering down hill toward Cool Run and the head waters of the Alloways Creek.

A country wagon trail climbs down at the other side of the surfaced roadway, rutted and picturesque. Across from the rough and hardened field that seemed to be hollowed with unexpected cavities, there is a farmhouse and before it is a mail box bearing the name of Marich. Foreign, you say, and should you doubt the hasty diagnosis, a woman may appear, as she did the day we were there, a woman in mannish denim among a lowing herd, restless at milking time beside none too comely barns and outbuildings.

Here, more than 200 years ago, on the Alloway-Daretown Road, was once a thriving town, founded by foreigners intent on an industry that gave it distinction in the new world. This was the site of Wistarburgh, earliest of the successful glass-making villages of the Colonies, political football in days when pioneers were building toward a nation's independence. Here where we saw cows crowding together was the "glass house" itself.

If you should come here armed with a spade you could

dig a few inches beneath the surface and find glass fragments, indisputable evidence of the exact location. And if you examine the stones and bricks of the Marich farmhouse closely, you will observe that they were collected from some earlier structure, surely the foundations of the Wistar manor house which once commanded the promontory. Otherwise you may find it difficult to believe that this was Wistarburgh; the Biblical axiom of "ashes to ashes and dust to dust" is visibly proven.

Wistarburgh was founded by Casper Wistar, whose glassware in authentic preservation is to be found but rarely, nowadays. There is but one piece of Wistar-ware, they told us, in the Metropolitan Museum of New York, despite the avid claims of collectors in sundry places. Wistar purchased the land that was to rear his famous establishment from Clement Hall, a tract of about 100 acres two miles from Alloway and six from Salem.

Wistar came to America in 1717, a native of Heidelburg, Germany, the son of Johannes Casper Wistar, electoral huntsman of the Duchy of Beden. Following his arrival in Philadelphia, Wistar worked variously for a few years and in 1725 became a member of the Society of Friends. Shortly after, he married a young Quakeress in Germantown, Catherine Janson, and two years later a son, Richard, was born to them—a son who was to have a part in his father's glass-making dream which grew and flourished through forty-one years. It was not until 1780 that conditions compelled Richard to close the enterprise.

With the rise of the Colonies there came a natural demand for table and glass ware. It was in 1738 that quantities of sandy soil favorable to the manufacture of glass was discovered in country described as lining the highway connecting Salem and Pilesgrove. It is also noted about the same time that the Alloways Creek—then spelled "Aloes"—was navigable as far as Thompson's Bridge, a cross-roads village nearer Salem, which today bears the more compact name of Alloway.

Wistar made an agreement with James Marshall, a sea captain, to transport to Philadelphia, for the sum of fifty-eight pounds, eight shillings, four experienced glassmakers. These men took ship at Rotterdam and through the years a controversy has waxed and waned as to whether the emigrants were Belgians, Germans, or Dutchmen. At any rate, Wistar, having worked hard to finance his under-taking, worked most efficiently in carrying out his prepara-tions. He signed the four experts, Casper Halter, John Halter, John Wentzell and Simon Greismeyer, to show and use their glassmaking formulas, with all expenses, liv-ing, servants and conveniences, cheerfully paid.

Whatever those original four were, Walloons or Flemish or what have you, they set to work for Wistar who, with the actually beginning of his operations, became known as "Casper, the Palatine." Just as one wonders how much the sea captain, Marshall, knew about the Marshalls of Marshallville, one reflects on the village of Palatine, not far off, in this connection. Such a reference to the famous glassmaking pioneer is made in records bearing the date of 1740 and it is supposed that the business was highly profit-able at this time.

The success of the enterprise, however, was chiefly in-dicated in papers and incidents of the day and in the political machinations which preceded the complacent years of colonization under the rule of England. Much attention seems to have been paid Wistarburgh by collectors of His Majesty's customs and even Benjamin Franklin himself was a party to the campaign of misinformation carried on in the mother country.

Franklin, in writing to his son, William, then a Governor of New Jersey, advised that the King should be told little or nothing of the glass operations, taking the attitude that what His Majesty didn't know wouldn't hurt him. Specifically Ben advised that reports to the Crown should state briefly that a Glass House was progressing, making coarse window glass and bottles but adding that "duty fine glass" could still be imported profitably from home. In 1768, this propaganda belied the real situation and it is not too much to imagine that Wistarburgh's success was kept under cover from overseas agents.

The bustle and activity of the Glass House, however, had built a goodly community, with a large plant in operation every day and with shallops carrying its products down the creek from Thompson's Bridge and beyond. Workmen's houses stretched along the road as far as the eye could see.

Advertisements in newspapers of the day were full of the news of runaways, bound-out boys and men who had fled from "Mr. Wistar's Glass House." Young women of Philadelphia and the vicinity who disappeared, apparently in the company of young Germans in blue coats with metal buttons, were reported to have eloped with employes of the establishment. Many of these runaways founded many of the glass towns of Southern New Jersey with varying success.

It must have been about 1760 that the enterprise saw its zenith. Then, from old Salem County, there poured a constant stream of flasks, demijohns, sweetmeat and pre-

is log cabin, not far from Wistarburgh, pioneer glass-making village, was the
ter of many arguments before it fell down—age, authenticity, almost every-
ig. Below, Joseph Sickler, of Salem, told me about his great grandfather
gler, co-worker of Caspar Wistar, and showed me some rare Wistarburgh glass.

Swedesboro, once New Jersey's center for bear meat and since then celebra[ted] for sweet potatoes, tomatoes, and other garden produce, was one of the ea[rly] Swedish settlements in the state and first was known as Raccoon. Here Tri[nity] Church, standing high over Raccoon Creek, where Swedish Lutherans buil[t] in 1784, became the stronghold of Episcopalians shortly after. It has a fine colo[nial] interior, and the church still uses Communion plate bought by the Swedes in 1[...]

serve jars, spice jars, mustard pots, snuff canisters, medicine phials, tubes and globes, in such colors as light green, golden amber, opaque white, and smoky brown.

We had as our guide to the site of old Wistarburgh Mr. Joseph Sickler, historian, author and postmaster of Salem. It is doubtful if, without his help, we could have found the place. Surely there was nothing then to indicate that any town, let alone such an important one, was ever here at what seems to be just another turn in the road. But Mr. Sickler, armed with such data as he had gathered in his own investigating, as well as family connections with the Wistar place, moved about, pointing to such evidence as could be found, with unquestioned authority.

It was Mr. Sickler's great-grandfather, Theodewald Ziegler, who became one of Wistar's trusted employes. The name, you see, was Ziegler then. Later, for reasons which must have been practical, Theodewald became David and Ziegler Sickler. Sickler it has remained to this day.

Another family identified with the rise of Wistarburgh were the Laurentzes. It was in the Laurentz house that the first Roman Catholic mass was said in Salem County, the Jesuits coming there under the George II interdiction.

As has already been pointed out, Thompson's Bridge has become the town of Alloway. Thompson was one of Wistar's managers and it is thought that with the closing down of the Wistar establishment, he moved up the road, took over the inn and gathered around him some of those who did not wish to remain on the site of a blighted town. Others say that Thompson's Bridge was in existence before the Wistarburgh debacle. It may be that Thompson managed the plant and ran the inn on the side.

We paused to look at the inn at Alloway, a building that has become somewhat the worse for wear. It has had its gay times and its feastings, its nights of hilarity when stagecoach guests were passing through and its nocturnal disturbances through the better part of two centuries. It was here that our guide told us a story that developed a controversy linked with the final part of our Salem journey.

It seems that Alloway, in 1861, was alive with "Copperheads," according to the legend that is disputed. Even those who felt strongly in accord with the South and the Secessionists were to be found there, Mr. Sickler said. Dr. John R. Sickler, the postmaster's grandfather, undertook to address a "Copperhead" rally at the inn in 1861 and was pursued out the back door by some infuriated negroes. There are other residents who will tell you that negroes were not welcome at the time anywhere in that vicinity.

Along the line of travel we had been inquiring concerning an old forgotten cemetery which, according to information supplied us by some hunters, was in this immediate neighborhood. Passing homeward through Fenwick, now a colored community that honors the name of Salem's pioneer, we asked questions at farmhouses and received a variety of replies.

From one dusky belle we were directed to "a man who knew all about cemeteries." From this gentleman, who seemed to have been interrupted in the midst of a convivial celebration, we were directed to at least four "lost" graveyards. On our own, we found such a place, but even now we are not sure it was the one we sought.

In a tangled mass, back from the gravel trail that once

was celebrated as the Salem Road, it is a motley assortment of graves, many decorated with tattered flags, some indicative of digging as if bodies had been transferred elsewhere. On the many stones, to be observed at all sorts of drunken angles, we saw that soldiers were interred here, their rank prefixing an abbreviation that is interpreted differently.

"U.S.C.T."—what does it mean? We came to a stone whose lettering we read in the combined light of a pocket torch and the rising moon, there among the shadowy cedars, sticker-vines and cavernous excavations. The military man's allegiance was proclaimed in full: "United States Confederate Troops." Perhaps these men enlisted from Alloway and at last, were buried apart, as veterans who fought for a questionable cause. Others, as we have recorded elsewhere, declared the initials mean "United States Colored Troops" but we have our doubts. Perhaps the South is not the only section of the country still fighting the Civil War.

And so you have a choice—the kind of oblivion that is now the inn's, a shabby mien that hides ragged memories; the soldiers, with faded flags now and then waving across an enigmatic inscription disputed by false patriots, or that of Wistarburgh, with nothing but bracing air, the melancholy bark of a dog and a farmer in his barnyard to solve the mystery of "conditions" that dropped a sudden pall on progress. Surely Wistarburgh's, with a few scattered specimens of early American glass for epitaph, is preferable.

XXIV

HERMIT OF HUNTER'S LODGE

HUNTER'S LODGE hardly merits the name of a town. The best classification to which it ever attained was "a place." But for all that, Hunter's Lodge, between Brown's Mills and the abandoned rifle range of Camp Dix, has had a singularly colorful history, antedating the Civil War.

Discovering it, or rediscovering it—whichever you choose—involved all sorts of surprising things, an unintended and unexpected visit to the rifle range of war-time, over wind-swept acres of white sand now cleaned up by a C.C.C. encampment; the passing of a road gang, glistening with sweat,—and refreshment in a Wrightstown café operated by a captain who, after soldiering, served sandwiches, and the rest.

In the unofficial Who's Who of Southern New Jersey, the name of Black has more than ordinary prominence. From the founding of East and West Jersey, the Blacks have been linked with important developments of history and progress. Many members of the Black family still are prominently identified here and there and many, too, are living in or near old homesteads of yesteryear.

Somewhere in the vicinity of 1850 two brothers named Black, John and Thomas, became the first dwellers in that little clearing on the lake shore which became Hunter's Lodge. They were wealthy, for in those days, and years that followed after, a man did not have to acquire a cold million to give him financial standing. The Black brothers were men of medium height, of stocky build and according to the recollection of a few, bore a marked resemblance to the Smith Brothers of cough drop fame.

The Blacks were devout members of the Society of Friends. Their lives were as regular as a well-oiled clock and to them the eerie silence of the woods was angelic music of paradise. John and Tommy, as they were called by those who frequented the backwoods trails in those days, purchased about five hundred acres in a tract of virgin forest divided over the line of New Hanover and Pemberton Townships in Burlington County. Here, in the midst of their woodsy hideaway they erected a log cabin as their home and called it Hunter's Lodge.

Just what the two brothers did to pass their time, or just why they chose such a primeval life, keeping to themselves almost entirely, making occasional journeys to town only when provisions were needed—all this is one with the enigmatical uncertainty of the country. And, with the same lack of show or warning that marked their appearance, the Blacks disappeared one day and in their stead was a caretaker, William E. Corey.

Mr. Corey soon became as familiar a figure to the cabin and the lake in front of it as the Black brothers had been. He was soon known as "Bill" to all who chanced that way. It was whispered that Bill had been a colonel in the Civil War and that he had high family connections. And, it was said by those who dealt in gossip, Bill's wife was well-to-do and something of a society personage in Philadelphia. Bill had tried, the gossips said, to spend his wife's money too quickly and so had been cast adrift.

All that was known was that Bill Corey was now at the lodge where the Blacks had been. He had left another life behind him and he never referred to it. He had been a soldier? Yes, but why bring that up? This was Hunter's Lodge, he was caretaker, and no questions asked, if you please. And with his establishment, Hunter's Lodge became a different place.

While in the days of the Blacks it had been a woodland shrine of solitude, it now became a center for whoopee of the Victoria era. For the most part, Bill made it such. He meant to live, perhaps, the life which his people had forbidden him—laughter, life, and plenty to drink. Even so, Bill was an educated man and ingenious as well.

He soon labeled the lake before his cabin as "The Dead Sea," with a sign in large letters.

In the same manner the stream which still feeds the lake became "The River Jordan."

The fruit and vegetable garden which soon were blossoming and bearing, despite the barren country around it became "The Garden of Eden."

The well was placarded as "Rebecca's Well." The sign on the spring house and fruit cellar was "Where Lazarus Dined On Snapper Soup." An ordinary ladder was soon glorified as "Jacob's Ladder." One particular work of art was a board, fastened between twin oaks, over which was nailed the inscription, "The Old Bachelors' and Old Maids' Courtship Seat."

Bill Corey's sign fancies faded and were revived from time to time. He was a dog fancier, too. He had so many dogs that some were always being born while others were dying. As fast as they died Bill buried them in a carefully planned rustic cemetery. Little graves were made with a headboard for each, on which Bill painted an appropriate rhyme. Bill always had dogs for sale.

When the animals didn't die fast enough to suit him, Bill provided yawning graves so that he could exercise some sudden inspiration for an epitaph.

Bill began writing for the newspapers. His style was as unusual as his ideas, it is recalled, and soon, subtly invited by the hermit's airy description of his lodge, many persons were presenting visitors' cards. Callers called again. Parties were arranged. Writers, malcontents, society men and politicians began gathering beside "The Dead Sea" to smoke, play cards, lose money, and sip rib-rocking applejack.

Here in the woods there were no troublesome spies. Bill asked no questions and gave no answers. These visitors could get away from the lives they had to live to please society with no fear of tattling. But there was one understanding, one unwritten law for such gatherings and that was: No Women. In all the stories we have heard of Hunter's Lodge, there is no mention of coy feminine smiles, rustling skirts, or a Dorothy known temporarily as Sue. There was wine and there was song but there were no women.

Snapper soup well flavored with sherry was the dish that made Hunter's Lodge famous. Poker was the chief indoor and outdoor sport. Warner Hargrove recalled that at one time the ground of the little clearing was virtually covered with bills, as the stakes ran high.

Gunning parties were organized and guns were toted to the scene. Few were ever fired. That was so much camouflage. There were too many other things to do at Hunter's Lodge. There was too much laughter, too many good stories, too many jugs in the cellar. Hunters got used to coming home with explanations as to how the deer that were sighted got away.

Long tables were erected for banquets and card games.
There were gay political jamborees. The best blood of
Burlington County attended. Let not the descendants of
Pop Williams, Brazilla Shreve, Gus Grobler, Bert Seeds,
Al Seeds, Ivy and William Lippincott, John Antrim,
Thomas Early, John Lemmon, John and Henry Irick,
Mart Haines, Charlie Joyce, and Andrew Fort think their
ancestors were criticized for attending the festivities at
Hunter's Lodge.

Things went on for years at such a pace and then Bill
Corey became ill. He was taken away one day, unsmiling
and with eyes closed on the many signs he had tacked up,
to the Old Soldiers' Home at Kearney, where he died in
1885. The property was sold. Some of the timber was
cut away. Bungalows were built here and there through
the near-by woods.

But the ghost of the hermit, Bill Corey, came back not
so long ago. They say he did a lot of wandering and a
great deal more mumbling, through several visitations.
Probably he didn't like the fact that his signs had been
taken down and that "The Red Sea" had become "Fallen
Leaf Lake."

Few will admit that they have actually seen the
phantom.

"But I've heard him, for nights on end," said Joseph G.
Browning, of Moorestown, who was the occupant of
Hunter's Lodge when we were there last. "He seems to
be looking for something. If he wants something, I wish
he'd find it. If I only knew what it was, I'd give it to him
so he could give me a little peace."

Mr. Browning showed us the quaint interior of the

house and a desk which, he declared, had as much history as the lodge itself.

But no one, to this day, has been able to tell us how Bill Corey came to be there and where the Black brothers went so mysteriously.

Much has changed on the old rifle range at Camp Dix since we saw it then, deserted, forlorn, forgetful of the days when it prepared an army for fighting overseas. Makeshift sand platforms were distinguishable but trenches and mounds made like shell-holes were falling away. One range butt was still in condition with its numbers and greased elevators intact. Behind the butts were pictures clipped from "art" magazines and pasted on the cement.

Gerhardt Crate was with us on the trip. He was much interested in the Number Five on the rifle range.

"I was in Dix three weeks," he said, reminiscently. "But I was out here only once. I fired five shots and was picked for the next entrainment of men for France. Afterwards they told me I had made two bull's-eyes and three fours on the clip. I always wanted to see what the camp was like and now I never will."

XXV

SWEDES BEYOND SWEDESBORO:
NEW STOCKHOLM

MENTION Swedes in New Jersey to ever so many people
and they'll say, "Oh, yes, Swedesboro." Then they'll tell
you about the town, how it was founded by Swedes, how
it used to be spelled Swedesborough and how, from either
of the roads that follow the turnings of the Raccoon
Creek, you can see the houses from far away, clustered
around the spire of Trinity Church.

They may tell you that over a hundred years ago there
were more than a hundred houses, that a gentleman by the
name of C. C. Stratton, Esq., operated a woolen factory
that's disappeared, that once there was a fine academy and
finally, that you can call the Raccoon Creek the Narriticon, if you like. But they won't go any farther than that,
for the most part, and they certainly won't tell you much
about New Stockholm. And that's not very thorough, or
thoughtful of them, either, for Swedesboro couldn't have
come into being until long after New Stockholm had
disappeared.

The trouble is that no one knows a great deal about
New Stockholm. The nearest community today to where
it was located is Bridgeport, a town, which, if we were
content to accept the opinions of some who live there, is
chiefly celebrated as the home of the Chester-Bridgeport
ferry. And although such an estimate of the past and present may not be fair, it has a prophetic aspect: Bridgeport

isn't at all what once it was and, with its new ferry road down to the very point the Swedes called The Landing Place, it is doubtful if yesterday's importance will be reclaimed.

The old road to the ferry turned sharply at the drawbridge, extending inland along the bank of the Raccoon and veering obliquely toward the slips for boats bound across the Delaware where the Swedes once rowed to church in Pennsylvania. The new road turns traffic to the right almost as soon as it attains the village, or else hurries it through from seashore resorts, and little of Bridgeport can be seen at all.

Insofar as we could determine, for there's nothing at all to celebrate the fact, the new highway passes directly through what once was the New Stockholm Plantation, a tract of six hundred ninety acres which has been also referred to as "The Town Lands of New Stockholm." Both old and new roads are alike in that they reach the river shore along the line of a town site set up by the Swedes at least three hundred years ago.

We went to Bridgeport in the hope of discovering something handed down about New Stockholm and, at least, finding out why Mr. Gordon made no reference to Bridgeport in his century-old Gazetteer. Solution of such a puzzle has often come in the discovery that in Gordon's time the town in question was known by some different name. Not so with Bridgeport.

First we accosted a policeman at the crossing of the new road. A man with a badge is often good for something more than odd means of confusing uncertain wanderers. "Was Bridgeport always Bridgeport?" He said that it was. We told him of our old books and maps, pointing out that Bridgeport appeared on neither. "There must be something wrong with them," he said. "All the oldtimers say that Bridgeport was always here."

Much of Bridgeport would confirm such a conclusion. There's an old stone house down by the creek that used to be an inn; now it serves as a dwelling. There's another old tavern across the road, although it's a little of everything except a hotel now. On the main street itself are several buildings and a Methodist Protestant Church, closed and falling into ruin. The bell in the church tower hasn't rung since the Armistice.

Down the stumbling trail that passes the stone house, we found some sheds on the creek bank and a couple of small river freighters. These, owned by the Wright brothers who also own the stone tavern, were tied up at the littered wharf for repairs.

"Bridgeport?" snorted one of the bystanders. "Always *was* Bridgeport. New Stockholm? Never heard of it!"

And so we explained where the Swedes were supposed to have laid out their town, down by the river shore where the walkable ground plunges off in reeds and marshy hummocks. "They's been farms out there for years," objected one of the men. "One's been known as the John Cadwallader place for hundreds of years. Then there's the old Lawrence property—used to be called the Raccoon Island farm; Andrew Hitzelberger had it—or was that the other one? Maybe that was the Peter Carey place, I don't know for sure. I live on the island farm—only there ain't no island since the channel filled in. But Bridgeport was always Bridgeport."

We let him have it so. We did tell him that some of those names he had mentioned reached back into the past, perhaps with a Swedish connection. "Bet they knew where New Stockholm was," we said. "Why, there was an island then of appreciable size." And there was. The inner channel was used by ships plying the Delaware when skippers avoided the long bend of the river. "Sure," chirped another bystander, "my grand-daddy used to tell about that. He used to sail through." But the speaker was more interested in some Indian relics picked up in the neighborhood, hastily recovered from aboard one of the boats and dumped from a rusty tobacco tin.

Bridgeport, we discovered later, was a name adopted after travelers referred to the point, for many years, as Raccoon Lower Bridge. It was just a ferry crossing, with houses going up around the two or three tavern stops. And in spite of the seeming lack of interest on the part of those we happened to see, the best authority on New Stockholm used to live in Bridgeport—a Camden lawyer, Samuel H. Richards, who became properly excited when, in clearing a property title or two, he came upon deeds plainly indicating the whereabouts of the lost Swedish colony.

Much has been written and much more will be said of what happened when the Swedes went to the other side of the Delaware, but as far back as 1842, Isaac L. Mulford, an authority on history, referred to New Stockholm, on the Jersey shore, as "our Delaware Plymouth."

New Stockholm was a ferry crossing in earliest days. Writing an introduction to Mr. Richards' little pamphlet regarding chance and painstaking discoveries, Frank H. Stewart declared that up to 1704, with the establishment of the Swedish church in Swedesboro, Swedish settlers had to row to Wilmington for service. Mr. Stewart pointed out that in a law suit of 1687 one Andrew Robeson brought action against Lacy Hooman, giving his address as New Stockholme, and his birthplace as Clonmell, Ireland, a name he undoubtedly bestowed on the creek that lies opposite Tinicum Island.

Burlington's Samuel Smith, writing in 1765, was one of the few writers who must have spent some time finding out what he could about the earliest settlers from Sweden. He recounted the arrival, in 1677, of the good ship, *Kent*, with two hundred and thirty passengers from London and Yorkshire, who disembarked at the mouth of the Raccoon. These pioneers made use of what was left of New Stockholm before moving up to Peter Jegou's Dutch settlement near Burlington two months later. The Swedes for the most part had either moved across the river or inland to Swedesboro.

Basing his enthusiasm on the two deeds he discovered, one under date of 1702 conveying land by metes and bounds designated as "a certain tract of land or plantation called New Stockholme," Mr. Richards made undisputed location of the forgotten colony. As he has said, the very name, New Stockholme, says a great deal. "Named for their capital in Sweden," he declared, "it requires little imagination to vision the plans and purposes of those who established the settlement."

There are records to prove the plans and purposes. Where imagination is required is in picturing, back of Bridgeport, a fort and early town where the land slopes down to lowlands, where a gnarled and decaying tree stabs at the sky from a rise surrounded by stagnant water, where long lines of automobiles, heading to or from the South, compete for places of vantage on wide ferry decks.

It was Peter Minuit who led the first expedition to the mouth of the Delaware in March, 1638. Some say he had been commissioned to use his own good judgment in selecting a place for a town, to build a fort and to fire a cannon as part of the ceremony in which the place would be named New Stockholm. Old Peter came up the Delaware for provisions, according to the writer of an old Dutch book and, instead of going on his way to the West Indies, went ashore and built a fort. Minuit's Journal could have settled the point but unfortunately it was lost, with its owner, off the Island of St. Christopher on the next trip homeward.

The Dutch author says that Governor Kieft, who succeeded Van Twiller in New York, told Minuit he didn't like that business of making believe he wanted food and setting up a fort while he obtained it. Kieft wrote a letter under date of May 6, 1638, saying that the Dutch had been possessors for years, had built forts up and down the Delaware and had carried on operations whose evidence must defeat all possible argument. However, Campanius disputes such a view, charging that either Kieft was ill-informed or he exaggerated. The Swedes, he wrote, had bought title to holdings in the area from the Dutch as far back as 1631.

There have been rumors, of course, that the Swedes were on the New Jersey side of the Delaware at an earlier time, perhaps between 1627 and 1631. But even the redoubtable Mr. Gordon expressed a preference to believe that writers who were credible in this regard took the will for the deed. The plan for colonizing the Delaware had been talked up to, and by, Gustavus Adolphus but that Prince fell at Lutzen in 1632 in the German war. It took the ministers of his daughter, Christina, some years to get around to such ideas again.

Viewing the success of the Dutch West India Company with more than ordinary interest, the Swedes began dreaming of projects that would extend through Africa, Asia, and America. William Usseling, a Hollander and an agent for the Dutch company, had prevailed on Gustavus to take stock in his reports on prospects for a Delaware colony and these reports, extensive and highly colored by a man looking for a job, are what made some early historians conclude that Swedish adventurers had arrived previously. "The South Company" was formed but it stayed at home till the wars were over.

Gordon is conclusive in his declaration that no European interests set foot on the Delaware shores between 1633 and 1637, the period of Swedish reconstruction, "unless, during the time, Sir Edward Ploeyden commenced his ephemeral palatinate of New Albion." Here again the name of Palatine and Albion on modern maps will start many to wondering. But the Dutch paid visits to Delaware Bay, anchoring their ships and trading with such Indians as came down the river from the vicinity of Fort Nassau, the Gloucester of today. Many who know Gloucester would prefer that something of Fort Nassau be dug up from wherever it has vanished.

By 1640 emigrants were leaving Sweden by the boatload for the Delaware shores. Old Swedish documents have been quoted to show that Captain Jacob Powelson, among others, brought several quotas, well equipped to found more permanently what Gordon calls New Sweden. But something had happened since the time, in 1637 or 1638, when "an expedition, consisting of the *Key of Cal-*

man, a ship of war, and a transport named the *Bird Grip*, carrying a clergyman, an engineer and many settlers, with provisions and merchandise for trade with the Indians" landed under Peter Minuit's command.

Minuit liked the Jersey shore. John Printz, a colonel of cavalry in Swedish service appointed to succeed the drowned commander in 1642, "had different ideas" when he arrived a year later, as Mr. Richards says. It seems very likely that Minuit's charges looked over the western shore first and then took refuge on the banks of the Raccoon, where they set up New Stockholm. They called one place Paradise Point but that was not because it looked like the promised land. They were probably glad to see land of any kind. John Printz declared for the paradise of what today is on the Delaware and Pennsylvania side and that is why New Stockholm may be overlooked in the celebrations over the way.

Printz set up his capital on Tinicum Island. Accompanied by John Campanius—this was in 1643—he directed the anchoring of the ship, *Fame*, and her transport, *The Swan*, off Tennekong, the old name of Tinicum. Later he built New Gottenburg fort, erected a church and curried favor with the Indians who were pleased to remember the friendly terms of Minuit's old agreement. The Indians liked everything but the church services. They couldn't understand how large groups of people listened to one man talk so long without refreshment.

Long before Printz left Sweden it was common knowledge that an English group had established itself on the eastern Delaware shore, "sixty persons having settled near Oitsessing, Assamohocking, Hog or Salem creek"—you read your maps and took your choice of names in those days, too!—"at the close of the year 1640, who were, probably, pioneers of Sir Edward Ploeyden, or squatters from the colony of New Haven. The Swedes," the narrative further declares, "purchased all the lands from Cape May to Narriticon or Raccoon Creek, for the purpose of bringing the English under their dominion. Printz was instructed to either attach them to the Swedish interests or to procure their removal without violence."

Printz didn't do what he was told. He and the Dutch joined forces to oust the English and as a result of the squabble there came into existence Fort Elftsburg, or Elfsborg, known today as a point below Salem dotted by summer bungalows, and also recalled in the name of Elsinboro Township, Salem County. Unless it is the Swedesboro women's pronunciation of Narriticon as "Narra-ty-kon," there is nothing quite so picturesque as the language used to describe how occupants of the fort were driven out by mosquitoes, just as insect hordes have driven us back from some of our most inviting undertakings.

"All authors agree," Mr. Gordon says, "that the Swedes were driven out by an invincible, and sometimes invisible, foe,—that the moschettoes, in countless hosts, alike incomparable for activity and perseverance, obtained exclusive possession of the fort, and that the discomfited Swedes, bathed even in the ill-gotten blood of their enemies, were compelled to abandon the post, which, in honor of the victors, received the name of Moschettoesburg."

When the *Kent* sailed from England, loaded with those Yorkshiremen and Londoners, she passed by Salem and landed her pilgrims at what had been New Stockholm. Considering that there wasn't must left of the Swedish town and that the newcomers lived in cow-stalls, caves, and a tent made from the *Kent's* sails for two months, it might be well to inquire why they passed up John Fenwick's town. That is Salem's story and fairly well known. Fenwick had been manipulating finances so as to fool Edward Billing's creditors and had been scolded by no less than William Penn for his schemes. Avoiding the law courts, as Quakers do whenever possible, Fenwick's title to the land around Salem was somewhat clouded and the Englishmen passed it up.

They had three other landings to choose from, New Stockholm, the Indian town of Gloucester, and Jegou's Dutch settlement near Burlington. Two months must have persuaded them that they had guessed wrong, for not long after the *Kent* set sail for London, the good folk were moving inland along the Raccoon or up along the Delaware shore toward the Rancocas. Names in that party of Englishmen are well known today along the Delaware. But of them all we have always found interest in that of William Woodmancy, who is recalled today in a lonely pinewoods station on the Jersey Central.

Today, except for the names on old parchment and in scattered cemeteries in and around Bridgeport and Swedesboro, New Stockholm has vanished. Few, even those on the scene, will believe such things happened just around the corner, down the ferry road. Old Trinity Church, in Swedesboro, the little Moravian church down the road out of Swedesboro toward the Seven Stars Tavern, the King's Highway that runs through Haddonfield, Westville, Woodbury, and Mickleton to Swedesboro—these must do their share to recall the strivings of Swedes of Peter Minuit's day.

Near the site of the Moravian church, now the property

of the Episcopal Diocese of New Jersey, was an earlier log church, dedicated in 1749 by Bishop A. G. Spangenburg. The present church, delightful in its quiet crossroads setting, was begun in 1768 and completed three years later when it was dedicated by Bishop Ettwein. Conveyance to the Episcopal Diocese came in 1836 but in recent years only occasional services have been held, usually meetings of an historical nature.

In the graveyard, where the weeds are usually cut in time for visiting delegations, are Shutes, Gills, Woods, Vannemans, an Appling, a Linmark, and a Crawford, with dates varying through the middle and late 1700s. Few of the Swedes' descendants buried here lived beyond middle life and many stones are at the head and foot of graves of little children. Perhaps their kin know who they were and how they traveled across the old Quaker Road, connecting with the King's Highway, from Mickleton, past Solomon's Graveyard and over Moss Causeway to The Landing Place.

When we were there last, some unknown "archaeologists" had discovered what they must have concluded was an Indian mound, or burial place, for in elaborate diggings they had uncovered innumerable relics, we were informed. We found the excavations deserted. Tramping the fields where no monument but a ferry road exists, we emulated the English colonists who dug down and found Swedish coin and hatchets long after Fort Christina was a myth.

We found, as those directing the operations had done, the broken stems of deep-bowled clay pipes, possibly Dutch, more probably Swedish.

XXVI

SHINPLASTERS: CHEW TOWN'S MONEY

PEOPLE from Panama living down the old Batsto Stage Road at Chew Town.

Persimmon trees from Texas thriving at Iron Mills.

A gentle black cow grazing among the ruins of the stagecoach inn that once provided a chapel, paneled in walnut.

These were but a few of the observations we noted on an excursion to Chew Town, arranged as a result of letters that followed an earlier book. We were informed, in no uncertain terms, that in passing through Chew Town and Pestletown, on journeys beyond, we had missed much that would prove unusual. And our informants were quite right.

"I have read of your travels with much interest," wrote Mr. J. Melvin Chambers, of Elm, "and when I read about West Mills, Pestletown, Spring Garden and Bates Mills, they reminded me of Iron Mills and Chew Town.

"Chew Town is one of the old stage roads running between Waterford Works and Batsto. There was an inn there where the stage stopped to change horses and passengers to refresh themselves. And there was a cemetery where Civil War veterans were buried, I think."

Previously, after visiting West Mills, we had doubled back on the old stage road as far as the Jersey Central, turning to the left along the track on what we were assured in all seriousness was the Whoopee Road, from which we swerved into Pestletown. Iron Mills, surprisingly enough, is still marked on automobile maps, even though there's nothing there now to give it away.

The way is over the high spindley bridge which crosses the shore-bound railroad tracks back of the Spring Garden Hotel. Taking a narrow trail to the right, we drove close to the plantation house of a large cranberry bog and found out that Iron Mills was far at the end of the straggling path. This meant prayers for no traffic—otherwise, one of us would have had to do some backing.

In our pocket was another letter, as well as a crude map, provided by Mr. H. K. Bodine, of Pennsauken, a descendant of the glass-making Bodines of Squankum and Marshall's Mills. The map traced the way to Pestletown and beyond, to Iron Mills, but the letter said that only a sluiceway would indicate the forgotten town's site.

The day we went there was sunny. The undergrowth, through the woodland patches, with its rich reds and golden yellows, contrasted the crisp brown of the oaks, the mottled green and yellow of the maples and the silken saffron of the field grass. A car can be driven all the way through to the railroad, at the edge of a field where some industrious soul has planted raspberries and other canes, but from here expeditioners must go through afoot.

The undertaking is worth while only for those who enjoy such wandering, no matter what turns up to reward the search. There are one or two overgrown but distinguishable trails through the woods on the other side of the track where the sluiceway meanders on. We found the sluice and a canal that cuts through a patch of bramble-choked woods and a mound that must have been the site of the mill itself but we were compelled to turn back without finding the juncture of the canal and the Albertson Branch of the river. A swamp will now defeat any approach in this direction for years to come.

We walked back the two miles to the parking place, a circle around a large maple tree, and set off again along the tracks to a crossing marked by a sign, "Chew." Turning to the right here in the direction of the concrete highway into Atsion, we sought information at one or two houses but found them deserted, abandoned, apparently, for some time. At a third house, also unoccupied, a weather-beaten note was tacked to the door. Someone had reminded the owner, should he return, that he expected to collect two dollars on sight.

Then we drove up to the house of Mr. and Mrs. John Fink, formerly of Panama, and now the guardians of what is left of Chew Town. The Fink house, also occupied by the family of Robert Cleghorn, is known as the Fruitdale Farm. Before it was repaired with composition shingles, it still bore the outlines of one of the more imposing Chew houses. Mr. Fink had suffered two strokes, they told us. So much of the land has not been cultivated in years, he said wistfully. He said he yearned constantly for a return to Panama.

It was a brother of Mrs. Fink who planted the persimmon trees at Iron Mills and she told us they were doing quite well. In front of the Fink home was a broad maple which, we were told, is one of the oldest in this whole area—a native who died recently at eighty-seven said the tree was a century old when he was a young man. Mrs. Fink proudly boasted that she is a second cousin of the late Mrs. McKinley, wife of the president. Her grandfather was a judge in Cumberland County, Pennsylvania, for years, she said, living in Carlisle. No doubt we would have heard more family history if we had lingered longer there.

Chew Town was the settlement of Contine Chew, whose grave we found in a cluster of stone in the enclosed Chew's Graveyard, in which nearly all the markers bear the family name. Endres and Moss seem to have been names equally well known in the vanished village. Down the road from the burial plot is the site of the inn—today just a heap of stones. The taproom, the chapel with walnut paneling, the elegance of an oldtime roadside hostelry, all are reduced to a scattering of meaningless foundations. The inn burned down fifteen years ago. Now, with stones from the ruins, Stephen Rusnak has built a home for his family.

Mrs. Rusnak, no more than thirty when we were there, browned by work in the fields and wearing a man's blue dungarees, came out of the lean-to that was temporarily serving as home. Four years before that, she said, Mr. Rusnak had bought forty-two acres including the site of the inn for $1100, and since then, a living had meant a daily battle against adversity. Unable to obtain a loan, apparently because he was a stranger in Chew Town and its vicinity, Rusnak was working on the cranberry bogs in the hope of gaining money for his own place by Spring.

When the Rusnaks reopened the well of the inn they found the water beyond description. "More than a dozen skunks had been trapped and had died inside," Mrs. Rusnak told us. "It is work, work, work. I am very tired. There is no town here no more."

And she was right. Just as the stage road itself has lost significance, the whole of Chew Town has lost its identity. Once in a long while there is something to recall attention—as when Mrs. Fink saw to it that Legion men and boy scouts gave old Charles Leary, a Civil War veteran, a military burial in the Chew plot.

We thought of Mr. Rusnak and wondered about him. At least he was working in times when the bog owners couldn't pay him in bog currency, as they used to do. The glass-making towns thrived on the practice, too, until comparatively recently, paying workers in "shinnies," good only at the bog or glassworks stores. "Shinnies" was the term used to describe little home-made coins that were used, possibly a mixture of "shillings" and "pennies." The paper bills used were called "shin-plasters" and Mr. Bodine showed us examples of both.

Mr. Bodine also showed us, in his collection, an old deed, "a tri-partite indenture" dated August 30, 1774, bearing the names of Thomas Gage, John Tyng, William Kneeland, and John Varnum. It assigns to the heirs of John Alford, of the Massachusetts Bay Colony "portion of the Squankum Settlements," land now somewhere between Williamstown and Chew Town. Three Bodine brothers, John, William and Alfred, sons of Joel Bodine, of Wading River, went to Squankum in 1839 and operated a glass-plant there.

Bog town and glass village currency lost out when the National Bank System came into full operation after the Civil War, with a ten per cent levy on all such private monies.

J. A. Thompson, of South Westville, another who wrote a letter to us, later showed us a chest, made from pine cut in the vicinity of the New Brooklyn of today, and dated 1626. Mr. Thompson, who used to haul sand from Cross Keys to the glass houses at Marshall's Mills and

Squankum, said the chest was that of his great-great-grandfather, passing from Abraham Park to Jacob Park to Leara Park and thus to his daughter, who is Mrs. Thompson. In the chest there was a secret compartment which did not reveal itself until a few years ago when Mr. Thompson began comparing outside measurements with dimensions inside. Inside he found a silver dollar, dated 1787, he told us proudly.

"It was all wrapped in flannel," Mr. Thompson said. "I should have left it where I found it. I carried it around for a pocket piece and then it disappeared. Whoever has it now doesn't know that it saw a Chew Town that will never come back, a Squankum that has nothing at all in common with Williamstown, and a Wading River when big wooden ships were being built in the river there."

This giant oak was celebrated for miles around when Chesterfield was Recklesstown.

XXVII

RECKLESSTOWN AND FOOLTOWN

WHEN CHESTERFIELD was Recklesstown and George-town was Fooltown, Sykesville was Plattsburg and Wrightstown, Penny Hill.

Thus when an earnest Forgotten Towns hunter sets out to locate lost villages of long ago, he is first confronted by a scramble of "new" names, provided half a century or more ago.

It makes no difference that the reckless aspect of Reck-lesstown derived its significance from a man's name and not from foolhardy characteristics. Nor does it seem to matter that Fooltown gained such distinction from a first citizen who was fool enough to start a house almost two hundred years back without enough money to finish it.

Although it might be said that some confusion could arise from a Plattsburg in New Jersey and another in New York, Penny Hill is surely more picturesque, if more penurious in sound, than Wrightstown. However, al-though Recklesstown ceased to exist as such all of forty years ago, there is a crossroads sign not far from Borden-town, plainly indicating the direction and mileage. If you take it seriously, as we did, carefully measuring distances, you will arrive, in some bewilderment, at Chesterfield. The conclusion is, as inquiry will authenticate, that Reck-lesstown is no more and that the new name of Chester-field was found suitable since the village is the geographical center of Chesterfield Township, Burlington County.

Fooltown became Georgetown and Plattsburg Sykesville at the same time. George Sykes, a bachelor who had
been both school teacher and surveyor, was elected to
Congress. When the establishment of post offices was
brought to his attention, he agreed that Fooltown didn't
sound at all dignified.

Since postal authorities have always objected to dupli-
cations of names in the same State and since many towns
have changed their names in order to get post offices, it is
reasonable to believe, as some have told us, that an attempt to avoid duplication with the New York town was
also made. Congressman Sykes solved the puzzle in one
action. He gave his own first name to Fooltown so that it
became, and now remains, Georgetown. He donated his
last name to Plattsburg so that it became Sykesville.

"Nothing simpler than that," said Thomas W. Ridgeway, of Chesterfield, when he told us about the queer
shifting of names, talking reminiscently in his little woodworking shop. Why Wrightstown preferred dropping its
earlier name, Penny Hill, he wasn't certain. "I don't know
why Black Horse became Columbus, either," he said.
"Somebody just had ideas, I guess."

Descriptions from the New Jersey *Gazetteer* of 1834
offer helpful information for comparisons. Here they are:

"Recklesstown, post town of Chesterfield t-ship, Burlington co., 12 miles N.E. of Mount Holly, 5 S.E. of
Bordentown, 11 from Trenton, and 177 from Washington Capital; contains a tavern, store and 10 or 12
dwellings, in a very fertile country of sand loam."

Georgetown is listed by its present name, indicating
that Fooltown may have been an ancient nickname and

that the more dignified title was used even when it was not official. The description reads:

"Georgetown, hamlet of Mansfield t-ship, Burlington co., near the N.E. boundary line, 6 miles S.E. from Bordentown and 9 N.E. from Mount Holly."

Wrightstown had abandoned "Penny Hill" in 1834 and is described as having two taverns, two stores, a Methodist Church, and some fifteen or twenty dwellings. Its taverns, one of which was operated by the father of Detective Chief Ellis Parker at one time, were put out of business by the establishment of Camp Dix in war-time, for the law forbade operation of such establishments within set boundaries of military camps. The whiskey served in Wrightstown was as potent, they say, as Penny Hill was picturesque.

Columbus, described one hundred years ago, was said to contain a tavern, a store and about thirty dwellings. Recklesstown and Bordentown are the only "villages" listed in the Chesterfield Township of those times, with assets described as follows: "Population in 1830, 2386; 75 singlemen, 1030 neat cattle, 510 horses above 3 years old; 10 stores, 1 saw mill, 2 grist mills, 40 tan vats, 6 distilleries for cider, 2 coaches and chariots, 3 phaetons and chaises, 7 four-horse stages, 10 two-horse stages, 41 dearborns, 58 covered wagons, 8 chairs and curricles, 17 gigs and sulkies, paying a state tax of $1216.32 and a township tax of $1000."

This township description is interesting from many angles, the careful record kept of articles tending to show progress and good business prospects, as well as the loss, today, of many colorful terms for means of transportation.

The neighborhood of Georgetown and Chesterfield is attractive today because of its well-kept and profitable farms and, too, its fine examples of unspoiled Colonial architecture. We had seen some of these fine old houses, with their chimney dates in the 1740s and 1750s, and our requests for recollections and information on the area brought a letter from Miss Kate Sitgreaves, of Pemberton, sister of a well-known physician there.

Miss Sitgreaves told us that she had taught school in Georgetown in trying days there. Despite the fact that the schoolhouse leaked, with pupils bringing pieces of cloth and zinc to mend it, Israel Kirby, then school trustee, felt there were better uses for money.

"See here, Miss Katie," said the old Quaker when Miss Sitgreaves went to see him, "I taught in that school forty years ago and if it was good enough for me then, it ought to be good enough for anybody now."

Miss Sitgreaves taught at Georgetown about thirty-five years, after work that began in the pine towns of Hedger House, Sooy Place, and other points where she kept classrooms open six months a year in order that the schools might get their State aid.

"I liked to fight," said Miss Sitgreaves, "and I decided to overcome the obstacles they put before me. I told Israel Kirby I didn't want to fight him but I'd use my own methods if he made me go on with things as they were."

And she did. "I wrote to the parents of the pupils I had," the former teacher told us, "asking them to invite me to supper. Those who were too poor for that, I merely called on. Everywhere I went," said Miss Sitgreaves, "I preached my sermon. Leaking roof, plaster off the walls, bricks on the floor to keep the carpet from blowing up

ot to be confused with a more modern development of almost the same name, eorgetown is known for its old houses of colonial brick, many bearing the tes of their completion. There were fourteen houses in Georgetown when ese chronicles first appeared, most of them owned by a dairy farmer or those o worked for him.

The forgemaster's mansion at Atsion as it was long before New Jersey purchas[ed] it as part of the Wharton Tract. Atsion's days of making household wares [of] bog ore are recalled in Crosswicks, where the meeting-house has an Atsion sto[ve].

The late A. K. H. Doughty, of Collingswood, was the author's first guide [to] Bulltown, where rubble of the old glassworks was still to be found.

when the wind was high, the necessity of excluding children from the room so I could assume the undignified posture required to rake the stove—I told everybody all about it. Then we found out that $200 had been appropriated for repairs and that old Israel had never ordered the money."

The upshot of it was that the smoking stovepipe and the use of pigpens for kindling, offshoots of conditions in the McKinley administration, were forgotten when Montrey, the village blacksmith, was put in as a trustee and $400 was voted for repairs and general improvements. Old Israel must have torn out his hair, if any.

Miss Sitgreaves recalled old family names and manor houses, with some of the characters in and about Georgetown, when we responded to an invitation appended to her letter, to visit her. As a teacher she boarded in the home of Dr. Patterson and although there was a Methodist Church more conveniently located, she attended services in the Presbyterian Church at Sykesville. One resident who remained vivid in her memory was Dr. Main, a country practitioner who went about in a buggy crowded with beagle hounds.

"The sentiment we had to fight then was that the country was too hard and that the city life was easier," said Miss Sitgreaves. "I used to keep on saying, over and over, that those countryfolk ought to be thankful they were where God seemed to have put them." And it seemed, at least from her appearance and good humor, that Miss Sitgreaves had practised all that she preached.

We had heard of the Hutchinsons, Blacks, Newbolds, Marters, Burtises, and other prominent families of this, an area which was known in earlier days as the richest agricultural land in the State. But Miss Sitgreaves informed us that the Marter farm was visited by George Washington and that the Newbold mansion, surrounded by beautiful trees, had been graced by them, as saplings brought from the Continent, when the mansion was new. And when we saw the Newbold Hutchinson house for ourselves, we heard even more.

There were fourteen houses in Georgetown when we were there, most of them owned by Newbold Hutchinson and occupied by those who either work in his dairy or on other farms near by. There is a huge old house, once the trading post, now an antique shop where even the proprietor doesn't know what he has for sale. Across the way, up the rise of a wooded hill, is the ancient Colonial house that inspired the first title of Fooltown as the dwelling begun but laggardly completed. Georgetown has an old, and yet forgotten aspect—today the main road manages to skirt the village altogether.

It was from Mr. Ridgeway, over in Chesterfield, that we gained the facts for most entertaining reminiscences.

"Anthony Bullock, who lived across the way here, was the fellow who had most to do with the dropping of the name Recklesstown," he told us. "Bullock was a rich man, with many friends in Washington. I think it was Colonel Stone, of Pennsylvania, who said to him one day, 'Why don't you change the name of that town of yours? That "reckless" part of it sounds ridiculous!'"

Recklesstown had been founded by Joseph Reckless, who ran the old mill. There is no more reason to suppose that he was reckless than that Gabriel Morris was, who, down at the mill that was still in operation then, and may be still, told us we were in Recklesstown without knowing it.

One of the unusual features of Chesterfield is a button-wood tree, standing in the middle of the roadway, half-way between the store and the old hotel. The tree, according to our informants, has been there more than a century.

"It was being planted," Mr. Ridgeway said, "when they heard about Joe Clough stabbing Mrs. Hamilton, down in Bordentown."

That seems to have been a rather famous murder. Mr. Ridgeway's grandfather served as foreman of the Grand Jury at the trial which followed and so he recalls the details rather graphically. Clough was an Irishman who came to Bordentown as the foreman on the railroad line then going through. He was enamoured of Mrs. Hamilton, a widow who seems to have had a number of admirers in the neighborhood of the times. One of these was Jim Lippincott, of Recklesstown—and that's where the buttonwood tree comes in.

Lippincott was helping plant that tree. A flask of whiskey was placed beneath it in the accepted tree-planting style. Then word came of the murder. Naturally, since he was personally interested, Lippincott went to Bordentown at once to learn the details. Clough had killed his sweetheart in a jealous rage. But from that day to this, speculation has been rife as to whether Jim Lippincott's bottle stayed under the tree when he went away or not. Some say he dragged down the contents when he heard the news and tossed a "dead soldier" among the roots before striding away.

Once there was a wheelwright shop, a blacksmith shop, a harness-making establishment, two shoemakers' shops, and a tailor, in Recklesstown. Now that it's Chesterfield—"There have been just three new houses built here in forty years," Mr. Ridgeway declared.

Bullock, who changed the name of the town, has a lonely station named for him along the Jersey Central, deep in the pines where he once operated some of the first cranberry bogs. With his death, the old toll road he built went to perdition because the prospective customers found so many other ways to get where they wanted to be, avoiding it.

Mr. Ridgeway himself is a descendant of the Recklesstown pioneers. His grandfather, John C. Ridgeway, his father, John, Junior, and he, the youngest son, never lived more than a mile from where the little woodworking shop may be found today. No one can say the Ridgeways were reckless.

Haines Bog still is one of the centers of the cranberry industry, the bogs crossed and recrossed by man-made "causeways."

XXVIII

GLASS AT BULLTOWN

WHEN WE were in what is left today of Hermann City, someone said there had been a huge blast furnace in Bulltown. They insisted, however, that nothing would be found of the town itself, inasmuch as builders of deer hunter's cabins had been hauling stones away from the site for many years.

Each time we have come to a conclusion based on such passing information, someone comes along to produce new evidence and directions on how to find the lost village in question. So it was with Bulltown. Mr. A. K. H. Doughty, who since has died, wrote a letter to say that he was certain that traces of a grist mill, a smithy, and the Bulltown glass works could be found.

We went to see Mr. Doughty and as a result made arrangements to take him along as a guide. He was eighty-seven at the time. He said he had been born in Pleasant Mills, near Sweetwater, and that he would enjoy leaving his home in Collingswood for a time and journeying over the trails he hadn't seen in fifty years.

We chose a way down the old White Horse Pike, turning off on the old clay road to Atsion where Joseph Wharton planted a grove of imported pines at a time that is beyond the memory of any natives we found in the vicinity. Pausing in the cathedral aisles of these trees, with a brown carpet of needles sending up a pungent aroma, Mr. Doughty expressed the opinion that planting the trees was the best job Mr. Wharton ever accomplished. Mr. Doughty's views of Mr. Wharton and his ideas were not very complimentary.

Mr. Doughty could not forget that Mr. Wharton was once offered $250,000 for some acreage at Atsion by the Singer Sewing Machine Company and, according to the story, refused the bid, saying that if the ground was worth that much to a sewing machine concern, it was worth quite as much to the owners. The sewing machine interests went to Elizabeth, and Atsion, with its background of failures in iron, paper, and other ventures, is just another forgotten town.

Going on across the concrete highway at Atsion, we took the winding woods road that plies between the old mansion and Batsto, through Quaker Bridge. We had been along this roadway many times en route to points beside the Mullica and Batsto Rivers but it was not until our new guide bade us stop here and there, in apparently empty landscapes, that we heard there had once been houses and farms along the road. Now the trail is grown over and all but owners of rickety cars object to traveling through that way.

In two of these halts we found evidences of foundations, old iron stones, and bricks, with crumbled piles of plaster. Back toward the Sleepy Creek and Ball Run, we saw that there had been tilled fields and tended bogs, as well as orchards. Surely this road was once an important one, with more than one or two cars going through each day, the traffic of these latter days.

The road to Bulltown may be found on the opposite side of Atsion Lake, up beyond the fire tower where George Adams maintained his vigil against the greatest menace of the pinelands. There is a half-moon road that swings into Tylertown, a village of a half dozen dwellings, and back, if you follow it through, to Hermann City. A garage being operated in Green Bank today was built of bricks from the dynamited glass factory chimney in Hermann City.

Bulltown is now a bog center, the cranberry plantation operated when we were there by Charles DeLong, of Egg Harbor. There are 500 acres of cranberries and several bogs of blueberries being tried. William Wills, caretaker of the bogs and road supervisor for Washington Township, took us very kindly to where the smithy and wheelwright shop stood, marked by piles of charcoal, an old axe head, some fragments of horseshoes, and a sheltering grove of ancient oaks which, it was evident, had been damaged by every severe storm.

"There used to be some other relics lying around," Mr. Wills said. "I remember wheels and such. But along came a junk man one day and he carted them away."

The grist mill was beside the dam where the cedar water that passes through the bog sluiceways is blacker than we have ever seen it anywhere else. The glass works was beside the road, where it bends around the bog. Fragments of brick kilns, as well as bits of Jersey glass, litter the sand on the road and the mounds of earth through thickets beside it. Mr. Doughty knew of Bulltown and how it might be found but he could not remember how the glass works appeared when it was operating. He stood there, trying to recall the scene, examining the particles of slag and glass residue he picked up.

Up the road beyond the smithy was a store, in the old days. It is a mere hole in the ground now. One of the dwellings you may find near by was built to replace an earlier house destroyed by fire, a fire which probably burned the store as well. All in all, there was something of a town but nothing to be found today will prove it.

Our way home lay through the leftovers of Hermann City, down to the Green Bank bridge over the Mullica, and back through Crowleytown and Pleasant Mills. At Joe Mulliner's burial place, we saw that our interest had evoked a kind of tombstone rivalry. We had done so much talking about Joe Mulliner and how they hanged him as an example to the other Refugees that in addition to the original "J.M." stone, there was a cross erected by Audubon gunners, duly inscribed, and a new marker of painted concrete.

We paused at the deserted and unkempt St. Mary's Cemetery in Pleasant Mills. It is all that remains of a Roman Catholic Church that burned down beside it. Today huge limbs of trees have fallen among the stones, already hidden by weeds. Mr. Doughty told us he had known many who were buried there.

"I remember the day when I stood up there above 'The Forks,'" he told us, "and counted one hundred and fifty-two ships in the river, all loaded with wood. I remember the old barracks, erected on George Washington's order—they stood just over there. They were near where Judge Higbee's summer place is now.

"Seems to me there was a town called Bernalda around here, too, but I could never tell you where. I remember it had a dozen houses or more and lots more people than you would think could live in them. The ships, the houses, the towns—they have vanished all together, you see."

It is heartening to remember that we took the old gentleman along with us to revisit the scenes of his boyhood, even though he discovered, as we did, that he couldn't remember quite as much, on the scene, as he expected to. Mr. Doughty was a disciple of progress all his life. He could not understand why and how these lost towns sprang up and then fell in ruin so as to be without trace, in many cases, today. He was one of a group of pioneers who wanted Haddon Avenue, through Collingswood, Westmont, and Haddonfield, spread to a width of sixty-six feet. Despite his efforts thirteen feet were cut from each side— much to the regret of traffic experts today.

Towns are not concerned with the days ahead—at least, many of them haven't been. Perhaps if some of these forlorn hamlets had known people who could have dipped into the future without rose-colored glasses, we would find them different today. Perhaps there would be no ruins, no bits of glass, no fragments of rusted iron, for such towns might never have been begun. Even Westmont, concerned with an event of the moment, dropped its former name, Rowandtown, for Westmount, the monicker of a racehorse that brought its backers big returns.

XXIX

BUCKSHUTEM'S FERRY OF 1812

Down among the marshes and mosquito choirs beyond the Panther and Berryman Branches of the Maurice River is a tiny town which, in the earliest histories of New Jersey, identified itself as Buckshutem.

When we climbed the old wharf behind the Josiah Brick mansion in Bricksboro, below Port Elizabeth in Cumberland County, we looked across the flats and river to where a little white school and smaller white church were visible. These, we were told, were in Buckshutem. The name and quaint appearance from a distance inspired a resolve to find out more about them.

Buckshutem has nothing of the distinction which identifies Elizabeth Bodly's town, Port Elizabeth, or of Bricksboro which, as Bricksborough, laid claim to from twelve to fifteen dwellings on the confluence of Muskee Run, a century ago. Buckshutem, described in 1832, was "a hamlet, near the meeting of Buckshutem creek with Maurice river, Milleville t-ship, Cumberland county, containing eight or ten dwellings, a grist and saw mill, and store."

In the historic writing of the same period Buckshutem Creek is pictured as "a fine mill stream." But the millers of yesteryear have gone to their reward, the mills of which they were so proud have crumbled and the mill streams, their time of service likewise past, have become sluggish, grass-choked ditches.

Neither the church nor the school, viewed from across

the river, are as old as Buckshutem, nor are they as picturesque when the traveler arrives in closer proximity. The village itself, a scattering of houses along the road to Mauricetown, may have divided some of its charm of antiquity with the development of Laurel Lake. It was at the head of the lake, where the stone bridge and dam have been enlarged, that the mill once stood. Known as "the old windmill," it either burned down or fell apart some years ago, present dwellers are not certain which.

Most of those who recall Buckshutem, as it used to be, have died. Many farms in the vicinity are owned now either by strangers who know nothing of the area's history or kin who remember little of what they have been told.

The day we chose for our first journey to Buckshutem was a poor one from the standpoint of weather but a good one for finding farm folk at home. On the way down to Millville we ran head-on into three thunderstorms, weird flashes of lightning zigzagging from angry clouds whipped by the wind across the sky.

Our first inquiry was at a farmhouse where a phonograph of ancient vintage was wobbling a popular song out of tune. A woman who told a child to silence the music until she had finished talking spoke sketchily of the neighborhood and said there had once been a ferry across the river there. She pronounced it "fairy" just as some others to whom we talked called soot "sut"—but she was right when she directed us to the old Mayhew house.

Patty Mayhew, last of the Mayhews to own wide domains along the river, died in 1932. Since then, the house in which she was born and in which she died has been occupied by Leslie G. Woodruff and his wife, Mrs. Woodruff a cousin of Martin Mayhew. Later still it was the home of a bachelor hermit. This old dwelling goes back to Revolutionary times but there is little left to prove it now. It isn't so much that these assertions must be taken on faith as the small attention given hereabouts to houses and objects which have an obvious traditional value.

The Woodruffs said confidently that their house was 150 years old, at least. Mr. Woodruff, a raw-boned farmer, and his wife, a slight, small woman, were the only ones among us who didn't seem to be worried by the mosquitoes which, in great singing clouds, soared from the marshes and hovered over the rain-drenched grass.

Standing on the brick-floored portico at the back of the house, just beyond an adjacent chicken hatchery, the Woodruffs indicated to us where soldiers of a guard placed on the Maurice River during the War of 1812, rested after crossing the ferry.

"The marshes weren't there then," Woodruff said. "In fact, they haven't been there so very long. We used to be able to walk out on firm ground to the river. That's where the ferry used to be, making regular crossings from Bricksboro and Port Elizabeth. That was the only crossing of the river until the bridge was built at Mauricetown."

The road that led up from the ferry wharf is all but lost on the Woodruff side of the hard-surfaced road to Mauricetown. On the other side, use for other purposes has kept it in evidence. But it is difficult to conceive that here was a river worth guarding against enemy ships, that men in uniform were ferried across under orders, and that the countryside ever boasted greater prominence than it does now.

Mrs. Woodruff proudly opened the door of a back-kitchen, since then piled high with wood, in which the high wide fireplace with a rusted side-oven is still intact, disused and little changed in more than a century. It was around this fire and in this oven that the soldiers prepared and enjoyed tasty fare of long ago.

The Woodruffs showed us a kettle, too, which once hung over the fire. They procured it from behind an outhouse where it had become almost as forgotten as the ferry. But there was fitting climax to that visit, there in a house that had been pegged together prior to days of a scarcely mentioned war-time, for we heard how Buckshutem was named. The explanation is so simple that it is bound to leave many as dubious or as incredulous as we were.

"I remember that a teacher in the schoolhouse up the road once asked us how Buckshutem got its name," Mrs. Woodruff said. "All we could do was repeat the story as we had always heard it. They had told us that when the first houses in town were being built, a large buck deer ran across the road.

" 'There goes a buck!' someone cried. 'Shoot him!' And so the town became Buckshutem!"

There are others who say the name has an Indian origin and that it came from one of the streams near by. However, the other variation, with "Buck! Shoot him!" becoming "Buckshutem" will stand for the present, for the teacher was apparently satisfied with the explanation. Why shouldn't we be?

XXX

NOTHIN' IN NOTHIN' IN ROCKWOOD

THIS IS the saga of Rockwood, of West Mills, Pestletown, and Spring Garden, and a rather sad saga it is.

For at Rockwood they told us that cranberries weren't so good, that farming was a washout, and that "there ain't nothin' in nothin'!"

At West Mills, the lone farm and sawmill that distinguished it is recalled merely in a brace of rusty wheels and at Pestletown a forlorn and curious cemetery recalls earlier and more auspicious days.

Finally, at Spring Garden, descendants of a hotelkeeper who saw stagecoaches stop at his front door and later pioneers who witnessed the coming of the first trains to the seashore, find themselves cut off from all save occasional auto travelers.

Rockwood is on the State map and may be located not far from Atsion, once Atsiyunk, on a road that leads from the concrete of Route 39 and ends at the "village." West Mills is not located on recent maps but was perhaps two miles to the east. Pestletown is on the "Whoopee Road" toward Waterford and Spring Garden and in the same neighborhood, not far from Blue Anchor and Ancora.

From appearances, as they are indicated on maps, Rockwood would seem to have importance equal to some of the other towns. Following the woods road cut through the scrub oak and pine, protected by cedar water ditches on either side, we found a cluster of buildings, perhaps three or four of them dwellings, a mere cranberry settlement.

The pickers were in the bogs the day we visited there, and then, driving carefully along the narrow causeway through flooded lands adjacent to the drained cranberry vines, we met Mrs. John Ford. Mrs. Ford came out of the largest dwelling of the group to find out what we wanted. We had a great deal of trouble persuading her that we were not minions of the law, looking for stills, and that we were merely trying to dig up forgotten history, instead.

To any number of questions concerning saw mills, old houses and any particular detail in Rockwood's long-ago, Mrs. Ford gave us the same guarded reply:

"You won't find what you're after here. From what I hear, they're up in the other direction, near Waterford."

It was not until our excursion neared its end and when we had heard of "the Whoopee Road," that we realized the cause of such unnatural wariness. In the past we had remarked the lack of suspicion among the people with whom we talked. Any number of them have climaxed interviews with refreshment, even offers of Jersey Lightning. But not Mrs. Ford.

Reluctantly she took us down to talk with her husband who was foreman of the bogs, owned by Frank Haines, of Medford, for more than twenty-five years. Mr. Ford was district fire warden, too. He proved more amenable, easier to convince that sane wanderers could actually travel about the country looking for Forgotten Towns.

"There ain't no money in cranberries," bemoaned Mr. Ford. "If you're making any money in the bogs, tell me your name. There ain't no money in chickens, either. The false-blossom has got the berries and the hens just ain't no good. There ain't nothin' in nothin'!"

The Fords knew little of the history of Rockwood. They had never bothered to find out. What they told us, they assumed after surveying a marker bearing the name of C. G. Rockwood, the original owner, with a date of 1871. We couldn't resist putting one facetious question and we were immediately hushed up with the reply.

"Are you any relation to Henry Ford who makes the automobiles?" we asked Mr. Ford. Soberly, and without a smile, he replied:

"I'm his uncle!"

Here at the plantation, adjacent to the Clark Branch, there were 244 acres of cranberries. The yield was 17,000 bushels in balmy days but Mr. Ford said they would be lucky to get 400 that year. Heavy rains and this false blossom they said so much about, had blighted the crop.

West Mills is another bog settlement. Once it was connected with Rockwood by a road through the woods. Now the road has gone to pot and is open only to persons who go on foot and don't mind muck. Its muddy way is indicated by a swath cut through the trees.

West Mills was the scene of much activity the day we were there, pickers combing the bogs in formation and walking in line along the causeways with boxes numbered in black to where the trucks were waiting. Mr. Ford's son was in charge there, dumping the red and green berries in long containers for removal to the sorting and storage houses.

Here there was once a mill and a farm, as we have said, but evidences of them have long since tumbled down to be covered over. Long Indian grass waves desolately through clearings in the pine woods and two rusted wheels, from a cart that once hauled logs along narrow-gauge tracks, jut from sand near the dam. The water is murky and swirls away in eddies through the crisp and dying ferns, yellowing weeds, and red sumac, toward the mystery of the cedar swamp.

Pestletown is off on the other side of the road, along the trail to Waterford, and then off on a bumpy road that follows the tracks of the Jersey Central for a time. Another turn is made to the right, as this path loops back to the Waterford route. Then, quite suddenly, there is a scattering of fields and houses.

Our questions in the vicinity as to how Pestletown got its name indicated that it is of Indian origin. There is a Pestle Brook in the neighborhood and unquestionably the name, given first to the brook, came from the well-known stone Indian utensil used for grinding corn. A few informants maintained that there had been a family named Pestle when the town was carved around and from the Garwood farm, but that is doubtful.

The artistic sense of natives expresses itself in Pestletown in unusual ways. One of the plastered houses, whitewashed, has home-made gargoyles at either end. There is a cemetery, too, which demanded closer inspection than could be obtained from the road. The crosses and "monuments" are home-constructed, of wood and cement, and on many of the graves are what appear to be small houses. They have glass doors but otherwise look much like dog kennels.

These are some sort of shrines, no doubt, in the eyes of Italians and others who put them there. Old dried-out wreaths and strange ornaments can be seen inside. We were treading on dangerous ground, it was obvious, when we asked what they were for and what they meant—

ground just as dangerous as that trodden when we asked a man what he meant by "evil spirits" when we asked him about the gargoyles he said his neighbor provided to keep "such things" away.

Spring Garden is on older maps but it lost significance altogether when the new White Horse Pike passed it by, over the Ancora bridge further up the road. Here you will find the old Spring Garden Hotel, built in 1826 by David, son of Josiah Albertson. The hotel, an 18-room dwelling when he were there, is still a part of the Albertson Estate. Mrs. Claude P. Chew, who now lives there with her husband, was an Albertson, a direct descendant.

The property, as part of the Blue Anchor Tract, saw lively days when hotels were necessary to the operation of stage roads. It was Josiah Albertson who operated the Blue Anchor Hotel. At Spring Garden, stagecoaches from Cape May made a stop-over, changing horses and stabling them across the road where today there is nothing to show where the huge barns once stood.

Later, when the first wood-burning trains started down to the first Atlantic City, a resort reared from a swampy island, passengers stretched their legs on the platform behind the hotel and had a drink or two at the bar while the cars waited for them. This was a long journey in those days and time out was necessary without the modern conveniences we know and so little appreciate. Today only a few cinders remain to show where the platform and the adjoining beer garden were.

The road on which the hotel still stands was the old White Horse Pike. The new road cuts directly across the field that lay behind barns and stables across the way. Down the road was a mill pond that became, in later years, a cranberry bog—now it's just a swamp. There was a tenant house or two, as well, but these, with the mill, are gone.

This old hostel, sturdily built of wood, laid over brick, is a monument to the line of Albertsons who saw this particular section of Southern New Jersey grow up. There was Josiah, of Blue Anchor; his son, David, who built the hotel at Spring Garden; his son, Josiah, who lived on there; and now Mrs. Chew, his daughter.

"The stagecoaches stopped coming when the trains pushed through," Mr. Chew told us. "Now, there aren't many trains. Did you come up by way of the 'Whoopee Road'?"

We told him how we had blundered through and he said that was the road we had followed. "Why do they call it the Whoopee Road?" we asked him.

"Why," he said, "everybody down that way makes moonshine. They've had a few raids. Government snoopers have been ducking in and out. But they still carry on. There's plenty of whoopee, from what they tell me."

Then we knew what Mrs. Ford, of Rockwood, meant when she kept insisting, believing that we were revenuers making believe to look for towns:

"You won't find any town thisa-here way. From what they tell me, the stuff you're after is up thata-way."

XXXI

OLD FORT BILLINGS

Fort Mercer, at National Park, with its well-clipped sweep around old trenches and mounded earthworks and the Ann Whitall house close by, has become a shrine well known to persons who consider themselves history-minded.

However, further down the Delaware, its stone wall crumbling and one of its turrets a hollow sentinel on the river shore, an old fortification whose battery sank at least two British ships in the Revolution, remains desolate, un-honored, and unattended.

The notation in Gordon's *Gazetteer* carries this descriptive paragraph under date of 1834:

"Billingsport, more properly written Byllingsport, named after Edward Bylling, a merchant of England, the purchaser of Lord Berkeley's undivided Moiety of the province. It lies upon the river Delaware below the mouth of the Mantua creek, and 12 miles below Camden, and was rendered famous by the fort erected here during the revolutionary war, for defense of the channel of the river, remains of which are still visible. It contains a tavern and a ferry and some half dozen dwellings."

The historian of more than a century ago seems to have boasted that there was evidence of the fort in his time. For that reason it is an unusual privilege to record that the remains of the fort are visible now, even though no effort has been made to preserve them. More remarkable still, no interest has been shown in protecting the old fortress tower and its adjoining wall from those who enjoy themselves best in destroying whatever they can. Beyond the turret and the wall there is a high promontory, covered by a second or third growth of trees, among which are stumps of venerable forebears which, we were told, were cut down by the unemployed of the first depression.

Earthworks are plainly visible. Up the river a short distance from the turret and crumbling wall is a deep, stone-lined road, sloping up from the river shore where the lapping water constantly moves fragments of shell to make a musical tinkle. This roadway either led into the fort from the rear or, possibly, was used by a later ferry. Off the beach are the rotting timbers of old wharves and slips and down the river are two houses on the bluff, one more than 100 years old, and the other part of the plant which, appropriately enough, makes smokeless powder.

It is curious to reflect that within so close a proximity of the old fortifications, munitions are being made and powder is being stored against a new war, compared to which the old battles of the fort will seem child's play.

Despite the manufacture of instruments of conflict, however, folk in this part of New Jersey have continued to live, generation after generation, in spite of disasters, family upheavals and other wars. A letter written us by Dorothy Chessman revealed, first of all, that she was a descendant of one of the officers who manned the fort in the old days and that she felt she was touching the past every time she beheld the magazines and the chevaux-de-frise at low tide.

"I am a lineal descandant of one of the officers stationed there during the Revolutionary War," Mrs. Chessman wrote. "One of his letters written at the time is now in the possession of the Gloucester County Historical Society, at Woodbury.

"Billingsport was once quite well known as a shad fishing village until that industry died in this section. Old Lincoln Park, an amusement center of the early eighteen-nineties, was also located here. When roads were cut through for the park, many revolutionary cannon balls and Indian arrowheads were dug up."

It was Mrs. Chessman's letter that spurred our search, for very little is said about Billingsport and the fort that can be reached so easily. It may have had a thrilling part in the war of long ago but few remember any of that. Interest is centered instead at old Red Bank, the National Park of today, where Fort Mercer has been restored through Government funds. Much of the history that has been written skips over Fort Billing or Billings, unless it is the kind that has been privately printed for persons who, for one reason or another, have the reputation of being old fogies.

If anyone has made a thorough study of the Delaware River campaign in Revolutionary days, it is I. P. Strittmatter, M.D., LL. D., whose home, remodeled from a Colonial house, is just off the shore, down toward the site of a forgotten railroad station known as Paradise. As late as 1933, Dr. Strittmatter revised his researches on the campaign for a pilgrimage of the Medical Club of Philadelphia.

Dr. Strittmatter has pointed out that the Delaware cam-

author's record of the discovery of old Fort Billings has been disputed and
haps rightly so, although the ruins present every evidence of military design—
t least they did. Some say they were part of an amusement park constructed
g the Delaware River at a much later date. Tom Gordon, in his *Gazetteer*,
that Billingsport, named for Edward Byllinge, was "rendered famous by the
erected here during the revolutionary war. . . ."

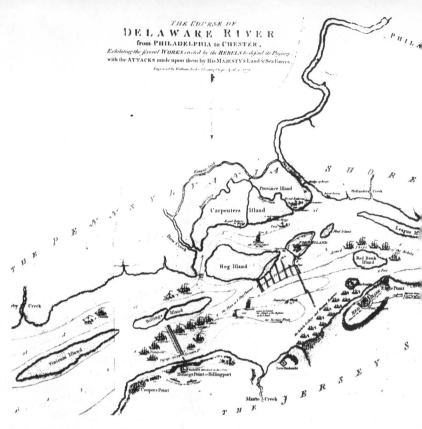

THE COURSE OF
DELAWARE RIVER
from PHILADELPHIA to CHESTER,
Exhibiting the several WORKS erected by the REBELS to defend its Passage
with the ATTACKS made upon them by His MAJESTY's Land & Sea Forces
Engraved by William Faden Charing Cross April 30 1778

This 1778 map shows Billings Island across from Billings Point or Billi
with an abandoned redoubt above it and with the channel of the Delaware
obstructed by stockados. The Tench Francis house, below, no longer stan
the fortifications where patriots fired hot cannon balls to blow up powder
zines of His Majesty's ships, the *Augusta* and the *Merlin*, in 1777.

paign, part of the occupation of Philadelphia by the British in an effort to join the forces of army and navy, was one of the most expensive experiences of the whole war and least productive from a British standpoint. The largest loss of Hessian allies, the deaths of about 1100 men and the destruction of the *Augusta* and the *Merlin,* all were tied up with the operations in and about Forts Billings and Mercer, and, of course, at poorly situated Fort Mifflin.

Ten times the amount of man power and war equipment were needed for the offensive than were employed in the defense. Even so, there was no formal surrender in the end, but only an evacuation. Despite its importance and the fact that the *Merlin* and *Augusta* were blown apart by red-hot cannon balls heated in a field not far from Dr. Strittmatter's property, and that their hulks lie even today at the bottom of the river where they grounded at the mercy of the fort garrisons, much of the campaign is in the dark.

Dr. Strittmatter says that the lack of information is due to the fact that much of the fighting was done by men who were not residents of this section, because Friends in the neighborhood didn't like war and wanted to forget all about it, and because of Tory influence. Many so-called patriots carried water on both shoulders, many others condoned such acts as the murder of Colonel Greene, heroic defender of Fort Mercer, and still others sought their own glory first and the success of the war from freedom last.

One cannot think back to the days of the forts and their operation here without recalling Robert Whyte, to whom was intrusted the placing of obstructions in both the Hudson and Delaware Rivers, who, with intimate knowledge of the forts and their weaknesses, sold out to the enemy.

The garrison at Fort Mifflin could have held out much longer, Dr. Strittmatter claims, if the conduct of Captain Whyte had not given the British singular advantages.

Armed with Whyte's information, a British ship, the *Roebuck*, was able to raise the chevaux-de-frise in the face of fire from Fort Bylling, or Billings. The fleet on the Delaware was of considerable size, as far as the Continental forces were concerned, with ammunition sloops, floating batteries and galleys stubbornly on the alert. On October 23, 1777, Commodore Hazlewood, in command, wrote General Washington that he had no reinforcements for the fleet and hesitated to take men from the forts, as weakly manned as they were.

On October 26, two days after the *Augusta* and *Merlin* were blown up by the unique fire from the forts, Hazlewood wrote Washington that the enemy could be seen crossing at Webb's ferry, massing for a grand attack on Fort Mifflin. These were real heroes, manning a fortress that was badly situated and in a state of dilapidation, a force that was still small despite the borrowing of every sailor from every frigate lying near by. Congress was laggard in acting, there was insidious apathy in the ranks of those in second command and Fort Mifflin's fall, which needs no recounting here, was no compliment to either British maneuvering or courage.

When the *Merlin* and *Augusta* became fast in river mud, the American gunboats opened up on them. There was feverish forging in the pits near Tench France's (this name is sometimes given as Francis) house, as well as a furious cannonade from the battery on the promontory of the New Jersey shore. Thomas Paine, writing of the event a few days later, said:

"The cannonade, by far the most furious I have ever heard, ended in a tremendous noise, as a peal such as from a hundred cannon was heard. A volume of thick smoke, rising like a pillar, spreading on top like a tree, was seen ascending to heaven. The region for miles around rocked as if riven by an earthquake; windows miles away were broken."

This was the *Augusta* going up. The *Merlin* soon followed. Only three boatloads of men were saved. After the ships had gone to the bottom and the engagement had been officially reported, England contended that the crews of the grounded ships blew them up deliberately with consummate heroics.

Dr. Strittmatter's conclusion is more to the point and infinitely more picturesque as one stands among the ruins of the forgotten fort, or high on the promontory where such amazing events went unsung so long ago. The medical historian, whose research has provided proof of his ideas and doubts on popular opinions, declares that hot shot, heated in Tench France's forge and fired from a battery of three pieces somewhere in the Billings fortifications 1330 feet from the *Augusta*, penetrated the port magazine. A second shot may have struck the *Merlin* but it is possible that the second explosion was caused by the first. When Dr. Strittmatter doubts his theories, he goes into the fields and digs up another cannon ball or makes more certain of the cavity that held the forge.

Today these events are mostly forgotten, except by farmers who live along the Delaware, and many of these pick up a ball, smile, light their pipes and toss it aside until they remember again. Two or three balls were turned up by plows only a year or two ago. Some of the ammunition that Dr. Strittmatter picked up reposes in a box exhibited in the McConkey ferry house at Washington's Crossing, far, far from home.

Thus the remnants of a gallant fortress stand on guard, as legends run through the countryside concerning old houses damaged by chance shots, while many live in the shadow of what ought to be a shrine and forget its name, and as hulks and bits of chain sink deeper to oblivion off the river shore.

Yesterday was yesterday. Today forgets. Tomorrow there may be nothing, no one left to remember, as the world picks up new speed toward a dubious future.

The lines of the mill at Spring Mills indicate that it was there long before the town's name was changed to Grenloch, long before Ed Bateman made flatirons, long before the Civil War.

XXXII

TETAMEKAN: SPRING MILLS

SOME PEOPLE say they want to live to be a hundred years old.

Some of them mean it. Others say it because they know it will please members of their families. Still others mention it as often as they can because they know it will displease those about them.

Even from those who are beloved, the hope, when openly expressed, fails to please, sometimes. So often those within earshot will say, or think: Well, I wouldn't want to live to be that old. No, sir. Why, all his relatives and friends are gone. The places he knew best have changed so that he doesn't recognize them. What has he to live for?

Grandpa Bateman wanted to live to be a hundred and he had plenty to live for. Ninety-two when we saw him for any prolonged conversation, he seemed but eighty, and far younger in spirit. That many of his generation had died didn't bother him. Nor did he grow dull, crabbed, or morose amid the decadence all about him. With his little white beard, his penetrating eyes that peeped over his half-moon spectacles, his neat self-tied bow tie, and his gold-headed cane, he was as agile as the young man he said he was—at ninety-two!

And because he said he didn't want to die before having a few airplane rides, we told everybody, and it was arranged so that he enjoyed his last two birthdays in the air, in open-seater planes. "It's more fun that way, demmed if it ain't," he said afterward. He died at ninety-four.

But the town that Edward S. Bateman knew so well, despite its change of names, was one of the many that grew down in South Jersey, in his case, perhaps, because he decided to sit back, closing the factory that had given it life. Many of Grandpa Bateman's dreams had been realized, triumphing over the ruins of Spring Mills, once Tetamekan, and now Grenloch.

Tetamekan was the name the Indians bestowed upon it, there beside what they call Grenloch Lake today. It isn't far from Blackwood, once Blackwoodtown, where there was an academy in Grandpa Bateman's youth, but railroad experts thought Tetamekan sounded Armenian and that Spring Mills was too long, even without considering the New Jersey duplication. So they looked down at the lake, saw that the water at the time had a greenish hue, and called the town Grenloch.

Grenloch was the name they painted on the sign tacked on the station. Grenloch was the name given the branch peanut line that came out through Mt. Ephraim and what, today, is Runnemede. But the railroad experts are probably dead and if they aren't, their railroad is, for it's years since a train puffed from or to the city, and the rails, where you can find them, are rusted.

Mr. Bateman was born in Spring Mills. Perhaps as a youth he had his eye on the old building that had been a mill and forge. At any rate, when opportunity came he bought it, along with the surrounding lands. He boasted to us that he had bought his factory site and the lands adjoining it for $200.

He started, with his brother, Frank, in the manufacture

of flat-irons. That went well enough. Some folk forget the flatiron days of Spring Mills until, in kicking up the scrub along the creek, a wanderer will find a couple of the irons, tied together and thrown away, just as "Sud" Norcross told us he did. The Batemans and Norcrosses were among the chief families of Spring Mills.

Throwing the irons away would indicate that the venture was a failure. It wasn't. Frank and Ed collaborated on the designing of farm implements. Of their many designs and products in farm tools and machinery, their hand plow was the outstanding success. The Iron Age hand plow, the first hand plow made in this section of the country, brought prosperity, long hours, and bookfuls of orders. The flatirons just had to be forgotten.

Plows, cultivators, every sort of helpful machine for the small farmer, these became Spring Mills specialties and soon they were making Spring Mills famous, even though many of the newcomers and those outside insisted on saying Grenloch. The business was started in 1865 and it prospered through many years with three hundred and fifty hands at work, coming from houses in town as if it had been organized as a Guild village. Everybody worked for Mr. Bateman.

In 1892, Grandpa Bateman incorporated a new firm. Frank was withdrawing. The workers, with whom the lives of the brothers were so closely entwined, gave him a loving cup. Edward continued until 1908, deciding then that he, too, would take it easy. The company was forthwith dissolved. Perhaps larger and more celebrated competitors had come into the field but it is more likely that the Batemans, with the start they had on the rest of the country, could have kept things going much longer.

A variety of other enterprises came to town afterward and sought to use the old buildings. None was successful very long. One was the operation of an alcohol re-distilling plant and it appeared to thrive for a time. Along came Prohibition and knocked it out. With Repeal, its existence seemed to have been forgotten.

Grandpa Bateman told us he was a temperance man, even so. "I voted for Prohibition," he said, "but they're not going to make a 'go' of it." And of course, they didn't.

For years the oldest man in town, Mr. Bateman used to think back on the days of the Blackwoodtown Academy and try to hunt up members of his class. He didn't find many. He said he had probably outlived them all, when he talked last to us. "The school building's still standing," he said, not long before he died. "They're probably afraid to take it down until I get out of the way. Although Joe Bruce was living in it last, I heard, and finding it right comfortable as a house. Many a day's schoolin' I've had there and many a rattannin' for monkeyshines."

Reporters used to lay seizure to the Bateman home each year the sage of Spring Mills had a birthday. The last two years, they interviewed him at airports. Asked the customary questions about the old town and what his recipe for longevity was, he would inevitably respond:

"Hard work and being cheerful!"

Grandpa Bateman had worked hard. And he had been cheerful all his life. Once, when he was talking about his views and Prohibition, he began: "There hasn't been a drop of liquor in this old house in—" And his son interrupted.

"Why, Dad," he said, "there's a jugful of good liquor upstairs!"

Mr. Bateman smiled, his eyes all a-twinkle. "Terrible when the man of the house don't know what's going on inside it!" he declared.

Every day was reception day at the home of his son, Roscoe, when Mr. Bateman was there. Those who knew something of Spring Mills saw the old buildings and came there to ask for more. He would usually take them for a walk down where he had dreamed his dreams and realized them, telling a different story every time he came along.

Today the old plant is in disrepair and ruins. Parts have been removed altogether. The sturdy building with a hip roof and cupola in which there was once a bell with which to summon the factory hands—this was the chief center of activity. It went back to Revolutionary times, Grandpa Bateman was sure.

Whenever Grenloch's sage went away for a vacation, the factory closed down early. All hands were called together, perhaps with that bell in the cupola. Mr. Bateman insisted on shaking hands with every worker, giving his personal good wishes in a quaint old-fashioned way. "I'm going away," he used to say. "Maybe I won't be back. You never can tell."

Just as at Isabella, the workmen's houses at Spring Mills proclaim themselves for what they were. Even now, long after the factory days, they remain, even though they may be occupied by those who never knew Spring Mills and have no recollection of what went on there. No one would dream that down this road, beside Grenloch Lake, near the present park and picnic grounds on land that was Grandpa Bateman's once, there was an enterprise that was a pioneer in its field.

It was "Sud" Norcross who acted as our guide. "Come

along with me and meet a nice old gentleman with some wonderful memories," he had said, smiling. "I'll buy your lunch." We forgot all about the lunch until much later, so unusual were the recollections, contrasting experiences in other forgotten towns.

Somehow Spring Mills sounds better than Grenloch. Tetamekan—well, that would be a fancy one to get around, for some people. But what it was and what it did ought to be interesting at least to the next wanderer who kicks up a couple of flat-irons and asks how they got there. This was where Grandpa Bateman knew but two disappointments: He wanted a trip in a dirigible and, he didn't round out a century.

Seeking the old narrow-gauge line out of Weymouth, the author and his friends came upon a viaduct to carry water from one lake to another, a project that could not succeed because of the law of gravitation.

XXXIII

LOST IN THE WOODS: ONE RAILROAD

Down in the country back of New Lisbon, where Burlington County natives run for cover when the suggestion is made that they have their pictures taken, there's a long length of rail, a few ties and the submerged uprights of a trestle to recall the old Kinkora Railroad.

We went down to look for them after a lover of the woods wrote a letter in which he said he had come upon the trestle by chance and wondered what it was. The journey that resulted might not have been quite as unusual, even so, if it had not been for a telephone call.

An inquirer asked what we remembered of Head-of-the-River. We looked up some faded notes, provided the information very briefly, for it was a busy day, and were prepared to say good-bye. Then the voice, owned by someone who admitted afterwards that he screwed up his courage, asked: "What's the chances of going with you on your next trip?"

In the protracted conversation the gentleman inquiring gave his name for the first time: William L. Farrand. Long years came crashing down with the sound of it. "Mr. Farrand," we said, "do you know who you're talking to? Don't you remember being a Sunday School teacher years ago? Don't you remember taking a group of boys out into the country near Haddonfield on Sunday afternoons?"

Bill Farrand said he did but he asked what any of that had to do with his question. "You're talking to one of those boys," we told him. "You probably knew him as little Harry Beck, the boy wonder violinist, or something, the lad who carried the cross in church . . . and wore bow ties and knee breeches and . . ."

So the trip was arranged, even though it was a little difficult, as it is with many, to persuade Bill Farrand that little boys grow up and that they sometimes become interested in decadent things and forgotten history before they grow the whiskers that real historians are supposed to have. Later on we talked of others who were in that class of boys to whom Bill subtly imparted the information that there was much in the out-of-doors that often escaped attention. One boy was a patient at Saranac, we said. Another was a priest. A third had been married, divorced, and married again.

Bill proved an amiable companion on many of our journeys, after that. That first trip, however, was to New Lisbon and its vicinity, and it began with an examination of the scene of another in a long series of pine woods murders and the gruesome discovery of a piece of scalp, left in a thicket where a victim had been dumped in the climax of a gang war.

We set out through Pemberton, turning down the old Barnegat Road at the water tank opposite the Burlington County Institutions. On the maps of a century ago, the town was a mile down this road, as what's left of it may be found today, but its name was Lisbon. The name seems to have come in a natural way, for many years ago, when a group of Portuguese came to Burlington County to cut virgin timber, they gave the community the name of their far-away city.

Crossing the railroad tracks, we turned to the left along them, beyond the piles of coal and other Government property serving as a base for C.C.C. camps in the neighborhood. The trail is narrow and the driver must be careful not to take a branch that swerves across the railroad line, to emerge at forgotten Brown's Mills Junction. We made sure about this detail and then went back to try again, discovering with pleasure that the trail to Mary Ann Forge, Upper Mill and Lower Mill, is marked now with directional signs that did not exist before we wrote about forgotten history there.

This trail through the pines leads on and on in country which is at its best in October. Early frosts had killed the ferns and tinged the maples and birches scattered here and there. The sunlight trickled through to vie with the lately arrived tang of autumn air. In the sandy paths there were hoofprints of deer, too alert to linger with our approach.

We came to a sequestered crossroads beyond the path leading to Mary Ann Forge, with signs directing the wanderer to the Four Mile Colony, Chatsworth, Upper Mill, and New Lisbon. Most of these villages existed as little more than name spots and remain on maps today because of taverns established in them, for such hostelries thrived at four-mile intervals along stagecoach trails.

We turned about to reconnoiter toward New Lisbon for there had been no trace of a hidden railroad thus far. We had gone back perhaps three miles when a small bridge confronted us, over a creek bed in which there was less than a trickle of water. Creek bed? It was nothing of the sort. Careful examination revealed that it had been a ditch dug by human hands and that it led to a trestle, or what was left of one. The posts of what "must have been" a narrow gauge line were still in place; new uprights had been installed to replace those burned in a forest fire long ago. We went back to the bridge and followed the line in the other direction.

This entailed a walk of more than two miles. The diggings led deep into the woods. There were twists and turns but the cut held to the same width and depth. We tried to picture a tiny engine on a narrow track making those sudden swings and somehow the reconstruction didn't hold together. Our theories sagged hopelessly when, after the cut dropped down into muggy spagnum moss, we climbed the bank and saw a lake, marked with charred tree stumps and limbless trunks, ahead. There beside the reservoir was a waterfall which, with a noisy splashing, whipped the cedar water into a froth below. All was mystery and quiet, except for the splashing of the water. Only an old footprint or two betrayed humanity.

We took an old wagon track back to where our cars were parked. Before we got there we heard the horns honking. Although there is scarcely any traffic on these backwoods paths, a car parked in the middle of a trail for a few minutes may block passage of the only vehicle that will come that way in months. We discovered that we were holding up a truckload of cranberry workers.

In a way, it was well that we blocked the road. For we found out definitely that our railroad cut was no cut at all but a sluiceway which had failed to work. On the truck, in a group of several men, were a woman and two small children. We learned only two names, for the others refused to disclose their identity. One was Samuel Herbert and the other Harry Sweet. It was Sam who told us about the sluiceway, but Harry, whom they called "Sweetie," ran away giggling when we suggested taking his picture.

The sluice was dug, it seems, for the cranberry bogs of Harry Black, near Lower Mill. The water was to carry from the reservoir to where we had seen the trestle—here the rush was to be carried across the stream in a wooden trough. It was somebody's brilliant idea, figured out in detail, but forgetting all about the laws of gravitation, that water won't run uphill.

Our informant directed us to where he said we might find the abandoned railroad. This, he said, was the Kinkora Railroad, the section at New Lisbon being out of service for the past thirty years, at least. We were advised to take our choice of two routes to find any relics that might remain, one through somebody's pigpen and the other back of the old dance hall on the other side of the Brown's Mills track of the Pennsylvania line. We chose the path back of the dance pavilion, which may have added fuel to somebody's stove by now.

On the road there is a picturesque house, now called Fenwick Manor, although it is far from Salem County where the name might have greater significance. Here a woman, who was pleasant enough after she had scolded us for trespassing, went into details about old Lisbon, the iron furnace that was there, the saw mill, the grist mill, and the old house, built in 1745. Samuel Scoville has a cabin up on Mount Misery Brook not far from here, and here he has written of woodsy creatures, botany, and the Continental soldiers who, according to tradition, paused at the Lisbon grist mill.

The Kinkora Railroad, running up through Lewistown to Kinkora, cut over part of the manor property. Beyond the dance pavilion there was a path that led to all the evidence that will be found of the railroad branch. It may be that even this evidence is gone now.

Here was an elevated embankment, overgrown with trees, but with cinders still scattered across it and easily kicked up from the moss and muggy ground. Following this down to the Rancocas Creek, we found one lone length of rail, a few ties and, down under the flowing cedar water, the snagged uprights of the old trestle our inquirer asked us about. But back of these fragmentary mementoes, all that remain after raids by campers and canoeists, lies a long and high-sounding history.

First there was the Columbus and Kinkora Railroad Company, incorporated by a special act of the Legislature April 2, 1866. The name was later changed to the Columbus, Kinkora and Springfield Railroad Company through another special act and the company was finally incorporated December 15, 1870. With Kinkora and Lisbon the terminals, fifteen miles apart, construction was begun in 1871 and completion effected in 1872.

The line was sold on foreclosure October 19, 1901. It was reorganized as the Kinkora and New Lisbon Railroad Company under the general laws of New Jersey April 27, 1903. It was consolidated and merged with the Philadelphia and Long Branch Railroad Company, as well as the Pemberton and Hightstown Railroad Company, the old U. T., February 25, 1915. This action made it a part of the Philadelphia and Atlantic Railroad Company, as it operated from Pemberton through Lewistown.

But in spite of all this organization and reorganization, the New Lisbon spur is already forgotten today. As for those days when a band of Portuguese bestowed on the town its original name—they're using a Portuguese kris for a stove poker at Fenwick Manor!

Bill Farrand said he wouldn't have believed a quarter of it if he hadn't come along.

XXXIV

FROM CROSSWICKS TO CABBAGETOWN

MANY worthy stories have been written about the neighborhood of Crosswicks, Allentown, Imlaystown, and Cox's Corner. The historical importance of these towns and the roads connecting them, colored by accounts of skirmishes in the Revolution, has been immortalized by many scholarly writers.

However, since our chief concern is with "lost towns" or villages which have lost their earlier identity in one way or another, we must use an approach that is quite different. Our history is not the revision of material which has already merited the attention of those who are scholars of events and dates. Ours is a history remembered by those we have talked to or, in some cases, those to whom priceless folk lore has been handed down. Such information has been in grave danger of being lost forever.

So let us talk for a moment about the wandering cannon ball of Crosswicks, what good old Quakers were doing with their penknives while waiting for the Spirit to move them, that road which has hairpin turns because it was an Indian trail following a creek and finally, the little hamlet which has protested ineffectually against the name of Cabbagetown, by which it has been known since long before 1834.

To linger in the vicinity of Crosswicks—called "Crossix" by natives who have inherited the first English pronunciation—is quite worth while. There is a charm that clings to the town with venerable houses and that splendid meeting-house, one of the largest in Southern New Jersey and home of the Chesterfield Meeting.

In the New Jersey *Gazetteer* of 1834, which follows Thomas Gordon's History, it is explained that the Crosswicks Creek on which the town is located, gets its name from the Indian word, Crossweeksunk, meaning "a separation." In the subsequent description of the post-town, it is disclosed that there were:

". . . from 40 to 50 dwellings, a very large Quaker meeting house and school, four taverns, five or six stores, a saw and grist mill" and that "the village is pleasantly situated in fertile country, whose soil is sandy loam. Near the town is a bed of iron ore, from which considerable quantities are taken to the furnaces in the lower part of the county."

There are more dwellings now but otherwise Crosswicks is much as it always was. Cabbagetown, however, is glorified beyond its present-day distinction:

". . . hamlet of Upper Freehold township, Monmouth county, on a line between that county and Middlesex, 17 miles from Freehold and 12 from Trenton, contains some half dozen dwellings, a wheelwright, smith and joiner's shop."

The wheelwright, smith and joiner died many years ago and presumably no one carried on their trade at the road junction which the tiny village boasts. One will look in vain for evidence of their shops today, unless a rickety shed we saw, and that no one knew anything about, was the remains of one of them. While quoting the old-time authority it would be well to give Mr. Gordon's estimate of the Imlaytown of his time against the Imlaystown of today:

> "It contains 12 or 15 dwellings, a grist and saw mill, tannery, one tavern, one store, wheelwright and smith shop."

Imlaystown has many more houses now although it is not one of those communities which boasts any remarkable increase in ratables from year to year. Allentown a century ago was much more imposing than Imlaystown, more impressive, perhaps, than it is today. "It contained from 75 to 80 dwellings, a Presbyterion Church with a cupola and bell, handsomely situated on a hill on the West; an academy, two schools, one Methodist Church, grist mill, saw mill and tilt mill on Doctor Creek, and saw mill on Indian Run, below which, at a short distance west of the town, is a cotton manufactory. A considerable business is done in town."

All that is hidden from many eyes in the present day. Too often travelers hurry through, unmindful that although the schools are shut up, academies gone, churches a bit weather-beaten and old mills and manufacturies mere holes in the ground, foundations were laid in and about them for what is happening now and what lies ahead for tomorrow. Such is the fate of Allentown, Imlaystown, and Crosswicks, although the State Commission on Historic Sites has distinguished the Crosswicks area with a road-side inscription:

"Crosswicks creek, three miles east of this point, was the scene of a skirmish June 23, 1778."

When General Clinton and his Redcoats were retreating toward New York, the patriot militia destroyed the bridge across the creek. Job Clevenger was killed as he cut the last piece of underpinning. There was considerable excitement, several exchanges of fire by the militia and the invading soldiers as well as the discharge of small field pieces, all of which make the background for the story of the wandering cannon ball.

Several years ago a reporter went to Crosswicks to write an article about the old meeting-house and the legend of the cannon ball, said to have lodged in the meeting-house wall. Everybody said the ball was there, that it had been written about before and that most people knew the story. But the reporter discovered that the ball was not in the wall and reported that the legend was a pretty one, but unfounded.

The day we trudged through slushy snow to browse in the Quaker outpost, built in 1773, a young man who accompanied us from a garage across the street pointed to the ball, about as big as a small-sized grapefruit, imbedded in the wall between two upstairs windows.

"That's funny," we said. "We know a reporter who came up here two years or so ago and said the cannonball wasn't anywhere in evidence, that the story was a fake."

"Maybe the ball wasn't here then," our informant suggested.

"Now, listen," we said, "the story was supposed to be that the ball crashed into the wall in a skirmish at the

The eighteenth century Moravian church near Oliphant's Mills, below Swedesboro.

Walter Golden, the last miller at Imlaystown.

The Atsion stove in the Chesterfield Friends Meeting at Crosswicks is m
prized by the community, as is also a cannon ball lodged high in one of the o
brick walls during the Revolution. The ball was surreptitiously removed at l
once, and taken home for safekeeping by a custodian who used it as a doors
but years later the trustees recovered it and put it back. It may be noted that
cushions on the benches in the paneled interior would not have been toler
in the old days.

bridge down there. That was in the Revolution. What do you mean, maybe the ball wasn't here two years ago?"

"They put it back since then," the man told us soberly. "You can see the plaster around it from here. It was this way: One of the residents up here was a trustee or something. He thought the ball was much too valuable to leave it where the Revolutionary cannon fired it. He had it gouged out and took it to his home where he guarded it.

"Maybe the other trustees didn't think much of the idea but they didn't do anything about it. They waited till the old chap died. That wasn't so long ago. Everybody agreed that the place for the ball was where it had been for over a century so they went and got it and put it back. They got a stone mason to do the job. That's why the ball wasn't here when the reporter was, see?"

Before we went down to the bridge itself, a thirty-year-old structure that was erected beside an old-fashioned covered span that was later removed, we borrowed a key from a caretaker across the street from the meeting-house in order to see the well-preserved paneled interior. The quiet of the lovely place would have been other-worldly except for the smell of old books and dust. There was something impressive, however, in the realization that here on the wooden benches, up in these galleries, apart from the world outside, generations had sat since those pioneers who had been linked with the earliest beginnings of New Jersey.

We made a real discovery in the men's half of the downstairs assembly room. In the midst was a huge stove which saw service at that time and perhaps still does. A large box-like and unbelievably solid article, the name

"Atsion" appears on the face. Unquestionably this stove was constructed of Jersey bog ore down at Atsion, old Atsiyunk, when the furnace there was going. The stove was the first of its type we had ever seen and the only one known to be in use, although we have been told that many farmhouses of the area work them.

There is a framed letter hung near the stove, stating that it cost eight pounds, four shillings and tenpence, and that Stacy Potts was named to collect the costs from members of the meeting. The date seems to have been 1772 and if it was, this stove has been on duty since that time. The furnace towns which made stoves near by went down about 1810.

There is no difficulty in telling which is the men's side of the assembly chamber. Up in the gallery, on the backs of benches and on the deep window sills, are the carved initials of long ago. K.F.N. carved his in 1838. B.C. made his mark in 1793, G.L. in 1819, and a host of others at various times before and since. There are no initials on the women's side. They didn't carry penknives and, obviously, paid greater attention to what was going on.

The old oak on the corner of the meeting-house lawn was there, they say, when William Penn visited various meetings in New Jersey, among them the Chesterfield Meeting. Seedlings of this tree were planted, according to information on various other inscriptions in the meeting rooms, by Richard DeCou and Herman Conrow, when the 150th anniversary was celebrated in 1923.

Another building of unusual interest in the vicinity is the Presbyterian Church at Allentown, whither we took our way via the bridge near which the bloody skirmish took place. This is the building whose cupola and bell is mentioned by the historian in 1834. The congregation was organized in 1725 but we were prepared for such an historic revelation by two old gentlemen who told us they had been in Allentown since "the Lord Himself was there."

There are many original rhymes for epitaphs in the ancient cemetery behind the church and several stones have the sinister skull and crossbones of the markers at Topanemus. Such old-stock names as Horspull, Pullin, Hay, Barcalow, Cowenhowen, Hepburn, and English are to be seen high on the promontory overlooking the lake. The church building goes back to 1756, was rebuilt in 1837 and enlarged in 1858.

Cabbagetown may have lost its original vegetable aspect but it has gained another. Most people call it New Canton, now. It consists of a cluster of houses, of which the largest boasts brick and frame construction obviously more than a century old, falling into ruin. Cabbagetown was named for cabbages, we were assured, but no one knows who called it that long enough for the name to appear on older maps.

We had the good fortune to find William Hendrickson, for 37 years the principal of the Imlaystown School, in the general store and post office there. The post office consists of a caged compartment as large as that assigned a cashier in a chain store.

Mr. Hendrickson said that Imlaystown is the only Imlaystown in the United States, although confusion arises sometimes because Emley's Hill is three miles away. "The Imlays," said Mr. Hendrickson, "trace their ancestry to

Scotland, the Emleys to the Indians. That old farmhouse over there was the first of any importance in the town and replaced an earlier structure, built of logs. It is occupied now by Allen F. Hendrickson, Sr. Peter Imlay was the first settler here and, when you are in Georgetown, ask for the Peter Imlay who lives there now. He is a lineal descendant, proud that there is a Peter Imlay on the scene after all these years."

We mentioned that it was rather curious that the main street of Imlaystown had so many twists and turns, despite so much traffic, however unwanted, being thrust upon it. "That's natural enough," said Mr. Hendrickson. "The first road was an Indian trail which followed the top of the bank along the winding Buckhole Creek. The trail was the first street here. The Imlays were always aristocratic. Refused any part of the Imlay farm, newcomers were compelled to build their homes on that one street or along the other creek bank."

Days when limeboats used to come up Doctor's Creek as far as Yardville are gone. With them, old Hogback Landing has disappeared. Even Hayti, pronounced Hay-tie here, forgets its palmy days on the old Amboy line in the meaningless station name of Shrewsbury Crossing.

XXXV

MOUNTAINS AND MOLEHILLS

HOWEVER hurriedly one refers to mountains in Southern New Jersey, one finds himself confronted by smirks or deprecatory argument from those who know the State much better than anybody else. But though it may have been an optimist who called them so, or perhaps someone with a gift for exaggeration, there are mountains, sure enough.

More than a century ago there were at least ten centers of activity, hamlets, villages or townships, with names that boasted elevation. Mount Bethel, up in Somerset County, is on Stony Hill. Mount Carmel, in 1832, was "a mountain hamlet" of Hunterdon County with soil that "is clay, cold, and at present not very productive but improvable by the use of lime." Mount Clinton was, even in those days, a village "laid out on the Palisade rocks."

Mount's Creek was and is a tributary of the Cohansey River. Mount Ephraim has kept its name through a hundred or more years although today its rise is hardly distinguishable and little there recalls the village of old Gloucester Township. Of Mount Ephraim one historian has written "the hill from which it has its name is, for this country, elevated, and affords an extensive view, even to the Delaware."

Mount Freedom, years ago, boasted a Presbyterian Church and a dozen dwellings in Morris County. Mount Holly, once The Bridge and Bridgetown because of the number of bridges over which the roads met there, took its new name "from a mount of sand and sandstone near it and some holly trees about its base." At Mount Misery, the old tavern continues to defy the fires that sweep the woods around it. There are three Mount Pleasants, all of them upstate.

Of one, Thomas Gordon said, "it is at least fifty feet above the waters" and this proud boast is the key, perhaps, to many of the towns and villages which acquired, through the years, a "mountain" aspect. All of it depends, certainly, on the point of view.

We remember pausing for the night in Caratunk, Maine, with the mountains frowning down from the sky in all directions. We asked a farmer their name. "Them's not mountains," he replied. "Them's hills."

The land in Southern New Jersey is so generally flat that the smallest climb gains comparative importance. Beyond the central area of the State there are mountains deserving the name but down in the country of bogs and barrens, few are more than glorified hills. There is one notable exception, of course—the Forked River Mountains, back from Waertown; these deserve a place of their own, for hemmed in by thickets and swamps that make them all but inaccessible, they boast at least one height, we found, from which, in one direction, we saw the hangar at Lakehurst and, in the other, Barnegat Light.

But our concern so far has been with the "mountain" villages which have been forgotten, for the most part, just as our queer ways have avoided those towns which, however historic, are better known to the traveler. So we went to Mount Laurel and Arney's Mount and Upper Springfield Meeting. There is an Arneytown, too, and because it seems to have moved away from the mount, it was a natural challenge. As for Upper Springfield, the "Upper" is more geographical than topographic.

It is possible, of course, that there was another name, for there is no mention of Mount Laurel, either township or town, in the older histories. Even Copany, we were surprised to find long after writing about it, was once Matacopenny. But early references to Arneytown indicate that it once was at the foot of the mount although today it is some distance removed, with the houses left behind owning no village name at all.

Not so long ago the Mount Laurel Meeting-house, one of the loveliest to be found in better known towns, was opened for the first wedding in years—the principals were the son and kin of the last couple married there. The most vivid of our several pilgrimages there is of a day when we had been to Hog Pond Corner, trying to discover how such a name came into being. The road sign with the name boldly blazoned upon it had long bothered us, standing at an angle out Church Road back of Moorestown, near a trail that swings into Evesboro. We found the corner a mucky field, despite recent tiling.

Inasmuch as it was the only pond in the vicinity up to seventy-five years ago, farmers set up a community slough for their hogs. "They used to brand the pigs," Mrs. Martha Ivins told us, standing in the dooryard of a farm near the corner, with blooming trumpet-vines all about. Mrs. Ivins said she remembered days when there was some semblance of activity thereabouts.

"When the pigs were branded," she said, "they were driven to that pond on the corner—it's all dried up now. Everybody knew where the hog pond was and this became Hog Pond Corner. There are a few pigs left around here now. See that rough-cast house up there? There's a piggery behind it. Polish fellow runs it. We call him the Pig Man because we can't get around his Polish name."

We went back to Mount Laurel. We took it for granted so long that for a long time we paid little heed to the 1798 stone in the meeting-house, unaware that the deserted road gets through, eventually, to Mount Holly. We had been so interested in the tiny brick tombstones with names and dates scratched into them in the graveyard not far away that we forgot to remark the oaks in the meeting-house yard, one of which is celebrated as the oldest in Burlington County. The legend persists that both the rise at Mount Holly and this at Mount Laurel served as signal hills but we have never been able to run that down.

At the crossroads is the Township Hall and down the road is a nondescript store but there is little activity, except on election day. Mount Laurel is chiefly a hamlet of colored folk around the crossroads now. Across from the meeting-house is a sign that proclaims the hill a State Reservation, surely the tiniest in New Jersey. Up the road is Springville, where, at another store, you may or may not obtain information about the mill towns that once made this corner of Burlington County hum. There were Christopher's Mills, Snyder's Mills, Ballinger's Mill, Little Mill, Braddock's Mill, and Kirby's Mill. Along came feed companies in Camden to put them all out of business, one by one.

Having followed a directional sign and spying a house under the shelter of some venerable buttonwoods, we asked a man who left his wife on a cool, white porch:

"Where's Oliphant's Mills, the town on the sign up the road?"

"This is it," replied the man, who said he was Sam Hinchman, once of Haddonfield, who was told he had to get deep into the country if he wanted to save his wife's life. That was thirty-five years ago and Mrs. Hinchman, who sat on the porch, had been given three months to a year to live.

"But where's the mill?" we persisted.

"Back there in the bushes," Sam answered. And so it was—and is—a broken pile of rotting timbers.

There are three or four houses at the foot of Arney's Mount, beside the intersection of two roads which are often bumpy, or used to be, one coming over from Pemberton and the other swinging in from the concrete Bordentown—Hammonton highway at Jobstown. The corner, when the houses fall away, will be distinguished still by the meeting-house on the rise, very different from the one at Mount Laurel, with the burial ground behind it ending in a point, farther up the hill.

The steep of Arney's Mount is made of stone, contrasting surrounding fields in which there are few, if any, stones at all. It is unusual, too, because of the great numbers of huge oaks that span the summit, ageless sentinels of active days that have gone and soon will be forgotten. The television experimental station higher up is well guarded and remains as much a mystery as the past that walls cannot reveal.

There was a quarry here long before railroads were thought of. Stone was hauled by mule teams over long distances. A store and blacksmith shop were soon established. The store closed up long ago for lack of trade. The smithy subsequently went out of business, not because of any increase in automobile traffic. Of the thirty houses which, they told us, once composed the town, some were moved away and at least two burned down. Perhaps those that were moved went to meet others in the Arneytown of today.

Squire Warner Hargrove, of Pemberton, the town undoubtedly named for Israel Pemberton, one of the early forge proprietors, recalled that his mother brought him to meeting at Arney's Mount and that it was here, among his kin, the Browns and Scattergoods, that he learned to remember the days of the month in the jingle of the Friends:

"The 4th, 11th, 9th and 6th,
     To each have thirty days affixed.
     All the rest have thirty-one
     Except the second month alone,
     Which has but twenty-eight in fine
     Till Leap Year gives it twenty-nine."

Picture the scene on a sultry day with the mount, said to boast an elevation of two hundred feet, stretching away to the woods atop the rise behind the meeting-house of native stone. Look at the graveyard, with stone walls following the contour of the land. Imagine the quiet scene interrupted, first by the noises of a far-away farmyard, then by the drone of a speaker in the meeting-house, with a hundred horses tied in the rambling sheds that are no more. The ringing of the hammer and anvil in the smithy have subsided for meeting day. Then you have Arney's Mount, not as it was when we saw it last with but two families remaining, but as it was on Quarterly Meeting day.

"Once," Squire Hargrove said, "we were quite late and we saw, as we approached the door, that the interior was almost filled. Good John Comfort, the usher, arose from his chair and calmly showed us seats. The room on the inside was thirty by thirty. Benches were all around with those that were elevated kept for those minded to speak. The rows were close together. When we knelt down we were knee to knee. Faces peered down at us from the gallery, closed off by let-down doors when congregations were smaller than they were that day."

The meeting-house was built in 1775. Gracing what is reputed to be the highest land in Burlington County, it is still the mecca, at least once a year, for Friends who come from miles around, in retreat from the world, in communion with kinfolk that worshipped here ages ago. The stone used in the building came from the quarry. It is partly covered with creepers and shaded all around by the tall trees. The interior seems always cool, even on hottest days. The woodwork is that originally placed inside, as are the benches, unpainted and impressive with simple lines.

Of the hundreds of stones in the climbing cemetery there are only a few that are more than a few inches above the ground. Many are stones from the mountain pit, rudely inscribed by relatives of those who lie buried here. The dates vary from those of the first meetings to present times. The stone of William H. Lippincott is dated 1782. Earles, Smiths, Woodwards, Haineses, Ridgeways, Ellises, Whites, Bryans, Newbolds, Doughtys, and Deacons rest from their labors in dated generations.

In the Deacon lot are John B. Deacon, once Burlington County clerk, and his wives, one at either side. On the stone of one is the inscription, "A True Wife—A Kind Mother." On the stone of the other is written, "A True Wife—Childless." Among the Houghs is the grave of

Brigadier-General Alfred Lacey Hough and that of Judge Charles Merrill Hough, whose funerals brought hundreds to climb the slope.

Joseph Engle, the caretaker, almost eighty when we were there last, rewarded our compliments concerning his care of the old shrine with permission to see some of the old books locked away in the meeting-house. One is a record called "The Mount Preparative Meeting of Women Friends." The first entry was "First month, 4th, 1824." The book shows clearly that meetings were held punctually and with great regularity and that through the week younger members were disciplined for being late and sleeping during sessions.

There are occasional entries, such as, "Sarah B. Davis, late Shinn, having accomplished her marriage contrary to the established order of the Society, on which account she has been treated with by one of the overseers. After consideration, the meeting united with her case being forwarded to the monthly meeting." Mrs. Davis must have forgotten to obtain approval or permission in the match or, perhaps, had acknowledged the authority of "hireling ministry."

This was in 1830 as was the case of Susan Leeds, who was disciplined for moving to Philadelphia without a certificate. Considerable space is given in the record to the affairs of Barclay White, clerk of the meeting, who married his first cousin "with the assistance of a magistrate." White was ordered to hand over all his books and was succeeded by one Benjamin R. Lamb who, the book indicates, had married with the aid of a magistrate himself, his disciplining being attested by White. These were days when justices of the peace were permitted to conduct wedding ceremonies.

Going across country to Springfield Meeting, perhaps with Daniel Smith and Elizabeth Hough, who, according to the signatures we saw, came from there to Arney's Mount to be among the subscribers to the proposed *Elwood's Sacred History* in 1821, we must assume that Upper Springfield long preceded the house on the mount. Squire Hargrove had a marriage certificate, signed there in November, 1735, and when we saw it we were told that it was eight years younger than the meeting-house itself.

The contracting parties on the parchment were John Croshaw and Sarah Antrim. The first signatures were those of the bride and groom. But the bride could not write her name—credit the excitement of the moment, if you would be kind. One of the witnesses wrote Sarah's name and Sarah herself affixed her mark. The clerk was perhaps a deaf old gentleman who was reluctant to ask for repetitions. Having made the certificate out in advance, as the careful penmanship indicates, with the names filled in and added on the day of the marriage, he couldn't have heard the groom's name very plainly, or if he did, the spelling stumped him. What he wrote was "Crusher" and not Croshaw.

Equally prized by the late Squire was a sampler, bearing the signature, "Sarah Croshaw, her work," indicating that the bride later recovered from momentary stage fright. Other names appended to the certificate, linking people of Arney's Mount with those at Upper Springfield, were Thomas and Mary Earl, John West, Thomas Scattergood, Job Eldridge, Rebecca Brian, Elizabeth Hance, Silence Butcher, Rebecca Ridgeway, Abigal Wright, Antrims, Croshaws, Bartons, and Smiths.

None we have found have been able to tell why the site of the meeting-house was called Upper Springfield. It is off the beaten track, northwest of restored Camp Dix on a tiny road that winds through Wrightstown, not far from the Stromboli stock farm mostly associated with the interests of Harry Sinclair. A frame meeting-house went up as early as 1723. Later, when Hicksites broke away from Orthodox members of the meeting, the quarrel was settled amicably, the story goes—the meeting-house was enlarged so that both sides could meet without either disturbing the other. Up at Arneytown they tell a different story, declaring that the Hicksites from Upper Springfield moved there.

The meeting-house today is as it was after restoration demanded by a fire in 1918. The original date stone was saved by Hillman Croshaw, great-grandson of the couple named in the certificate, who returned it at the rebuilding, with the original benches that were rescued from the flames. If you seek out the old meeting-house, remember, when you pass over the road from Wrightstown, that you are traversing an unusual highway—the divisional line that once separated the domains of the Indians and "the Christian people." Indians lived south of the line but there is no record of trouble caused by ventures across the border. Old Thomas Scattergood, who attended that wedding at Arney's Mount, thought the boundary line was silly and said so.

Renowned as a friend of the Indians, since the days when he and his family lived in a cave near Columbus, Scattergood fought the border idea and gave the Indians permission to use his lands in any reasonable way at any time, without thought of territorial restriction. It is recorded that when he died, Scattergood was mourned by chiefs and braves for miles around, hundreds of them assembling for the funeral.

We told you that Arneytown was a challenge and so it proved. After all, when you look for a town at the foot of a hill with a similar name and realize, suddenly, that the town exists, but somewhere else, you begin to wonder what has happened. But no matter how painstaking are your inquiries, you will encounter confusion in the minds of those who try to distinguish between the town that is and the sudden steep of the meeting-house.

Years ago the Arneytown whose name may have drifted down the road with the houses that were moved, had its post office, general store, blacksmith, church, and school, they say. The corner that was once the town is up a sandy trail that passes a group of unpainted houses in the shade of tall maples and then, skirting the ruins of a burned mansion and what we saw as the desolation of a deserted Colonial house, rolls swiftly down hill. It wasn't so long ago that prosperity made its last stand—the late 1890s. And yet but five or six families say they live in Arneytown, now, and that sets one to wondering how long it takes to obliterate such wayside villages.

The large white house is well-guarded against antique thieves, we discovered. The caretaker didn't make us very welcome but he did tell us something of George B. Wilds, who lived there and who, at the end of the nineteenth century, attained a skyrocket career in politics, being sent to the Assembly from Burlington County. George was tall, gaunt, bewhiskered like Uncle Sam.

In the days of his campaigning, he went everywhere, to harvest home suppers, farmers' picnics, anywhere to make a speech. Something of an agitator but an undoubted progressive in every way but one, he talked up ideas later duplicated by farmer-labor groups. Duly elected, he found himself out of his element among practising politicians. Fighting the use of the cranberry scoop in a manner that contradicted his advanced notions, he sponsored legislation that was laughed down. As a result he earned the sobriquet of "Huckleberry Wilds" and carried it to his grave.

John Bacon, the Refugee, called Arneytown home, and somewhere in the weedy cemetery that was partly a poultry pen when we were there, his body lies buried. Bacon was killed by militiamen, you may recall. John Steward, an Arneytown farmer, claimed the honor of having disposed of him. The body, they say, was examined at the hotel in Mount Misery for evidence supporting Steward's claim, but inasmuch as Bacon had been both bayonetted and shot, the "honor" went unawarded.

Bacon's body was taken up through the pines for burial. The grave was to have been in the middle of a road near Jacobstown so the spot would become obliterated and forgotten. But while patriots of Jacobstown were in the act of lowering the corpse, Bacon's brother appeared and begged for the privilege of providing decent burial. The pinewoods bandit was taken away and interred in the plot beside the turn of the road in Arneytown, where grave markers, concealed in rubble, show that the Lawries, kin of a New Jersey governor, are buried beside him.

Mountains, distinguished by town names after the towns themselves have faded, bring smirks and snickers. But it's a sad business. Men who were mountains in their day are less than molehills in current memories. Dead villages have buried both bones and recollections.

XXXVI

SOLOMON'S GRAVEYARD TO ADAMS CHURCH

BELOW MICKLETON, on the road to Swedesboro, there is a tiny road that meanders through the countryside, running between a deserted railroad station called Wolfert, and a corner known as Oak Grove. Here one of the oldest churches in Gloucester County may be found in excellent repair.

The name Wolfert is a misnomer. It ought to be Wolferth. Property in that vicinity is owned by Mrs. John C. Wolferth, a widow who still lives in the Wolferth farmhouse. John Wolferth bought the property from Christian Wolferth who, Mrs. Wolferth told us, took title from his sister. Mrs. Wolferth had no explanation for the change of name.

"It may be that the railroad sign painter ran out of paint," she suggested.

On this excursion you will learn, as we did, that pioneers along this road, as well as their kin, have been important people, even if the vicinity has gone to seed. Dr. Charles Wolferth, Mrs. Wolferth's son, is a heart specialist at the University Hospital. And yet, for all the Wolferths who have been and still are in the vicinity, that sign on the tiny depot platform has remained a mockery through many years.

Just up the hill from the railroad crossing is a small cemetery enclosed by a brick wall. This is Solomon's

Graveyard. A stone set in the wall proclaims the name and gives the founding date as 1850. John Gibson, who lives a hundred yards or so away, says that's as wrong as the name, Wolfert.

"That's the date they put the wall up, that's all," he told us. "The graveyard was there when King's Highway was cut through and the road was a short-cut to it."

Solomon's Graveyard, part of a property owned once long ago by a farmer, Solomon Lippincott, is now owned by the Mickleton Meeting of Friends. Inside are the graves of pioneers whose names can be easily traced in connection with important events in the vicinity. Vanleers, Warringtons, Goudons, Devaults, and Bennetts, as well as Keturah Gooden, Garret Clark, Chalkley Brown and many others owe the fact that their names are in evidence to the cows and sheep that are pastured in the enclosure.

Once there was a meeting-house, erected in 1740, but this was destroyed by fire in the late 1700s and was not replaced. The burial plot originally included the grove across the road and part of the land between the wall and the Gibson farm. The grove itself, which was once cut to obtain lumber sold to provide funds to keep the place in repair, has grown up again. Now the wall is crumbling and the owners of the cows will have to buy tethers.

Down the road is Warrington's Mill, as charming a turn in the wandering pathway as one could wish for. Well kept and protected from the careless invader—although few come here, not knowing, perhaps, that such hideaways exist—the mill itself has been in the Warrington family for more than 125 years. Albert Warrington, grandson of the original owners, lives comfortably in his grandsire's white manor house, on the brow of a hill that dips gracefully to the lake below.

The woods behind the spillway, where the old water wheel has been replaced by turbines, have been kept carefully in trim and are filled with birdhouses, all along the flooded stream. Warrington's Mill is one of four old grist mills in the vicinity still in operation, doing business that seems to defy the modern era. With Avis's Mill at Woodstown, Justice's Mill in Pedricktown, and Oliphant's, formerly Porch's Mill, near Swedesboro, it still holds the line for methods now obsolete, with but few changes.

All these mills grind feed except the Avis establishment where flour is ground by electric power, installed to replace the water wheel. Inside, the dusty cobwebs hang as they have for decades, centuries. Old beams are pegged and wheels tilted aside with a miller's apology, flanked by a promise to change nothing more.

The original owner of the Warrington mill and many who worked there lie buried in Solomon's Graveyard. It was the dull season for millers when we were there. Warrington's had operated only three hours on a Monday and on Tuesday not at all. There was something in the air, however, which rejoiced in the mill's being on a side road, something that raised its head proudly in the defending of a tradition, no matter what the cost.

"There'll be plenty work tomorrow," the miller said.

Further on, there is Hendrickson's Mill, not in operation now. Hendrickson's became a distillery in pre-Prohibition days and for its desertion of the ranks, is paying with tragic dissolution. Wilbur Hendrickson operated the distillery and his applejack was celebrated far and wide as Hendrickson's Whiskey. The place went out of operation with the adoption of the Eighteenth Amendment and did not regain its reputation with Repeal.

Those who went home with flour and feed from Warrington's in the old days used to stop at Hendrickson's for a drink or two but all that is forgotten now in a boarded-up building at the side of a little-traveled road.

Originally, Jacob Hendrickson was the owner. Wilbur Hendrickson, the tenant when we were there, sold the lake and adjacent land some time before but the buyer did not complete the deal. Later, when Mr. Hendrickson was compelled to take his holdings back, he placed the tract in the sheriff's hands. John Seegar, of New York, bought 105 acres, including the lake, and has established a country home there.

Alexander Swan, a nephew of Seegar, was tearing down the old homestead and we hurried away. A deserted house is bad enough but one being ruthlessly torn apart is a sight which, with every rip and tear, finds an echo in the heart. Workmen who boasted of finding an 1812 penny in a partition had the effect of rubbing it in. Someone has written that the mill pond is now Swan Lake, named for a man and not graceful creatures which will be sought in vain on the water.

Describing the old Adams Meeting-house, the little church building which stands opposite the abandoned schoolhouse at the end of the road, we can do no better than quote a few words from an article written by the late James L. Pennypacker, president of the Haddonfield Historical Society, in the almanac and year book of the Woodstown National Bank for 1916.

"Standing on a knoll under some large white oak trees," Mr. Pennypacker wrote, "at the crossroads on the north side of the Raccoon Creek about half way between Swedesboro and Bridgeport, is perhaps the oldest surviving Methodist Episcopal church building in West Jersey.

It is built of dressed brown stone, is architecturally interesting, and is in an excellent state of preservation. This building was erected in 1793.

"It was known in early times as 'The Adams Meetinghouse' and later has been called, colloquially, the 'Old Stone Church' and the 'Oak Grove Church.' The ground upon which it stands was a corner of the farm of Joseph Adams. Shortly after its erection Joseph, and Elizabeth, his wife, gave one acre of land about the building to a board of trustees and their successors for church purposes in perpetuity."

Mr. Pennypacker, whose scholarly interest in and writing of historical matters is often missed by many more fortunately celebrated, then went into the terms of the deed. The Adamses were among the trustees of the church at the time of the signing of the deed. The church, according to its records, once served worshippers from Clarksboro, Bridgeport, Centre Square, Pedricktown, Paulsboro and other smaller villages. From Centre Square they crossed in a barge, making their way over Raccoon Creek at the late Alexander Black's farm.

The church isn't used now, except for an occasional service which provides funds for its upkeep. Some day, however, those interested in such shrines, may awaken to the fact that Adams Church isn't as well-preserved as many think it is. For it is likely to be lost forever on a road that doesn't appear to be interesting at all but along which, at every turn and on every hill, there are monuments to a more unhurried time.

XXXVII

HEAD-OF-THE-RIVER AND TUCKAHOE

BACK IN 1780, during a blinding snowstorm typical of an old-fashioned hard winter, an early itinerant Methodist preacher, Mr. James, sought shelter at the home of David Sayres. Sayres, who had been a captain in the Continental Army, was living quietly at a point four miles from what was then called Tuckahoe, at a place referred to as Head-of-the-River.

Mr. James was an Englishman. He had arrived in this country at a time when the sentiments of patriots, especially ex-army men, were none too cordial to wandering strangers from overseas. Nevertheless, something happened on that stormy night when the pioneering parson found hospitality in Southern New Jersey. With sleet beating on the rude window panes and snow swirling in drifts outside, Captain Sayres warmed his guest with victuals and then listened to him talk beside the fire. And he became a convert or, if he had been a religious man in earlier days, he vigorously renewed his faith from that night on.

Baptists had been in the vicinity some time before but their attempts to establish a church had not been met by permanent success. But Pastor James and Captain Sayres worked shoulder to shoulder so that today, in the midst of a scattering of farms and near an old house converted into a roadside tearoom, Head-of-the-River remains distinguished by the church they founded, a white frame building of dignified Colonial design. Around it are tombstones of the first Methodists and across the road, all but lost in the thickets, are the graves of religious leaders who failed where Mr. James succeeded.

The Tuckahoe of those and later times had much more importance than the town of today—in fact, after two long talks with Mr. and Mrs. Anthony Parker in their quaint old house up the old Tuckahoe Road, there are doubts of whether today's Tuckahoe is yesteryear's town at all. A great deal of name shifting has been going on down along the Tuckahoe River, that's certain.

Tuckahoe, a hundred or so years back, is described as "a post-town, having some 20 dwellings, three taverns and several stores." It was a place of "considerable trade in wood, lumber and shipbuilding." The land immediately on the river was "good, but a short distance from it" was "swampy and low." The Tuckahoe was at that time "navigable for sloops, above the village of Tuckahoe more than 10 miles from the ocean."

Shortly after Mr. James' sojourn in the neighborhood, a class began meeting at Hunter's Mill. This class was later organized into a Methodist congregation by Caleb Pedichord and Joseph Cromwell, also Englishmen. As a result of the increasing attendance at these informal meetings, a church building was completed in 1813. However, the organization date still stands at 1780, when Pastor James was trapped by a blizzard—part of the building was being used, for there is a record of a dedication at that time.

The church building itself is unusual. It resembles in many ways the churches of New England and, as far as the interior goes, the old Presbyterian church at Fairton, Cumberland County. The general design is similar to that of a large, old-fashioned farmhouse, with no departures from austere simplicity as far as the exterior is concerned. There is a gallery around three sides of a large single room. A pulpit, resembling a magistrate's desk, with lamps at either side, is so high that between the pews of the lower and gallery floors the preacher may see each member of his congregation with a slight turn of the head. Although benches have been provided, the box pews are obviously older.

In contrast to many of the other historic churches of Southern New Jersey, this one was used every Sunday when last we were there. In 1933, a large congregation marked the establishment of the Sunday School one hundred years before. The graveyard is the burial place of soldiers of many wars, the Revolution, the Civil War, the Spanish-American War, and the World War of 1914-1918.

Across the road, where a faintly discernible path winds to where passersby brave the mosquitoes to examine chipped inscriptions, are the stones of the Baptists. A successful group of worshippers must have been content to forget those whose zeal brought temporary enthusiasm but no church to remember them by—it is unfortunate that the graveyard does not include these other stones.

Among those still visible are rude monuments to the memory of the Reverend Peter Groom and Anne Groom, his wife. If the stone did not point out that Mr. Groom was the pastor of the Baptist Church at West Creek in 1807, we might conclude, from his name, that he was a wanderer from the Swedish colony. Both were buried on the other side of the road, now grown over with brush and scrub, Mrs. Groom's stone bearing the date of 1796.

Other markers are imprinted with the fading names of

e Etna "stack" looked like this almost thirty years ago, but now a mere scat-
ng of bricks marks the site. I was told that the bricks that could be put to use
re long ago carted away to become part of a hotel in Ocean City. When
rbin City didn't exist except as Champion's Landing, Etna Furnace was often
led Tuckahoe Furnace. What is Tuckahoe today was Williamsburg, close by
ad-of-the-River Church.

The Methodist Church at Head-of-the-River, organized in 1780, remains too much as it did when the author saw it first. The annual service held there attended mostly by descendants of the founding families. In earlier days, name meant more—this was as far as the big ships could come up the Tuckah Across the road the Baptists started a church, and a few tombstones are still visil Below, Hendrickson's Mill, an old Gloucester County applejack distillery n Mickleton.

Isaac Bonnell, 1794, and Millicent Price, 1826. Millicent's grave is protected by an ornamental iron fence, rusty, effective, and out-of-place in the strip of woods.

There are many legends centering around Head-of-the-River but on all sides the people who live in the neighborhood accept history and tradition with greater calm than that of a mountain beholding the first sun of morning. One story given us by Walter Burley was to the effect that Head-of-the-River was the original Tuckahoe but no one to whom we repeated that conclusion felt that it made any difference now. Most of them were not aware that Tuckahoe is an Indian name for bread.

But Anthony Parker, who is eighty-two and living in the house where he was born, told us a great deal. Although our visits were far apart, we heard more of the details on our second call, perhaps because he invited us to sit beside him on an old settle in the kitchen, where clouds of mosquitoes didn't drive us away.

Mr. Parker's a well-preserved man, still fond of rambling down along the river that has lost its importance, picking up arrowheads anad Indian axes in the lowlands not far from Etna Furnace, or what remains of it. Mrs. Parker likes to chide him for parting with his relics when wanderers take advantage of him, departing heavily laden upon payment of a dollar.

"There are a great many Parkers along the shore," we said.

"Yes," he answered, "but they're no relation. There's a lot of them, especially up around Parkertown, but they're not the same—although I've got a brother who went up their way. George, he's at Beachwood.

"The old parchment deeds I've got refer to all this lowland country as Gravelly Run. This house? Plenty old, although this half's older than the other. Look at those old beams in there and you can tell. I've lived here all my life, since November 11, 1855."

Mr. Parker was a shipwright, as was his father before him, in the days when big ships were built and launched along the Tuckahoe River. Presumably, the house was built by a man named Steelman, who gave it to his son. Then the place was bought by a chap named Richman.

"After that the papers show Squire Benjamin Weatherby owned it—that was in 1809," Mr. Parker said. "Tuckahoe? Well, that's a funny thing. It used to be on the other side of the river from what they call Tuckahoe now. Where the village is now used to be called Champion's Landing."

Mr. Parker got up and went to a desk, built a century ago in the corner of the kitchen nearest the door. He brought out a book with yellow pages, presented to him when he went to Sunday School. "Presented to Anthony Parker, as a reward for faithful attendance at Champion's Landing Sunday School," was written on the flyleaf.

"That was this side, the Head-of-the-River side of the bridge down there," Mr. Parker said. "Over the bridge was Williamsburg, and that's what they call Tuckahoe today. This side's called Corbin City, though it ain't much of a city."

That Williamsburg had troubled us, and we told the Parkers so. There are two Williamsburgs mentioned by the old *Gazetteer*, one in Middlesex County and the other listed with the parenthetical "See Cedar Creek."

"That's wrong," said Mr. Parker decisively. "What they're thinking of is old Cedar Swamp Creek."

And he was right. For Gordon lists no town of Cedar Creek. There are two Cedar Swamp Creeks, one described as rising in Upper Township, Cape May County and flowing into the Tuckahoe River. So Corbin City didn't exist except as Champion's Landing, in early days, and over the bridge, what is Tuckahoe today was Williamsburg. And Tuckahoe must have existed as the old name of Etna Furnace and the vicinity around Head-of-the-River Church, from what Mr. Parker eventually disclosed.

He proved an unusual man to question. We asked a question and received an answer. Then he waited for another question. That's why there were two visits, the second arranged after a lapse of time in which further questions had been prepared, based on chance disclosures made to the tree-hunting forestry man.

"This country was all a-bustle, then," he assured us. "There was the glassworks at Marshallville, and another at Estelville. Etna Furnace, as you call it, was in full blast but it was Tuckahoe Furnace then, as a lot of people don't know and won't believe. I had three order slips given by Louis and Henry Howell, who ran it, and I've kept one of them to prove its name wasn't Etna. I remember showing the slips to Sam Champion, who knew nearly everything about these parts, and he said he had never heard it called Tuckahoe. Maybe Etna was the name they gave it when Tuckahoe became the name of a town."

The forge "went out" about 1832 but Mr. Parker knew Solomon Warner, who worked as a moulder there. And shipyards? "They were all over the place," he said. "There was James Lee's shipyard where they built coastin' vessels and some that went across. They took coal to Boston and came back with paving stones. They went to ports in Texas. They sailed down to Mobile. Built and launched above the bridge on the Cape May side, some of 'em went around the Horn on their maiden voyages.

"I can remember two ships being built up the creek. One was the *A. M. Bailey*—Cap'n Bailey sailed her—and the other was the *Three Brothers*. Why, one of the Baileys —Ralph, isn't it?—still keeps the store down by the old wharf.

"My father built two I can remember well—the *Mary A. Rhodes* and the *Mary A. Turner*—and they were good-size, too. Then, over on the Marshallville side, by Yellow Hill, Hezekiah Godfrey built a lot of ships. On this side, up River Road, Joseph Sheppard had another yard. My father's ways were on the Atlantic side. Why, there was still another yard right back of the house here." There was a slight tone of disgust as the old man added, "They call it Etna Drive now!

"My father went up to Pennsgrove to build two ships for a man named Bolton," he went on. "One of those went around the Horn, I know."

Shipyards, obviously were on every side, till nearly all the forest was cut away, replaced today by a tall second growth in many places. And there were more than ships.

"Why, in my day everything was activity," Mr. Parker said. "There were sawmills everywhere and charcoal was being burned on every side. The ships they made here set out right away with loads of cordwood."

The old stage road to Cape May went by the Parkers' door and over Tuckahoe Bridge. The Risley Road, paralleling the old Reading tracks and used by those who know of it as a shortcut to the seashore resorts, was a stage road, too. "The railroad moved it over and used the old trail itself," Mr. Parker recalled.

Then we heard of Ingersoll Town, for the first time. That's where Mrs. Parker and her people came from. Ingersoll Town was on a road from Head-of-the-River to

Doughty's Tavern. "There was John Ingersoll, Daniel, Jonas, and Carl—one of the Ingersoll girls married James Lee," Mrs. Parker put in. "All the Ingersolls, brothers and sisters, lived in houses all in a row—and that's how the town got its name."

The little one-room schoolhouse that isn't far up the road from the old Parker house used to be across the way from Head-of-the-River Church, Mrs. Parker said. "Up there beside the Teapot Inn," she remembered. "I had to walk to school and I had to get up and leave at dawn to be there in time," she smiled. "It was dark by the time I got home each day. Of course, there was a lot of us and we had companions on the long walk. But it was six or seven miles one way."

Then from his desk Mr. Parker brought out an old pamphlet in which voters of the vicinity, years ago, were asked to approve a plan whereby parents would pay two dollars a head "to have children schooled." "Two dollars per scholar for free schools," the proposal read.

Back of the house, still well preserved in the rising and falling waters of the old river, are wooden rollers which, Mr. Parker explained, were used in forcing the juice from sugar-cane.

"You promised to show them to Lizzie," Mrs. Parker said to her husband, suddenly, "and now she's gone back home." Lizzie was a relative, it was quickly explained, who had been visiting. "She lived down here a long while and never heard of those rollers. But Anthony knew about them all the time and didn't say a thing."

"Why, everybody down here had his patch of sugar-cane," Mr. Parker interrupted. "But the wooden rollers were the first—and they're still good. I used to grow some cane. When it was ripe, I took it down to Carl Ingersoll's, like everybody else. Carl had a place with vats where he turned it into molasses. We all made our own molasses for the winter in those days down here. And after all of it was cooked, Carl used to bring his rollers and put 'em back of the house, under water to keep 'em from splitting, till he'd need 'em again. When he died he didn't need 'em any more. So they're back there in the water where he put 'em—and that's more years ago than I can remember."

The Parkers are devoted to a stately old white oak in front of their house. Until what is thought to be the largest and oldest oak in New Jersey was found recently near Jacobstown, this grand old sentinel near Head-of-the-River was a record-breaker. Perhaps it still is. "Why, it's bigger in every way then the Salem oak," Mr. Parker said. "And it's certainly bigger than the one at Mantua."

They speak of it reverently as if it were a member of the family, an ancester who has become a patriarch of the neighborhood.

When first we met the Parkers, Mrs. Olive Erickson, who operated the Teapot Inn with her husband, said we should see them and stay long enough to measure "the oldest oak in Cape May County." So we went up the Buck Hill Road and counted over more Indian relics than Mr. Parker boasts now. He kicked some of them from around a flower bed where many have been stolen and then, with beaming countenance, he produced an eight-pound cannonball he found in the river mud, British to the core.

"It fits the British cannon they've got down in Ocean City," Mr. Parker declared, "for I tried it."

The old church must remember colorful days, standing as it does beside a road that's missed altogether as drivers speed by on the newer ribbon of concrete, forgotten with a veritable army of preachers, Cromwell, Everett, Joshua

Dudley, Richard Ivy, Woolman Hickson, John Magary, Samuel Rowe, William Partridge, and John Fidler. Head-of-the-River must have been hard on the pastors who undertook pioneering life there—or perhaps it was the mosquitoes!

Bishop Asbury preached in the church in 1809, coming from Cohansey, later Bridgeton, and Port Elizabeth. At the Tuckahoe chapel Bishop Asbury wrote in his diary that folk along the road told him he had not preached in that neighborhood since twenty-five years before.

One of the stories dug up for our benefit is similar to those which usually remain in an old church such as this. It concerns one Thomas Neal, a deacon at Head-of-the-River, who after conducting services during a severe drought, retired to the wood to pray for rain. Even as he prayed, the skies darkened. While he emerged to warn farmers to hurry home, there came a heavy downpour. One cannot help but wonder if Mr. Neal hadn't done his praying in among the Baptist tombstones across the road.

According to another legend, there were property difficulties in 1813 when the wife of the Reverend Joseph Pillmore was accused of not being of sufficient age to sign a deed relative to the church tract. A legal squabble ensued and the tangle hung over the town like a pall till a legal light of the county, one Coffee Jones, straightened things out. Inasmuch as Cape May County had boasted that no such "noxious animals" as lawyers were able to subsist there, perhaps Coffee's manipulations had something to do with such sentiments.

Ships, sugar-cane, charcoal, cordwood, glass—all are fragments of a Tuckahoe that has gone and a Head-of-the-River that will never return.

XXXVIII

OLD BATES' MILL

WE WENT down into the bog country when October's flags were flying, tawny field grass mingling with the crisp brown of dying ferns and scarlet splashes of young maples in the lowlands. Atop the rise of a little hill beyond a skimpy crossroads, among the initialed ironstones of a small square country cemetery, is one bearing the letters, "B.B." with a tattered flag beside it. So we found the resting place of Benoni Bates, founder of Bates' Mill and a soldier whose work is forgotten now.

Beside the crossroads, sinking out of sight forever in a tangle of thorny vines and scrub, is an old water wheel. Beside it are one or two rotting timbers, remnants of the mill. The stream that knew busy days rushes on, sways the water growths and tries to hide its unpoetic name, Pump Branch.

It is probable that we would have passed Bates' Mill by, unaware that there was ever a village, if it had not been for word from Edwin Reed of Newport who, he explained in his letter, had followed our travels through Rockwood, West Mills, Pestletown, and Spring Garden. "Why not see what is left of old Bates' Mills?" he asked, including a map to help us find it. And so we wandered into October's headquarters.

Bates' Mill is—or was—on the road between Waterford and Blue Anchor. On the State map, showing the improved roadway, there is a tiny lake eminently visible but there is no lake now. This was the mill pond, formed by damming the Pump Branch as it went its way to the Mullica River. The pump that gave the stream its name, familiar to stagecoach travelers in earlier days, has vanished, and so has the water of the pond where a cranberry bog has been in operation many years.

We have taken much chaffing for spending so much time in or near old cemeteries but there are few which have not given us information, or a clue, or a moment of amusement in some inscription or grotesque symbol. Here at Bates' Mill we came upon a gentleman dutifully trimming the plot where his mother and father lie buried. He told us his name was Christian Lehman, that he had come from Pleasantville and that he had lived "in that house across the fields there" when he was a boy.

The graveyard is a very small one. When it was established on land donated by the Bates, plots were given away. Now a plot costs five dollars. Here lie at rest the pioneers of a forgotten crossroads hamlet, the Bates and Beebes, Walkers and Clines, Wells, Crowleys, Lakes and Lehmans. There are a number of graves of Civil War veterans and in the back, in a small isolated section in which the rude Jersey-stone markers have a place by themselves, the history that can never be written lies buried.

Mr. Lehman told us that the man who could tell us all we wanted to know was David Bates. We were shown his name on one of the stones that bore the name of his wife, with the time of her birth and death. David Bates, we concluded, was one of those practical persons who pay as they go, leaving but a detail to be concluded after they have gone. We have often thought it might be a good joke if Gabriel should come ahead of time and with a toot of his trumpet make some folk suddenly aware that a final date would not be necessary. Perhaps some, if they have time, will ask a rebate from the stonecutter.

Mr. Bates, we were informed, was an old man, but he still worked in a mill. Following the directions given us, after pausing for a moment to see the moss-grown wheel of the mill that gave the village its being, we found the Bates home, with a ruined dwelling that had been joined by pegs near by. Members of the family, as it turned out, were pleased to see us, for one of the Bates had remarked that as long as we had been ruminating through the neighborhood, we ought to come to Bates' Mill. But even if we had gone on, unknowing, it is unlikely that there would have been an invitation.

We were told that, despite his years Mr. Bates was given to solitary wandering through the countryside, along the causeways of the bogs, down into glens where colors of Autumn were beginning to flash against the drab background of an in-between season. We gathered that members of the family didn't approve of such excursions and were in constant apprehension lest some night, when darkness fell, Mr. Bates should fail to come home. However, we waited, and he returned on this occasion.

David Bates proved a small man, with grayish hair and lively eyes. Except that he was a bit deaf, he boasted that he was in full possession of his faculties. Off he went by himself, night after night, he said, alone except for a nineteen-year-old Daschund which, because of infirmities, proved a little weak in the knees. Mr. Bates did not return, however, until we had gone to look for him.

Our return found the family assembled. An old newspaper was produced, giving the history of the cemetery and offering material that should have excited ardent Daughters of the American Revolution. We learned that although the mill was built by Thomas Coll in the middle of the eighteenth century, it was Captain Benoni Bates, an officer in the New Jersey line during the Revolution, who distinguished the vicinity.

Captain Bates' value to the cause of Washington, it seems, was, in addition to his active service, watching the Refugees, making certain of and reporting their movements and preventing their depredations as much as possible, horse thieving, farm raids, and the like. On many occasions, records show, the marauders were planning all kinds of hilarious excursions until it was discovered that the doughty captain was on their trail.

The Bates' mill was a saw mill, except for the negligible business it did in the grinding of grain for the family and a few friends. This we learned from Mr. Bates, who said he was the oldest man in town and grandson of the soldier whose grave is on the little green hill. The Bateses were sawyers and bosses and "everything important."

When the mill fell into disuse and the cranberry bog was begun, a family of Braddocks was behind the new enterprise. Though the Bateses were a bit skeptical that any success could be gained from something they declared a failure, the Braddocks were established long enough, it is evident, to give their name to a station on the old Reading line not far away. Braddock is the only depot of its kind we have ever seen—a baggage car, run off on a siding, with the name attached over the platform at either end.

Mr. Bates was proud to tell us that Reuben Heggan, who was freeholder from Waterford at the time we were there, was a member of the Bates family. So are many whose forebears are in the little cemetery which, Mr. Bates said, he repaired with his own hands. Here beside the Pump Branch of Albertson's Brook which, flowing into the Mechescatauxia, which no doubt meant something to the Indians, reaches the Mullica River, the Bateses go on, although the mill is silent and many in the family see no future for the section at all.

Mrs. Bates was more optimistic. She said: "All of us live back here in the middle of nowhere but it isn't far from anything important any more."

Our search for Burnt Mills was not entirely successful, although it was reassuring to hear Mr. Bates disclose that there had never been more than two or three houses and a cranberry bog there. The bog itself has been deserted many years. The bog over at Bates' Mill is operated by the estate of Henry D. and William G. Moore, of Haddonfield, whose holdings in railroads, mines, and other varied interests require the services of a field manager.

The road to Burnt Mills is probably approachable from the Pestletown end, down the Jersey Central, but the way in from the bridge near Atco is one that will defeat even the most ardent of explorers. After the first mile or two, what was once a wide trail is overgrown, winding in and out through scrub and dipping into inky pools. We crossed one small bridge, over the Wild Cat Branch, a name which may provide the final deterrent, and then pushed on through a swamp where a second span, broken and rickety, defeated us.

This section of the wastelands of Southern New Jersey is mysteriously ominous, more so than the pines, perhaps because actually it is close to some of the larger and better known towns. The trees are not all scrub. There are frequent scatterings of varieties which must have been planted in the area, giving rise to the certainty that this was not always a barren place. Everything else denies that, however: deep stagnant pools on either side of the road, such as it is; gloomy patches of brush in which there are wild colorful berries; the whir of wings and the scuttle of little animals in the clinging damp of the thickets.

Near the deserted bog and its red maple banners we found two broken water gates. Near one was an excavation which must have been the cellar of a house. One or two rusted pots and pans, a broken bedspring and other traces of habitation are massed just here. The rest is dismal and impassable. Far away we heard the baying of dogs, farther away the sound of a train. So near, we said, and yet so far. This was once Burnt Mills.

"They ought to have a monument on Captain Bates' grave, don't you think so?" asked his grandson, as we were leaving. "I'm eighty-four but I've got a few more years and I'd like to see it there before I go. Trouble is, back here isn't supposed to be important. What did you come here for, if it isn't?"

XXXIX

WEYMOUTH REVISITED

WE WENT to Weymouth many years ago, long before there seemed to be any call for writing about it. Those were the days when the old Weymouth Road was just a short-cut to the seashore, from Berlin, once Long-A-Coming, through Blue Anchor, to Mays Landing. Motorists wore dusters, boasted of clay roads, paraded gay vehicles with much brass and many guy-lines and got there like demons at all of fifteen miles an hour.

And we went back to Weymouth, not so long ago, impressed with the need of writing down something to recall its past, before the ruins are entirely lost in the trees and vines and brambles. No longer a short-cut from the White Horse Pike to the shore, the Blue Anchor stage road swings from the newer and wider Black Horse Pike. Motorists in slacks and halters, in sleek and silent cars, travel over a twisting hard-surfaced road that permits escape from long lines of drivers who refuse to go faster than fifty.

Anxious to quiet nerves frayed by driving in traffic lanes, they take the narrow curves at high speed and rocket across the bridge, caring little that Weymouth was a town of Revolutionary importance, that here among these broken ruins were fashioned the cannon of the War of 1812, that here paper was made for early books and finally, that this quick-moving present, so far removed from a lovelier past, owes it first allegiance.

Weymouth, when first we saw it, was a sequestered turn in the road known to a few picnickers who were orderly and liked to browse among the graves behind the old Indian church, as well as the ruins that were far more evident than now. Holiday seekers of today leave evidence of their flighty interest littered in the clearings, stir the bottom of the crystal-clear spring, and break the laurel and young trees to gain the edges of the old canals.

Little more than a century ago Weymouth was described as a blast furnace, forge and village in Hamilton Township, Gloucester County, "upon the Great Egg Harbour River, about 5 miles above the head of navigation. The furnace," says the writer of those times, "makes about 900 tons of castings annually, the forge having four fires and two hammers, makes about 200 tons bar iron immediately from the ore. There are also," he continues, "a grist and saw mill, and buildings for the workmen, of whom 100 are constantly employed about the works, and the persons depending upon them for subsistence average 600 annually."

How little there is to prove any of that now! Atlantic County has taken over much that was old Gloucester and Weymouth is more closely associated with the seashore area. The country store long since fell into a sad clutter. Stone-lined canals that supplied water power for the foundry and paper mill have filled with murky pools as the sand-edged stream swings in another direction, half-choked with broken timbers.

Old Samuel Richards operated the first furnace venture there and the paper factory rose on its ruins after abandonment following war days. When the paper mill, last in possession of the Cowells, went out of business, no one paid much attention to the land around it. Fountain Gale, for many years fire warden and operator of the saw mill, settled there with a number of those who lingered when the wheels stopped turning. No one asked for rent and, as long as no rent collectors came around, none was paid. For years on end, those who stayed lived there rent free.

Finally the Mays Landing Water Company took over the property, only to find it was impossible to oust the settlers by law. They had settlers' rights to their homes by then because of twenty-five years of rent-free residence. The water company officials were in a quandary. But the handful of folk who had continued to eke out a living among the haunted houses didn't want any trouble. The water company didn't rout them and they continued to stand by for payment of $1.20 a year.

Many of those to be found in Weymouth nowadays look furtively at invaders, out of habit. Not so with Fountain Gale. "It's gotten to be a fact," he told one of us long ago, "that all the folks here is so old, they're beginnin' to say you got to leave Weymouth to die."

As he spoke, Warden Gale pointed to a man of large girth and rosy jowls. "He's eighty-four," he said, "and he splits his share of kindlin' when there's need for muscle and heat. And he does his share of sleepin' in the Summer when the main job around here is to keep out of the sun and doze off where you won't be in the road. That feller ain't thinkin' of dying at all, no how. And the postmaster, wait till you see him! He's over eighty."

But few, with the exception of Fountain Gale, will talk at all, and he does his best to make up for everybody.

The workmen's houses, those that are occupied and haven't fallen apart in a mass of rubble, half hidden now

untain Gale, fire warden, game warden, and sawmiller in Weymouth, watched
e old furnace town collapse around him until New Jersey took over its ruins
d old houses. Here he stands with the nets that he used when he fished in the
reat Egg Harbor River. Founded in 1800, the Weymouth Furnace produced
nnon balls, parts for stoves, and water pipes, until fire destroyed it during the
vil War. The plant reopened to manufacture paper, but there was a second fire.
the graveyard of the Weymouth Methodist Church are tombstones made of
eymouth iron.

By the time the state purchased Weymouth in 1962, many of the old houses we
empty. Descendants of the pioneers had died or moved elsewhere. Samuel Ric
ards operated the first furnace venture with an output of nine hundred tons
castings annually in the 1830's, plus two hundred tons of bar iron. "There a
also," says an old record, "a grist and saw mill, and buildings for the workme
of whom one hundred are constantly employed about the works. . . ." All th
is over now.

by ferns and undergrowth, are dark and unpainted—it would be too late to paint them now. They have no conveniences except running water, and that spouts up anywhere. "Best water in the State," says Fountain, and with a name like that, he ought to say it. "Just sink a pipe about forty feet and up she gushes. Never runs dry once she sets off. Been recommended by doctors, too."

Water seems to have been Weymouth's theme song. The first water pipes that found their way to Philadelphia came from the iron works there. But its chief hospitality was always a beady glass of *aqua pura*, offered with a boast and then a teetering on the heels as the donor watched its effect. And so it is rather pleasant to find, after all these years, the spring that used to be commended for its health-restoring qualities, partly surrounded by shielding, though broken walls.

Deep down in a sort of trough, you can see bottom if some thoughtless trespasser hasn't been poking that way. The water everywhere about is of the same composition, the same perhaps as at Harrisia, the same that used to be identified with Paint Island Spring.

The high walls and chimney of the two main buildings which comprised the mill group recall the enterprise of pioneers who first located and built the iron works, while Indians, sometimes more hostile than curious, roamed the forest between the town and Mays Landing. They say the original forge building was of brick and that additions made in the paper-making days were similar, the bricks coming from England as ballast and finding their way down from Burlington. Most of the walls standing today are of the familiar native ironstone.

The experts seem to squabble about dates and figures

identified with earliest days of Weymouth. Many of them have written a mere rehash of the old records, adding to old account books which used to be shown with great pride down at Tuckerton. Surely the forge was in operation when the Revolution came. Then, despite dangers on every side, Weymouth set to making cannon balls and cannon for two wars, from the times of old Sam Richards through the days of Charles Richards Colwell. They say, too, that powder was manufactured there and transported on floats in bags supposed to be water-tight down the river to Mays Landing.

Although a great many of the stories are dated in the vicinity of 1800 the first furnace is said to have been completed as early as 1754. A "tablet" bearing that date is to be found there, surviving the changes of time and the disastrous fires. But before the fires, there had been those experiments with iron water pipes which soon displaced the old wooden conduits under the first streets of the earliest city planner, William Penn. But transportation hardships defeated Weymouth just as they had defeated so many of the earliest industrial centers of the State.

Charles Colwell was born at Valley Forge in the days when George Washington's ragamuffin soldiers were fighting the bitter cold of Winter there. He purchased the Weymouth holdings and sought gamely to make the town prosper. Now that's over and done with, buried in a few old books. The gate house that once stood near the Indian cemetery, the old Main Street indicated by the double line of old trees, the old road fenced off by Summer visitors, can be pictured only by those with vivid imaginations.

It took eight large wagon loads of charcoal to keep

the fires of Weymouth going. Two men were kept busy doing nothing else but dump charcoal and iron ore at the top of the blast furnaces. Each basket-load of charcoal and ore was called a charge. A soon as each charge settled sufficiently, another was dropped in. A blast of air from below forced combustion and maintained a smelting heat. Other men removed the molten metal as it ran out at the base of the furnaces. That is why, today, at Weymouth, Speedwell, Mary Ann, and other furnace sites, huge pieces of slag may be found with chunks of charcoal deeply imbedded in them.

Driven by 500 horsepower bellows, operated by the rush of water over a wheel, an air blast was forced through pipes made of iron and leather. It was compressed in huge tanks to make a steady pressure and today, what is left of the pipes and tanks may be mistaken easily for smokestacks, bent and corroding in the fast concealing vegetation of Weymouth.

In 1846, six years before the railroad came through Mays Landing, a wooden tramway was build from Weymouth there, for the use of mule teams. Some say this was a log road, designed to speed the passage of wagons to the shipping center on the shore of Lake Lenape. Others declare it was a rude railroad, with ties and tracks, and that the mules pulled early freight cars along it. There was much activity at both ends, for while, in Weymouth, they were digging iron from the bogs and fashioning it into all sorts of products, down at Mays Landing they were building ships, no less than six hundred of them, of timber hauled from the woods between.

It may be that there was as much traffic in the old days as now, for it was more evenly distributed then. Stages moved on schedule. Hauling from the village was done exclusively by mule teams, eight six-mule wagons leaving for Philadelphia at three o'clock every morning, to return laden with barrels of provisions and other supplies. One legend has it that Weymouth inaugurated the six-day week, honoring the Sabbath Day, suspending the mule-team trips and halting barges in the canals so that even the pole boys might go to church. Weymouth's name was known everywhere for it handled large quantities of ore from points in Pennsylvania and New York, as well as its own.

Now, with the old roads partly barred, with the last of the old houses along the stream and back in the green jungle, only the tall brick chimney, with a tuft of grass growing high at the top, recalls thriving days when Water and Vine Streets, Philadelphia, the old Philadelphia Water Works and Mark Adams, moulder and coremaker of note, were experimenting with pipes down at Weymouth.

We take everything for granted. If a turn of the tap doesn't bring an immediate rush of water, we hurry to a telephone and complain to somebody. It adjusts one's viewpoint to linger for a while in Weymouth, where today there is less than a handful of year-rounders in place of the six hundred hard-working men and women who looked ahead and knew what the old village might give to a world that would pass it by.

XL

CUMBERLAND WORKS: MARSHALLVILLE

TAKE AWAY a town's people, let its industries fall into ruin, move the roads, watch a river clog itself with marshes—and what happens? The town itself loses its identity, the ideas and energy that once gave it life become less than memories and the world moves on.

That, like the plight of so many forgotten villages, is Marshallville's, too. But Marshallville doesn't care.

Marshallville was described a century ago in these words: "Marshallville, or Cumberland Works, on Tuckahoe creek, Maurice Creek township, Cumberland county, 28 miles southeast of Bridgeton; contains 30 to 40 houses, some extensive glass works belonging to Randall Marshall, Esq., at which much window glass is manufactured, one tavern and two stores. There is much ship building carried on here in vessels of from 50 to 100 tons; soil, sandy."

Marshallville today is not in Cumberland County but in Cape May, just within the county line, shunned by the new State highway that skirts Tuckahoe through to the bend at Head-of-the-River. Back of Forrest Sherman's house, where poles jut from the marshes, were some of the boat basins in which some of the finest three-masted schooners once were built. On the bottom, when the tide's down, you can see the rotting timbers of a few that were begun but never finished.

Charles and Billy Sherman, sons of Forrest, the poultryman, listened that day we were down there, as Walter

Burley, whose house is across the old and deserted road, told of the old shipbuilding days. Few remember the stories of an earlier Marshallville better than Walter, for the Burleys have been living down there since 1730.

"My great-great-grandfather was married yonder in Tuckahoe," Mr. Burley told us, "and the rest of us have been here ever since—well, not exactly that, but you know what I mean."

"Yes," he went on, after his son had brought him from where he was harrowing a field, "there isn't much left of old Marshallville. That little house of mine there, and the one next to it, are among the few original houses of the smaller ones that were built in the old town."

It is more than fifty years since the last ship of any size was built in Marshallville. Then there was considerable lumbering in the vicinity.

"The last," disclosed Mr. Burley, scratching his head, "was the *Minnie Saunders*. There was a time when fourteen ships were being built out there at the same time—on the edge of the creek where it's now all glogged up. As for the glass works, that was a-goin' strong just up the road from here. You can doubt it if you want to but there are records somewhere that'll prove that Marshallville did $100,000 in business every year in those days."

They locate the site of the glass factory now by saying "it was over there by that chicken coop." In Marshallville now there are three houses of Colonial brick, all having been altered from their original appearance. One of these is the venerable farmstead, across the water, of Garret Garrett, well-known magazine writer. The smallest frame dwelling, home of the Burleys, is nearly 125 years old.

Mr. Burley, a gaunt, middle-aged man hardened by farm

work, isn't really a farmer. He tills a truck patch, growing enough for the family's use. If conditions were better, he said, he'd be painting houses somewhere, maybe in Ocean City.

No one we could find in Marshallville could tell us why the glass factory went out of business. Undoubtedly the plant was swallowed up by larger enterprises, operated in a field where raw materials could be obtained in greater amount, at lower cost and with less effort. That is largely the story of failures of lumber, glass, iron and paper activities in this forgotten frontier of Southern New Jersey.

"After Randall Marshall, Bob Stadler had it," Mr. Burley said, "and then came Jim Henderson. Jim closed the glass works down."

The shipping industry went to pot for similar reasons. "The smaller ships weren't wanted any more," our informant intoned dolefully, "and then, all the available timber had been used. Those ships took a lot of wood, you know."

The old shipyards along the Tuckahoe River have left no trace except for wharves and cradle timbers and those water-logged hulks on the muddy bottom, down in the marsh grass where mosquitoes swarm. Unless you were looking for what might have been ships, you'd pass them by as cast-off bits of wood.

Leaving Mr. Burley, we went up the road to where we found Charles F. Hilderbrand, formerly of Pittsburgh, a Spanish-American War veteran who lives in one of the houses along the river shore. He said he used to own more property but when pensions were cut down and since he contracted "rheumatiz" he sold all but the house which the Tuckahoe serves for a moat.

Hilderbrand recalled a picture painted by a wandering artist showing Marshallville as it used to be. He said the painting was left behind in one of several vacant houses and its discovery led to some spirited bidding and finally, a disappearance. "Last I heard tell of it," Mr. Hilderbrand declared, "it was over in Pennsylvania with a lot of people after it still."

Hilderbrand showed us a wharf back of his home. This, he declared, is a relic of old Marshallville, in service long before railroads took over the shipping of lumber from there. The old storehouse of the glass factory which, in its day, served as a post office, was later moved to a new location up the road. A sturdy brick building, covered over with weather-boards, it has the old pegged beams and fitted partitions. Even now it isn't far from where the creek bristles with glass slag fragments, close by what remains of the glass plant's loading pier.

An old road once flanked the creek, going past a line of storage barns. Allan E. Burchard, who owns the erstwhile post office now, using it for a barn, left off collecting eggs from his hen-houses long enough to talk to us. He said that the old Marshall mansion was changed after damage by fire in 1916. "The old chimney pots were removed to serve as gate-posts," he pointed out. "That was wrong but I had nothing to do with it."

It was Burchard who struck on what is perhaps the theme that lies in Marshallville's swan-song.

"You can't have everything," he said. "You can't keep up with the world all the time. By rights, I ought to be a mechanical engineer." Showing us a saw he had rigged up cleverly in the old glass factory store where the mail boxes serve now as a tool file, he went on: "When I should have been getting to know my father better, I was at school. When I should have been getting a start, the war came along and—oh, well, I've got four hundred chickens now and I'm going to have more next year. You can't have everything."

Hopes and expectations a little dashed, wouldn't you say? Mr. Burchard said that he had a collection of books four hundred years old but that he couldn't show them to us because he hadn't had time to make sure what they were as yet. The hens lay too regularly, perhaps, down in Marshallville, to allow time for little things like that. But Mr. Burley, as we bade him good-bye, promising to count all the stones with Burley on them in the Head-of-the-River churchyard, hit on quite another clinical note.

"In a place like Marshallville," he said, "depression times take a long while to come. And when they come, nobody pays much attention because they's always a depression around here. Maybe it's just that the first depression that broke things up never leaves."

He went back to his cornfield, never turning. There a bony horse, lashing at mosquitoes from the mudflats, saw no sense at all in his master's lingering over talk about scenes that can never be restored, especially when there was plowing to be done.

XLI

NAME TRADING: VINCENTOWN FOR QUAKERTOWN

A PATRIOTIC real estate man, fired with a fever that belied the cooling breezes of a resort whose fair name he sought to defend, once wrote us in nasty vein. The purport of his protest seemed to be that any implication that his town was in the forgotten village class was the product of an unbalanced mind.

It is no fault of ours that any number of New Jersey towns are headed for classifications which, when a wanderer with an insatiable curiosity starts stirring things up, reveals a wealth of forgotten material. In the years that have passed, governmental agencies have added concealment, giving names that add obscurity and bewilderment to those chosen in the beginning, as well as the incidents that marked their choice. Road builders, avoiding through traffic, skirt the old towns and bury their folk lore as effectually as present descendants have interred their dead.

There is a loveliness of the open country, of course, but there is no indication on the newer roads that not far from them are old trails with thrilling history, old towns that haven't changed despite new names, adopted by chance, or perhaps deliberately by those who would make them more "attractive."

Who remembers, for instance, that Vincentown was once Quakertown and who realizes that despite the change in nomenclature and skirting of modern ribbons of concrete its streets and houses have altered hardly at all?

Who realizes that the name of Barnegat goes back to the days of Hendrik Hudson and should be spelled Barendegat because it means "a place of breakers"? Who recalls that Bamber and Bamber Lake were named for an Englishman, of Barking, Essex, England? Who will tell you, without hesitancy, that Lakehurst was Manchester Furnace? Who will prevent the traveler in search of the old that founded the new that Mantua was first the name of a creek and that Mantua, the town, was first Carpenter's Landing? Who will explain why Byllingsport has become Billingsport, why Paulsborough and Barnsborough have dropped three letters from their original names?

Not lost towns? Why, each day spells some loss. Names are changed, shortened, varied. Those who know the answers or remember those who knew are losing their hold of recollections, even on life, with every week that passes. An interest in such decadence, then, seems defensible, even though apostles of the present may hope to forget the past for the good of what tomorrow may hold in store. It seems to us that what was, no matter how shadowy it has been, can be given much more certainty than what is to be.

Before Lakehurst was Manchester Furnace, named for Manchester, England, it is said to have been Federal Forge. We would like to think that it was Federal Furnace after the English name became, understandably enough, unpopular. Here a forge was erected in 1789. Such places as a hotel, the Federal House, the Federal Coaling Company's headquarters, and David Wright's coaling ground, came later. David Wright's establishment there is named as early as 1795 and 1800 in old surveys. There are discrepancies, however, for one deed refers to Dover Forge, as if it, too, were the name of Federal Furnace. The forge was one of a hundred or more, throughout the State, where bog ore was smelted to become ammunition, utensils, and stoves. There is a lake whose bottom yields particles of slag, now and then, to recall days with which Lakehurst, with its Naval Station and dirigibles, has no familiarity.

Whiting, erroneously referred to as Whitings on maps and road signs, was named in honor of Nathan C. Whiting, who came down from New Haven, Conn., to Ocean County, then part of Monmouth County, in 1852, erecting a saw mill and engaging in the lumber business for some years before returning to his home.

Bayville was once Potter's Creek, but it changed its name several times. Once it became Chaseford, in honor of a Secretary of the Treasury. The Potters were the principal family there at the time. The father of Thomas Potter, you remember, was the first Potter in this section of the country. Thomas was the founder of the Universalist Church in America. The first church of that denomination is at Good Luck, not far from Forked River, the name bestowed by a man who was saved from drowning in a near-by creek.

There are differences of opinion regarding the source of Toms River's name. Some say it was called after a noted Indian known as Tom, who lived for a time on an island at the river's mouth. A sketch made in 1740 of Mosquito Cove has "Barnegatt Tom's Wigwam" marked plainly upon it. Another story, accepted as more reasonable, is that Toms River was named for Captain William Toms, a figure well known along the Delaware from 1664 until 1674. Toms River is said to have been known in the days of its first salt establishments as Goose Creek and Dover Town.

ove Bridgeton is Deerfield's historic Presbyterian Church, erected in 1771.
e village was established by folk from Greenwich and Fairfield in Cum-
land County and oddly enough is still called Deerfield Street on the maps.
low, a rare photograph of Billy Speer, taken about 1867 to 1869 and copied by
thaniel R. Ewan. Billy was a hermit and lived in this cabin on what was the
k farm near Vincentown.

The site of a window glass factory of Dr. Randolph Marshall, established prior
1840. Marshallville is on Tuckahoe Creek on the Cape May-Atlantic County li

The Metedeconk River was once the Metetecunk, derived from the Indian words "Mittig-conck," meaning a place where there was a thrifty woodland. Cassville was named for Lewis Cass and was once known as Goshen. Later postal authorities got busy, refusing to have two Goshens, and allowing the one in Cape May County to stand. Manahawkin was once Mannahawkin and Mannahocking, meaning "good corn land."

Vincentown, once Vincenttown and Quakertown before that, is a pleasant little town today. Located on Stop-the-Jade Creek, it is made colorful in Summer by a profusion of old houses boasting tiger-lilies on every side. In the days of John Brainard, the celebrated Quaker preacher who built the Indian church at Indian Mills, the name of Quakertown was still used. The new name came with a post office in 1831.

Vincentown isn't far from many of the principal communities of Burlington County and is used by those who take a short-cut through Ong's Hat to the road over the plains and barrens to Barnegat.

On one of our visits to Vincentown we paused at the old marl pits on Route 40, diggings that gave Marlton its name. We had always thought of marl as a fertilizer but we learned on the scene that it is used principally today as a water-softener. There is said to be about a thousand tons to the acre still in the vicinity with a value of $100 per ton. The marl is dug and then screened and rescreened before it is pressed into bricks.

Today the plant, near which once stood Elmwood Station, is abandoned. There is no station here or anywhere along the old Marlton and Medford line for the tracks have been hauled up and the new concrete road follows the bed of the rails that spurred out from Haddonfield. The abandonment of the spur is said to have had much to do with the elimination of the marl plant.

From the marl diggings we went on to Sandtown, of which little remains but a name on a highway sign. There is one brick house and it seems to be old but its occupant could tell us nothing of its history. The cedar water of Bear Swamp Creek meanders through a picturesque meadow and under an ancient stone bridge. The road through Sandtown connects with Church Road, leading into Vincentown.

Joseph Burr operated a saw mill on the lake in Vincentown in 1775. The mill and surrounding property was willed to a daughter, Keziah, who became the wife of a governor of New Jersey. Kissie Burr was something of a reigning belle. But she was a strict Quakeress, too, and the gossips had it that she and Governor Howell, an Episcopalian, wouldn't make a go of it. But they were wrong.

Once there were two inns at Vincentown, operated by John Butterworth and Benjie Burr—their establishments were still operating in 1812. Opposite the "lower" tavern was Sam Beck's store—no kin of the writer, since his relatives were in England years and years after that. It is sometimes remarked by those who know the author well that his interest in these American frontiers is somewhat ironical because of something they impute to him as an Anglomania. Perhaps he should retort with something about heredity since his father was a native of the Island of Jersey, home of the first owners of East and West New Jersey. But this is an aside.

What's the story in Vincentown today? Many houses

stand just as they did long ago. The Sally Stretch Keen Memorial Library, opened to us by the postmistress, Miss Helen Ebert, the day we were there, is one of the few modern buildings on the old Main Street, but its design is Colonial. One of the ancient inns was damaged by fire in the late Prohibition Era, but the barber shop and bar-room were unscathed and, they tell us, are operating again.

Bill Dobbins, the wheelwright of long ago, is forgotten. Moses Bennett, celebrated minehost, is only a memory. The pits of the Vincentown Marl Company are deserted. To top it all, the railroad station has borne a "For Sale Or Rent" sign for several years.

Mantua, described as Carpenter's Landing more than a hundred years ago, was "a p-town of Greenwich township, Gloucester county, upon Mantua creek, at the head of sloop navigation . . . a place of considerable trade in lumber, cord-wood, etc., and contains one tavern, two stores, 30 dwellings and a Methodist church." Today, unless you have time to search about thoroughly, you won't find very much of Mantua that is reminiscent of Carpenter's Landing, unless it is a lumber business on the site of the old cordwood wharves. Old houses and inns have been transformed by proprietors of hardware and shoemaker shops and real estate agencies.

The Benjamin Lodge farm, down on the creek bank, seems to have been there in days when the waterway was navigable by large ships. Mrs. Lodge told us that she and her husband had lived there thirty years and that they had heard the story that the older section of the house was built in 1707, without troubling to authenticate it. The original owners were the Kaighns, she said.

We found another informant in Mrs. Ellsworth Conover, whose home was once a tenant house on the old Ogden farm, an abandoned mansion which once knew important days of industry there. Near the Ogden house, whose interior was damaged irreparably by a tenant who sought to establish a roadhouse, is the ruin of a square stone building, once the quarters of a gardener-coachman who served the Ogdens whose ghosts must weep over the scarred balustrade, the battered dining salon and the dance hall thrust upon the airy third floor of their old home. Sweeping drives outside are lost in high grass, weeds, and shrubs that fight their way through the tangle.

Mantua folk today can't tell you much of Carpenter's Landing. We soon found out that they were inclined to make up what they didn't wish to admit they didn't know and so, after invading several deserted farms and looking along the muddy creek for traces of landings, we came back to the bridge. Mrs. Conover said there was a broken-down brickyard in the woods near by and Mrs. Lodge said that a tannery once stood on the creek bank opposite the farm, but there were traces of neither. At the post office Winfield Smith, the postmaster frankly admitted his limitations and said his father, C. A. Smith, who held the job, before him, might prove productive. And so we found Mr. Smith, among his four hundred pullets.

"Carpenter?" he repeated our query. "Don't know what his first name was but he was a boat builder. There used to be a quarter-mile wharf down at the foot of Turner Street and down where the lumber plant is now. Scows and sloops used to take the water here, they say, and then serve in business that used to take cordwood and tanned hides down to the Delaware. But that was before I came along to take any notice of such things."

We went down to the foot of Turner Street, as well as further on along the creek. There are deep holes along the banks which are all that remain of imposing houses that once stood there. There is nothing of the quarter-mile wharf. Obviously there was a Carpenter's Landing, here where Mantua is, but Mantua isn't it. In the process of name-trading here, they've lost the old village altogether.

This pumper, part of the pioneer fire-fighting equipment of the Vincentown Fire Company, was discovered among the junk on an informal town dump. This photograph is credited with rescuing the relic from oblivion.

XLII

FORESTS UNDERGROUND

THE CLUE to it came, of course, from Captain Gandy. He had shown us the old Gandy saw mill in Dennisville and had told us he was sawing up logs dug from deep down in a marsh near Port Norris at Haleyville. What we did not know then was that this was the revival of a business that linked Cape May County with shingles placed on the roof of Independence Hall, in Philadelphia, in 1740.

Captain Gandy had said, characteristically, that the logs had been in the muck of the swamp "since the Big Flood of Bible times." Then it was that Mr. A. T. Cottrell, assistant forester of the New Jersey Department of Conservation and Development, asked us if we had heard of the return of "shingle mining." As if we knew all about it we inquired if he meant the venture near Port Norris. He said he did, but up to that moment we hadn't guessed the full significance of Captain Gandy's disclosure.

Much of Cape May County's history is already celebrated. Sea water was boiled in the making of salt near Beesley's Point in early days. As early as 1706 a road was laid out and built down to the point by Shagmar Hand and William Golden. New England Town, or Portsmouth, was a whaling center in 1685, and was abandoned 'way back in 1725. Our ruminations there gave indications of the experiment in manorial government by agents of Dr. Daniel Coxe who after two years abandoned his holdings at Coxe Hall in 1692. But our primary concern was with what remained to be seen and heard about on the sites of such early beginnings.

Thus the revival of something which had concerned pioneers of the area in the early 1700s and which, we were told, had been abandoned since days prior to the Civil War, was of great moment. Discovery of what it was all about involved a rediscovery of the methods used in "cedar mining" and an understanding of the conditions which made it possible two centuries ago and make it an actuality now. Involved, too, is the assertion that land along the tide-waters of New Jersey, if not the whole Eastern seacoast of the United States, is slowly but steadily being submerged.

These logs being dug from the marsh at Haleyville were huge. Their discovery was a side-issue. Those who found them were looking for peat and to get the peat, some twenty or thirty feet down, it was necessary to remove the logs—and this proved a big job. Peat production depends on the presence of so much water as to cover vegetable matter and hinder the full access of air. And so both underground forests and peat lie along the bay shore of Cape May and Cumberland Counties where the land through the centuries had been losing a battle against encroachment.

Leaming M. Rice and Maurice Beesley, in 1866, made up a map to show how the bay had been creeping in—and this in itself indicates that the probable site of Town Bank, the whaling community of long ago, is far out from shore and deep under salt water. Showing the wash from May, 1767, when the land along the bay was surveyed by Aaron Leaming, the map-makers avowed that a century later the water had crept in to fill 204 acres between the

West and East creeks, 127 acres between the East and
Dennis creeks and 350 acres between the Dennis and
Goshen creeks. By now the bay has moved in still further.

George H. Cook, New Jersey State Geologist, writing
in 1868, said: "The evidence for these changes is drawn
from the wear of the shores, the rise of tide-water on the
upland without wear, the occurrence of dead trees and
stumps in their places of growth and altogether below the
present tide-level, and from finding works of the early settlers in locations where they are now quite out of place on
account of the water." No wonder they say that New
Jersey is diving into the sea!

Dr. Maurice Beesley, who lived in Dennisville years
ago, had a map of Cape May, dated 1694, which gave Egg
Island, the western point of Maurice River cove, three
hundred acres. In 1868, the island was covered entirely at
high water. The new State maps indicate no Egg Island at
all in that vicinity.

"From the Cedar Hummocks to West Creek," wrote
Dr. Cook, "there are no sand beaches and the salt marsh is
exposed to the direct action of the waves. Several rods in
width of marsh are sometimes worn away during a single
storm. Some years since, a human body was washed up on
the shore near the mouth of Dennis Creek. It was carried
in forty rods from the shore and buried in the marsh.
Three years after it was found the shore was worn away
quite up to the grace, and the coffin was washed out."

"There was a common opinion," the geologist writes
in his record, now seventy years old, "especially among
the watermen along the Bay-shore, that the mouth of the
Maurice River was formerly down near Fishing Creek,
East, West, Dennis and Goshen creeks being its branches.

Their reason for this opinion, in addition to that derived from the present rapid wear of the shore, is that a line of oyster-beds is found out in the Bay, at different points, between the present mouth of Maurice River and Fishing Creek; and similar beds extend out from the mouths of the other creek for some distance into the Bay."

A glance at any modern map of New Jersey will give significance to this opinion. If these creeks were once branches of the Maurice River, then the whole shape of Southern New Jersey has been radically changed by the unrelenting encroachment of the sea through long years. Perhaps those older maps which seemed to have been drawn by someone who knew nothing at all of the Cape end of the State, were more accurate than we know. Shingle-mining, possible now, would indicate that once there were woodlands stretching down to the shore and that unknown settlements slid with them into the creeping muck of the marshes.

Aaron Leaming, writing about the grave of his grandfather, buried in 1694, said: "In 1734 I saw the graves; they were then fifty rods from the bay, and the sand was blown upon them. The town was formerly between them and the water. There were still some signs of the ruin of houses." Leaming was writing of Town Bank—seventy years ago there was no trace at all of the graveyard but there were legends of skulls and bones tumbling with sinister splashes, from time to time, into the bay.

As for the seacoast of Cape May County, as well as other counties, the encroachment and quirks of the sea are nobody's secret. Jetties are built and then the waves dash in from a new angle. Large buildings were recently abandoned as unsafe because, in spite of barriers, the Atlantic continued to move in. Summer resorts have built new boardwalks only to discover, not long after, that the ocean which had seemingly moved out, had come back again. But we were most interested in the marshes of the bayside, over which the Dennis Creek shipbuilders dragged their vessels with each high tide, to open water.

Dr. Cook has quoted innumerable authorities, citizens whose kin are to be found at every hand in these days, to show that "the salt water comes higher on the upland than formerly, by the killing of timber on the low borders." Dr. Cook himself found that "in most of the marsh near the upland, which is shallow, fallen timber is found buried; and the stumps of trees are still standing with their roots in the solid ground where they grew. The timber found in this condition is of oak, gum, magnolia, cedar, pine and other species, such as are now the natural growth of the country.

"Where they are of pine, cedar, or other durable wood, their broken and weather-worn trunks are seen projecting above the marsh which has overrun the place of their growth." Excursionists, speedily passing the marsh that stretches bayward as far as the eye can see at South Dennis, express no amazement and little interest, as they should, that it could have been written, almost a century ago— "hundreds of acres are to be seen about Dennisville all dotted over by cedar stumps, which are still standing where they grew, though the salt grass has long since taken the place of the living timber. The soft and spongy nature of the cedar swamp-bottoms would lead one to suppose that the mud, with the load upon it, was gradually going down, were it not for the fact that these bottoms are found

...ain Ogden Gandy, of Den-
...le, remembered the old
... and who sailed them, but
...asn't "up to building them
...more." At eighty-nine, he
...retired, as he put it, in 1936,
...perate the sawmill of his
...bears. The sawmill, below,
...e a specialty of splitting
...shingles" from cedar logs
...ed for centuries in Delaware
...muck.

There is a West Creek near Dennisville, but this one is on the coast a[t] Tuckerton, and few there today know of the other's existence. The engra[ving] is from *Harper's New Monthly Magazine* of the 1890's. Below, wrecks o[f] ships on Dennis Creek.

far below the tide-level, and the muck of which they consist, extending down to the gravel."

And so the peat-hunters, near Port Norris, were merely encountering a condition which, although it has been remarked near Port Elizabeth, at Bacon's Neck, back of Waertown, near Cedar Run, and elsewhere, has been known to the careful observers, and experts, for a long, long time. It may be that the discovery of seasoned and submerged timber, such as Captain Gandy has been sawing up, will lead to other enterprises, after this long interim. As long as Hickory Island, south of Tuckerton, is remembered as being covered with a thick growth of hard wood, as long as there are cedar swamps back from Leeds Point, Dennisville, Dukes' Bridge, deep in the Forked River Mountains and virtually everywhere in the mysterious pinelands, the challenge remains.

We wanted to know, naturally, what happened when the giant logs "of the Big Flood" were found and so we besieged Mr. Cottrell and many others with questions. Trunks are found, it seems, at all depths beneath the muck, down to the gravel. Some are so thick that a number of trials have to be made before sounding rods can be thrust down without striking against them. Tree after tree, from two centuries to ten centuries old, have been found lying across one another, extending in every direction. Some are partly decayed as if they were killed by the salt water and remained standing a long time before falling. Others were blown down but continued to grow a long time after.

Henry Ludlam, of Dennisville, sketched such a swamp for Dr. Cook where the timber had been cut off around 1800. There were stumps shown, left behind by trees which had extended their roots over trunks of an earlier growth, indicating "the accumulation of hundreds, or even thousands of years." In mining such primeval timbers, crossed and recrossed and tumbled together, skill and experience are necessary. The men must judge, sight unseen, the value of the logs they strike, or they will waste a great deal of time bringing to the surface some that are comparatively worthless. With an iron rod, the shingler sounds the swamp until he finds what he judges to be a good log; he uses his rod in determining length and size; then he takes means of drawing the log to the surface. Time was when such logs were dug, with sharp spades; now, at Haleyville, they slip a cable under the log, pull it back to the top of the muck and attach it to a motor operated on a truck. The cable grows taut, strains, and eventually drags the log from the depths.

It used to be that the shinglers chipped a piece from the log and drew it up first, knowing from the smell whether the log was a windfall or a breakdown, blown down or broken off. The windfalls are best, inasmuch as it is probable they were sound when they fell. Modern methods have made child's play of what was once a task requiring care, great experience and patient work, and no matter how crude they remain, they put a different prospect on the whole future of the business, with the current revival begun by a search for peat, and not underground forests.

Dennisville's Dr. Beesley startled the newspapers in the 1800s with an article that was widely quoted concerning his discovery of a stump with 1080 rings of annual growth, with a trunk buried beneath it estimated at fifteen centuries old. Nicholas Godfrey, who long ago operated a tide-mill not far from Beesley's Point, was linked with the earliest timber mining and had much to say about a tide that rose fifteen inches higher than when his mill first operated. Other pioneers of the locality have written of the raising and sawing of logs which came up "with as much buoyancy as a freshly fallen cedar; not being water-logged at all."

Dr. Cook's record declared that "the bark on the underside looks fresh, as if it had lain but a few days, and what is remarkable, the underside of the log is always the lightest; the workmen observe that when the logs float in the water they always turn over, the side which was down coming uppermost." When the upper logs and roots of later trees are removed, the lower logs in many cases rise to some extent of their own accord. Bolts or blocks are cut for splitting into shingles. Tools have changed somewhat with the methods used but the source remains as it was and the product, we were told by many, is even better than the finished shingles of long ago.

It is difficult to determine now if shipbuilding was of greater importance in Dennisville, near Goshen, and around the bend of Delaware Bay, below Port Elizabeth and over toward Port Norris, than was the mining of timber. It is recorded that a small part of a swamp near Dennis Creek, or Dennisville, yielded 20,000 shingles in a single year. When a well was dug at Dennisville a century ago, a shaft of eleven feet yielded blue marsh mud at the top, peaty cedar swamp earth a little lower down, cedar timber in logs and stumps beyond that, and, near the bottom, sweet gum and magnolia.

So, under the salt-marshes that fringe the Delaware Bay and Atlantic shores, they are digging up secrets of the past and much, we feel, remains unknown. Folk who live in the villages that were, off the road, known by different names, changed to all but those who seek them out and pause to put queries about this or that, "are very sensible of this change of level between the land and water, and are perfectly well satisfied that the remains of the timber found are in the places where they grew," as the State geologist put it just after the Civil War. The subsistence goes on, along the coast beyond New Jersey.

The pleasurable thought is that though some towns are seemingly forgotten, they may now reclaim importance through the very activity that gave them being on the edge of the swampland in days almost beyond recall.

XLIII

EAYRESTOWN: WITH TWO E'S

JUST BEYOND paths that were long familiar and yet in a world apart, unspoiled in its remembrances of the past and unaffected by magnified nothings of the present, lies Eayrestown.

We stumbled on it once, just after Autumn had come and when, in the vicinity of a sequestered lake, children were trailing home from school, despairing of the coming cold and hopeful for the return of warm and leisurely days. Then we did not know it as Eayrestown.

A string of electric lights had been strung across the end of the lake for night swimming. There was a diving platform, a few old houses, and a sign proclaiming the vicinity as Cedar Lake Park. None of this was akin to Eayrestown when it was Eayrstown, before someone added an extra E. There was nothing, on that occasion, to make a traveler pause and reflect on lost days of industrial activity.

To pause, however, when we went there later in the snows of Winter, was to know that in the old dams and bridges, in the empty raceway of the mill, the little store that is now a dwelling, and the manor house that has become a beer parlor, once there was something more in Eayrestown. So, in the old *Gazetteer*, we looked up and found this entry:

"Eayrstown, village of Northampton t-ship, Burlington co., on the S. branch of the Rancocus creek, near the junction of the Haines' creek with that stream, and at the head of tide, between 3 and 4 miles S.W. from Mount Holly; contains a cotton factory, a grist mill, a saw mill, fulling mill, 1 tavern, 1 store and 12 or 15 dwellings; soil, sandy loam, fertile and well cultivated."

Today, with all the rest, even the spelling has been changed, on maps and in occasional news items. The ruin of the saw mill, principally consisting of one of the arches under which the water rushed on its way to rejoin the creek, recalls an active yesterday. The structure of the fulling mill now rests on the foundations of the saw mill, long since destroyed by fire.

We had come along the road out of Lumberton. Seeing what we thought might be the old store, we knocked and then walked in, thinking it was still a public place. This proved a bit embarrassing for, surrounded by a strange miscellany of furniture, a piano, dusty bric-a-brac, and a parrot, was a smiling old lady.

"We thought this was still a store," we said, apologetically, seeing that this was her home, despite outward appearances.

"That's all right," she told us. "Lots of people do. It used to be the store before I came to live here."

She told us that she was Mrs. Mary W. Moore, that she had lived in Eayrestown since her husband died, so that she could be near a daughter and a son-in-law "in case anything happened." She said that although she visited her other children she really preferred living alone—except for the parrot. Mrs. Moore said the bird could be eloquent when he wanted to be, but this was obviously one of his off days.

The store was once the grocery that did a fine business when the mills were going. The miller lived on the other side, then, directly across from the store. There was a building across the street and to this Mrs. Moore drew our attention. "That was the mill office," she said.

Mrs. Moore said her son-in-law was David Dean, a tobacco salesman who came to Eayrestown some years before, purchasing forty acres and making an amusement park around the smaller lake. She urged us to call on her daughter, "just three houses up the road, for she knows more about old Eayrestown than I do. I like to be alone," she ended. "I like to do as I please. The weather has been cold, hasn't it? This is the first time they've known the lake out there to freeze."

We found Mrs. Dean indisposed. Her daughter sent us to see "Mr. Stricker, at the top of the hill. He's been there as long as the hill," she informed us.

George S. Stricker, a quiet-spoken man with a white beard, was at work. His house had once been brick but was marred somewhat by an overcast. There was no answer to our summons in the dooryard and we were about to take our leave when Mr. Stricker appeared, driving a mule up the snow-covered hill, drawing a birch log for firewood.

"Guess I'm the oldest in Eayrestown," he readily admitted. "I've been here forty-three years in the last stretch. Of course, I was born here. This was my uncle's place and after he died, I thought I'd like to come back. I'd been living up Jacksonville way—and so I bought it."

Mr. Stricker's father and grandfather were born in Eayrestown, too.

"This was once a hustling town," he told us, leaning against the barn as the mule champed and stomped. "This house and that one over there," he indicated a second dwelling of brick used by a Palmyra man as a summer hideaway, "are the oldest here, I think. They're well over a hundred and fifty years old for sure."

Mr. Stricker recalled Jacob Githens as the probable founder of the town. "He ran the mills for a long time—in fact, up to the day of his death. Then his son, Frank, took over. Some of the Kirbys came here but it was in their time that the mill failed."

There was a note of sadness in Mr. Stricker's recollections. There is nothing so disheartening as the lost glamour of a faded town and Eayrstown, or Eayrestown, lends emphasis to that reflection. Stress is further added by the swimming park, deserted as it was, in Winter. With the streams edged with ice, with the old barn transformed into a bathhouse, locked in snow, the sterility was unmistakable.

Up on the hill, marked by a beer sign, was the manor house of Jacob Githens, the town's founder. The scattered dwellings, some used now as summer cottages, have a knowing look, as if to say, "Just see how things have gone down. We can remember when—but you newcomers wouldn't care about that."

The old mills have burned down, have crumbled, have been removed and have been refitted. No one remembers the cotton mill in operation. "They said there was a factory but I don't remember," Mr. Stricker said, tugging at his beard. The lake that turned the mill wheel has a mucky bottom. Wheels that replaced those that first were used are still. Only Mr. Stricker and a few of his generation recall them moving at all.

Quietly the old man turned toward the red barn in the

distance. "There was a house down there that burned down. That's where I was born."

There didn't seem anything more to say. "We knocked at the door," one of us called after him, "but there was no answer." Perhaps this was a suggestion of further talk, out of the cold. "Do you live alone?"

"No," said the gaunt old man. "No. But my wife isn't able to be about. She had a stroke and has been in bed ever since. I've been dragging up this firewood while the snow holds. It makes it easier."

The icy blast whipped away the words. You know the poem about the man treading the deserted banquet hall, "with all but he departed." Our going away from Eayrestown was like that.

When they built the new Eayrestown mill, they erected it on the foundations of the old, which had burned.

XLIV

THE FORKED RIVER MOUNTAINS

No PORTION of New Jersey offers greater mystery than that area known, and yet not known at all, as the Forked River Mountains. Once they were in Burlington County, which goes back to 1681. But Hunterdon County took a part in 1714, Mercer County more in 1838, and Ocean County a third slice in 1850. Now the Forked River Mountains lie almost entirely in Ocean County.

Within an area bounded by Mount Misery, Buckingham, Whiting, Dover Forge, Double Trouble, Forked River, Waretown, Brookville, Cedar Bridge, Woodmansee, and Pasadena is a wide expanse of moors, barrens, pine woods and cedar swamps, crossed by an interlacing of winding trails first broken through by the teams and wagons of charcoal burners and bog iron men.

No one has crossed the plains on the straight strand of concrete from Ong's Hat Circle to Cedar Bridge, where the newer highway turns to Manahawkin, without owning a natural awe and wonderment at the vast expanse of stunted pines, scrub oak and such vegetation as will fight the white sand, extending for miles in every direction, as far as the eye can see. A few trails wander through the scrub. Several old roads have been improved by CCC encampments. However, as puzzling as the plains have been to scientists, writers and theorists of several generations, it is the Forked River Mountains which, today, present the challenging enigma.

It is difficult for those who live in Southern New Jersey, let alone those who live elsewhere, to realize that there is any area, so near to well-known and much-traveled country, which is wild, uncharted, and almost inaccessible. And yet, approaching from every direction and armed with geodetic charts and an array of maps, it took us more than eighteen months, at odd times, to find the way to the "peaks" from which, in one direction, we could see old Barnegat Light, and in the other, the Lakehurst hangar.

We could have consulted guides, those they call woodjins, in the beginning, of course, but then we would have spoiled the fun. We would have missed some of the thrills of tackling an unknown wilderness in the manner of an explorer, although after several journeys through, there is much to be located, reaching back into the past and reconstructing what was out of what is left.

To have attained those elevations described in the surveys as boasting from 175 to 182 feet above sea level seemed a notable accomplishment at the time. Then, after trying a number of trails that were all but blotted out or ended in the middle of nowhere, in spongs or at broken bridges, we concluded that we knew the way. Since then we have marveled that we did find the way, concealed as it is, and that we returned safe enough after any number of unsuccessful quests.

Although as we have said any reference to mountains in Southern New Jersey, notoriously flat, will bring a snicker up the best Sunday sleeve of most people, the sand hills of the Forked River Mountains are higher than many can believe without seeing them. From the road that cuts from Whiting to Forked River, the town, and its yacht basin, one can see the hills along the skyline far away.

From Wells' Mills and its broken-down saw mill, one can see the inviting line of beckoning blue. But to respond to the challenge in these directions is to be defeated, as we found out.

Our first try was from that Forked River-Whiting Road, through a brambly and hardly traceable road to what was Lacey Station. The name Lacey, erroneously spelled Lacy sometimes, appears on modern maps along the Tuckerton Railroad. There was nothing more than a name when we were there; the station is gone, as well as the dwellings that gave it consideration as a town. We crossed the track, after following what was once, obviously, a wagon trail, but at the end of a mile or so toward that elusive deep blue, a broken bridge and an added two miles left us far, far away.

Another time we tried by way of a trail known to natives as the Frenchman Road. This is a path that crosses a clearing opposite the ruins of a house and some imported spruces, later cutting through the brush and emerging beside the Tuckerton track in a ribbon of woods. There was once a crossing but this has been removed. We headed down the railroad as far as any kind of a road penetrated but then were compelled to turn, among the stumps. Once again we tried the Frenchman Road, easing the car across the track but a new growth of small trees halted the car and a dense swamp ended the journey afoot.

We came upon a native in Forked River. "Is there any way to the Forked River Mountains?" we asked. He mentioned the Lacey Road. We told him we had tried it and considered ourselves lucky to get out. He suggested the Frenchman Road and we replied that we had tried it twice, to no avail. "Then there ain't any way except along the fire-stop," he averred, referring to a swath cut through the woods to check forest fires.

We tried to follow his directions and, although in that instance we were not sure we had been in the mountains, our failure produced some information. Lacey Township, covering much of the impenetrable forest, derives its name from General John Lacey who, in 1809, built at Ferrago, later Bamber, a forge, dwelling houses, barns and stables, buying large tracts in that vicinity. In 1810, there is a record that General Lacey applied for authority to lay out a road from Forked River to Bamber and thence to Hanover Furnace, most of which has become the hard-surfaced and more frequently traveled highway of today. Woodmansee, we found out on that trip, took its name from David Woodmancy, one of the emigrants from Yorkshire who settled first on the site of New Stockholm, and later in Burlington.

Reuben Rockwell, who came from Vermont in 1843, tried to make something of Ferrago, whose name goes back to the Latin word for iron, but though he called it Bamber, it got nowhere. Cutting across country toward Dover Forge, we found ourselves traveling, unexpectedly, in country that was the setting for the first Mormon meetings, many of those who went to Utah starting their journeys at the edge of the Forked River Mountains. In 1837 Elder Benjamin Winchester preached the first Mormon sermon in what is now Ocean County, in the schoolhouse at New Egypt. Mormonism was also preached at Toms River, Forked River and Hornerstown, while at New Egypt, Joseph Smith himself was heard on one occasion.

After failures to attain what we knew were mountains, over the round-top at Chicken Bone, through Dutchman's

Lot, through Howardville and Brookville and from the
tiles and abandoned cemetery near Red Oak Grove and
Old Half Way, we received a letter from Lloyd Camburn, of Waretown. If Mr. Camburn had been at home
the day we went down to see him, we might have missed
the pleasure of gaining the Middle Hill by ourselves.

Knowing that we had been asking questions and getting nowhere, Mr. Camburn wrote that there was a road
in from Waretown that would take us up Middle Hill.
The old crossing near Chicken Bone, Mr. Camburn wrote,
was known as Frankie's Causeway which, if followed,
goes up the West Mountain. Since we had reached a point
known both as Isaiah's Bridge and Zare's or Sayre's Bridge,
he said we had been at the gateway we were looking for.
But Mr. Camburn was out on Barnegat Bay clamming
and, coming that far, we resolved to make one more try.

Turning in from Waretown Junction to Daniel's
Bridge, we were attended by the luck that rode along with
us now and then. We had been at Daniel's Bridge almost
a year before, we realized suddenly; that time we came
through Brookville and Wells' Mills. This time we came
upon a man driving a mule team homeward. We asked
direction. He drove on as if he hadn't heard. We didn't
blame him at all when we thought about it. What would
you do if two strangers jumped out of the woods near
sundown and asked you what place this was or had been?

This time on the way to Daniel's Bridge we passed two
or three patches where the brush had been cleared for the
drying of spagnum moss. This moss, gathered in the
swamps and baled, is used by florists in wrapping flowers
and making Christmas wreaths. When we got down to
the bridge, we realized that this was a base for the moss

"operations." We noted a landing made of railroad ties the year before but this time there was a home-made flat-bottomed boat on the landing.

We had begun to examine the boat, wondering what it would be like to take a ride down the choked swamp of pungent cedar water, when a man came out of the woods. He was a tall man, very erect, with a lined and weather-beaten face. He wore rough clothes, mostly torn denim, fastened around the legs with bits of string. We spoke to him in a self-conscious way, seeing as how we had been caught in the act—or, the boat.

We spoke of the moss business and asked how much there was in it for so much hard work. Then we asked the way to the Forked River Mountains. For reply the gentleman, who said he was E. B. Stackhouse, of Ware-town, knelt on the ground to draw a map with his finger. We offered our own maps and charts but Mr. Stackhouse said he had left his spectacles at home. So we followed his finger in the sand, by the camp of James Mercer Davis, turning to the right at Good Will Camp.

Mr. Stackhouse had been regarding us out of the corner of his eye. Suddenly he stopped drawing. "Say," he said, "I know you. You were in here a year ago." Thus are visitors remembered in the vicinity of Daniel's Bridge.

Our voluntary guide of the sand map said he was born in Brookville. His grandfather ran the hotel at Cedar Bridge, he said. Before that the family was down Millville way, in the glass business. "Brookville used to be quite a town," Mr. Stackhouse recalled. "Everybody there raised large families. I'm the youngest of twelve, and I'm sixty-four. Been here in the woods all my life—live in Ware-town, of course, but this moss business keeps me here."

The moss gatherer said the Forked River Mountains used to be thronged with pigs. "They used to brand 'em in the pine settlements around here," he told us. "They'd let 'em go wild in the woods. I can remember my father going up in the mountains to bring his back home. He stuffed his pockets with corn and fed the leaders. The rest followed home.

"If some little pigs were born in the woods and mountains and followed your sow into town, there was no quarrel. Those little fellows were yours. Imagine people getting along like that today!

"Yes, Brookville's mostly gone. There used to be lots more houses. That little school that's falling apart was where I got my schoolin'—now the Brookville kids are picked up in a bus and taken to Barnegat and Waretown. 'Tain't like it used to be at all, at all."

We reluctantly left Mr. Stackhouse to his moss-gathering and taking the road toward Wells' Mills, turned off on a trail just beyond the Davis bungalow. We arrived eventually at Chicken Bone, as we knew we would. Up to this point the track was fairly clear. Just beyond the Good Will Club we found the other trail, through a screen of saplings and tall straggling vegetation.

Here, almost at once, the actual climb began. There were several dips through swampy cuts, requiring speed and bumps. Beyond a ridge of low pines, with charred trunks scattered through them, the scrub drops down to four or five feet. The road, if it could be glorified as such, twists and turns in the lower hills until, after about three miles, the landscape is spread all about in lonely panorama.

We passed one hill and made for another which seemed to be higher. The car attained the top of a rise which was

Although Mount Misery was mostly gone, we found this cabin in the 1930's. Below, sphagnum moss-gatherer E. B. Stackhouse, of Waretown, drew a map in the sand to direct us to the Forked River Mountains.

This road to Calico was typical of those found down from the Forked Rive Mountains in earlier days when Forgotten Town hunters came equipped wit jacks, ropes, and axes. When spring set in, water oozed into the swamps an little streams so that we had to test its depth every foot of the way. Even so, th whereabouts of Calico remains obscure to all but a few who remember the pape plant at nearby Harrisville or have visited the site of Martha Furnace. Nam like Old Half Way and Chicken Bone appear on old maps of the area.

obviously an old fire-stop, with piled branches lying beside it. Here we mounted the pebbly, sandy, scrub-
carpeted ground on foot, pausing to make sure about what
sounded suspiciously like a rattler. Once on the tip-top,
we looked around. Sure enough, there was the Lakehurst
hangar, with a blimp diving toward it. In the other direction we saw the bay, the sea and Barnegat Light, all without the aid of field glasses.

This was surely the center of a mysterious, barren and
sinister country, we said, as we climbed down. Anything
could happen here. Anybody could wander here and vanish without trace. Perhaps there was truth about that
Sikorsky plane diving in the hills and zooming its passengers off the face of the earth, here in the Forked River
Mountains, so near and yet so far from everything.

Then, as our early wanderings had begun in Waretown,
it was fitting that we should return there. In the half dark
of the wide portico of the old house of Dr. Nelson E.
Newbury, we heard Dolph Arens, a woodjin of the
Forked River Mountains, recall what had happened there
and what might have occurred, indicated by hands and
arms and skulls and stones and vines and bits of crockery
that Dolph had picked up, through the years, in strange
and unrecorded places.

It is only from the perspective of Barnegat, Waretown
and Forked River and what they were, once long ago, that
one can see the Forked River Mountains of the old days,
with today's overgrown trails the deep-rutted road of the
charcoal and wood wagons, with Waretown harbor filled
with two and three-masted schooners and with the shore
line far different than it appears now. Then it was that pine
wood was being taken from the woods back of Waretown

to New York, when charcoal meant so much before the introduction of hard coal in the 1850s.

Dr. Newbury was born in the old house across the road from his present home, a house that was his grandfather's, where his grandmother came as a bride. The newer road was unknown and the old trail along the shore, with its later cinder path down from Freehold for the first high-bicycles beside it, wandered through Waretown.

"Looking up and down the road, when I was a boy," said Dr. Newbury, "we knew that every house we could see was that of an active or retired sea captain. There was Captain John Holmes, then Captain Enoch Jones, then Captain Bill Burden. That house up there with a cupola on top was Captain Jacob Birdsall's. My grandfather was Captain Corliss Newbury. My father was Captain Andrew Newbury. I can remember a captain in every house along the Waretown Road.

"Captain William Warren was across the street. Captain John Rulon was next, living with his brother, Steve, a bachelor, with whom he built and operated many ships. Then there was Captain Elias Chambers, Captain Charley Bowker, Riz Horner, and Henry Horner. Some of them are still around; all are over seventy, most of them ninety or more. I've always said that in Waretown, with about three hundred residents, there are more nonogenarians per capita than anywhere.

"Every one of them was a member of an American first family, rich Yankee stock—there were no foreigners anywhere around when I was a boy. They were big men who knew ships, who knew the sea and who stayed in Waretown and Barnegat when the world left them behind. As the age of speed came, there was only the Coast Guard and this business of taking out fishing parties left for them. I can remember when this road out to what they call the harbor went out into what is now deep water—there was room for a four-mule team, with its load of wood or charcoal, to turn around. Now the three rock-piles offshore recall what was the old road."

They sent for Dolph Arens and with word that "He'll be a-comin' " we waited. Dolph, one of the earliest foresters in the State, is of unknown age. He doesn't talk about it. He doesn't look more than fifty and yet he must be much more. Deeply tanned, weather-scarred, he was a youth from Germany in the early 1900s when he planted imported trees from the Continent that may be found in unburned groves up in the Forked River Mountains even now.

Dolph began talking of Red Oak Grove and its forgotten cemetery, the piles of tiles that indicate a lost industry near by, and the diggings at Old Half Way, now a favorite drinking place of deer. We had been there, of course. Dr. Newbury said he was sure that some of those old settlements in the hills had been wiped out by smallpox but Dolph said he wasn't sure of that. "That's what they say," he responded.

"There was a big flow of water in all these creeks, then," said the genial physician. "I can remember going down on the meadows with my father and, as far as we could dig, the depths under the mud were solid in chips. This must have been where Amos Birdsall's shipyard was. The bay has changed altogether, you know. Cranberry Inlet, out beyond where the first Universalist Church was built, has disappeared altogether."

Dolph began talking of what he called the principal

road into the mountains, the Bryan Road, perhaps recalled from Billy Bryan's place. "You go up through Daniel's Bridge," he said, "then to Cat-n-Rat, then over Cold Brook and the Ridge Road, then to Good Will Corner, over Sayre's Bridge to Cave Cabin Hill, to Star Tree, the Boom Road and up to West Mountain and Middle Hill."

It sounded quite simple. We recalled Cat-n-Rat and Star Tree, for they were marked. Dolph Arens said he marked them, years ago.

We talked of where Abraham Waer, said to be Waretown's founder in the days of the Quaker Baptists, was buried, up in the Presbyterian camp meeting grove. "He used to have a stone," Mrs. Newbury declared. "Somebody stole it for a mooring."

Dolph said that he had looked up old deeds and discovered that the name Waer, which has become Ware, had other spellings that we hadn't known. There was Weir, he said, and, at the very beginning, Wire. "It was Thomas Wire who first settled here at the edge of the mountains," he said. "That was in 1712. The deed's up at Perth Amboy. Thomas had a place back of Garrison's Crossing, probably a grant from the Crown."

Cave Cabin Hill is recalled today in the name of a stream, noted on maps as the Cave Cabin Branch. Factory Branch, Dolph declared, recalls one of the first bog iron forges. "Rutherford Stuyvesant had a big place back there," he said, "and once he brought over a lot of Frenchmen to live in the hills. They brought a lot of their own trees and shrubs and they're growing up in the mountains where the Frenchmen used to be."

Dr. Newbury has some of the imported grasses, soft, silky and odd, in his garden. Back of Waretown, in the ridges where Dolph lives and where the Stuyvesant estate still holds title, there's a grove of Australian pines that the woodjin planted as seedlings in 1901. That was before the Frenchmen had vineyards going in so-called barren ground, before they were making their own brandy and cognac, before the plans for tree-planting were given up. So often one thinks of reforestation as a modern idea.

There was a man named John Chamberlin back in the wilderness fastnesses, with a ten-acre tract, as early as 1740. Other early settlers were James DeBow, Marion Rutherford, Maria Bowker, the Sopers, Sally Brown who was Sally Griffee, and the Ransomes. The Ransomes were said to have Indian blood of the tribes that wandered the sand hills in pre-Colonial times.

"I can remember nine houses at Lacey," said Dolph, "and there's nothing there now. Then there was Aserdaten—and no one knows where such a name came from. Cedar Creek—I call it Chamberlin's Branch because it goes back to old John. There was Bullock's Farm—now it's just Bullock on the Jersey Central. No," Dolph concluded, "don't make up your mind that the place was always a wilderness. Plenty's happened back there in those Forked River Mountains.

"Now and then I find a hand or a foot or something. I bury it. There must have been a grave and other graves near the holes of the houses—I come across a new one once in a long while. The trails you've traveled over were cut through by charcoal burners and lumber men. Waretown and Barnegat were humming with doings, then. Boats were being built along the shore to join those loading up in the harbor."

Dr. Newbury said he could remember when over at Harvey Cedars, the cedar stumps used to show at low water where today, at any tide, there are shelving depths.

Both the physician and his wife recalled where over at Barnegat, the lighthouse keepers, three of them with their families, were housed under one roof. Solid land extended more than five hundred feet, near the Oceanic Hotel, where everything's under water now. There were three lighthouses in the history of the island out there. Two have disappeared, to become rock-piles for fishermen who know where to hunt sea bass, as Dr. Newbury and his father did, years ago.

Grover Cleveland, who liked to fish, knew Waretown well, where hotels were at every hand, replacing the numerous stagecoach inns. The old hotel at Barnegat to-day reclaims lost glories of years when the sea came close, when the tide flow came in with a rush, and when sea bathing was a new fad.

So, looking forward to a time when, with Dolph Arens, or Dr. Newbury, or Dr. Hovde, his son-in-law who first told us about Dolph, we can arrive in the "heights" of the Forked River Mountains in time to see more than the sunset, we try, as you must do, to picture the white sails of charcoal boats in the bay, the logging teams creaking down the trails, and sea captains, in uniform, mingling with Southern New Jersey's own mountaineers.

INDEX